# OUR MASTER MUḤAMMAD
# THE MESSENGER OF ALLAH ﷺ

بسم الله الرحمن الرحيم

IN THE NAME OF ALLAH
MOST GRACIOUS, MOST MERCIFUL

*May Peace and Blessings be upon His beloved, our Master Muḥammad, and upon his Family and all of his Companions.*

سيدنا محمد رسول الله

صلى الله عليه وسلم

# *Sayyidunā Muḥammad RasūlAllāh* ﷺ

# Our Master Muḥammad The Messenger of Allah ﷺ

## His Sublime Character & Exalted Attributes Volume II

**Imām ʻAbdallāh Sirājuddīn al-Ḥusaynī** رضي الله عنه

*Foreword by*

*Shaykh Muḥammad b. Yaḥyā al-Nīnowy*

Translated by Khalid Williams

SUNNI PUBLICATIONS

First Edition March 2009
First Print March 2009



ISBN 978-90-79294-07-7

Our Master Muḥammad the Messenger of Allah
His Sublime Character & Exalted Attributes
Volume II
Imām 'Abdallāh Sirājuddīn al-Ḥusaynī

Foreword by Shaykh Muḥammad b. Yaḥyā al-Nīnowy
Translated by: Khalid Williams
Design by: Abū Nibrās
Printed by: Mega Basim, Istanbul

Published by Sunni Publications
The Netherlands, Europe
www.sunnipubs.com
info@sunnipubs.com

# TRANSLITERATION TABLE

| | | | |
|---|---|---|---|
| ى/آ/ا | ā | ظ | ẓ |
| ب | b | ع | ‘ |
| ت | t | غ | gh |
| ث | th | ف | f |
| ج | j | ق | q |
| ح | ḥ | ك | k |
| خ | kh | ل | l |
| د | d | م | m |
| ذ | dh | ن | n |
| ر | r | ه | h |
| ز | z | و | w/ū |
| س | s | ي | y/ī |
| ش | sh | ة | /h/t |
| ص | ṣ | ء | ’ |
| ض | ḍ | أ | a/u |
| ط | ṭ | إ | i |

# LIST OF SYMBOLS

| | |
|---|---|
| عز وجل | Mighty and Glorious is He |
| سبحانه وتعالى | Exalted and Sublime is He |
| جل جلاله | Glory be to Him |
| صلى الله عليه وسلم | Allah bless him and give him peace |
| صلى الله عليه وسلم | Allah bless him and give him peace |
| عليه السلام | Peace be upon him |
| رضي الله عنه | Allah be pleased with him |
| رضي الله عنها | Allah be pleased with her |
| رضي الله عنهم | Allah be pleased with them |

# FOREWORD
## *BY SHAYKH MUḤAMMAD B. YAḤYĀ B. MUḤAMMAD AL-ḤUSAYNĪ AL-NĪNOWY*

IN THE NAME OF ALLAH, MOST GRACIOUS, MOST MERCIFUL. Praise be to Allah as His majesty and perfection merit, and benedictions and salutations be upon our Master Muḥammad and his Household, and may Allah be pleased with his Companions and loved ones.

Cast your eyes over the character of the Chosen Prophet ﷺ and you will see resplendent beauty; open your heart to the secrets of his attributes and you will see the springtime of life in bloom; immerse your spirit in the light of his remembrance and he will become for you a loved one and an intercessor; and devote your all to him and your breast will be filled with faith and noble character. Shed tears out of love for him, and learn from him despite his distance, and perhaps you will be honoured with reaching him, so that your heart will gain life through him, and your soul will find peace through him, and your spirit will find tranquillity through him.

Remember the time of the Companions, and the people of understanding and perception, and draw from your heart a beam of light that can cross the ages and guide you to a connection between us and them; and give your soul a teardrop that will shorten the distance between us and the Messenger of Allah ﷺ so that our souls might soften, and our hearts might beat, and our yearning might be roused; for the separation has been lengthy, and the time for reunion is nigh. Imām Ibn 'Abd al-Barr ﵀ narrated in *al-Tamhīd* that Mālik was asked when he first took instruction from Ayyūb al-Sakhtiyānī.

He replied, 'He made the pilgrimage twice, and I saw him but did not take instruction from him; but when he mentioned the Prophet ﷺ he wept until I felt compassion for him, and when I saw this I began to take instruction from him.' And Qāḍī 'Iyāḍ ؓ said in *Tartīb al-Madārik* and in *al-Shifā*:

> Muṣ'ab ibn 'Abdullāh said: 'When Imām Mālik mentioned the Prophet ﷺ, his colour would change, until those with him found it difficult to bear. He was asked about this once, and replied: "Had you seen what I have seen, you would not find fault with me for what you see now! I have seen Muḥammad ibn al-Munkadir, the leader of the reciters of Qur'ān, in such a state that we had barely asked him about a Ḥadīth before he would weep so much that we felt pity for him! And Ja'far ibn Muḥammad[1] used to smile much, but if the Prophet ﷺ was mentioned to him his skin would become pale! And I never saw him relate the sayings of the Messenger of Allah ﷺ unless he was in a state of ritual purity.

---

[1] This is the Imām, and inheritor of the Prophet's ﷺ knowledge, known as al-Ṣādiq (the truthful), one of the great members of the Household of Muḥammad ﷺ, Imām of the Imāms. The great Imām Abū Ḥanīfa al-Nu'mān studied under him for two years; years which had the greatest impact on his life, as he used to say: 'Were it not for those two years, Nu'mān would have perished.' And the great Imām Mālik studied under him, and said about this: 'No eye ever saw, no ear ever heard, no heart ever imagined, any man finer in knowledge, worship, and piety than Ja'far ibn Muḥammad al-Ṣādiq.' He was the son of Imām Muḥammad ibn 'Alī Bāqir ؓ, inheritor of the knowledge of the Prophets; his paternal uncle was the martyr Imām Zayd, the ally of the Qur'an who was martyred in Kunāsa; his grandfather was Imām Zayn al-'Ābidīn 'Alī ibn Imām Ḥusayn al-Sibṭ, upon his grandfather and his Household be blessings and peace.

> And I went to see him many times, and found him either praying, or in silent meditation, or reciting Qur'an; and he was one of the true worshippers, who feared Allah Almighty. And when 'Abd al-Raḥmān ibn al-Qāsim mentioned the Prophet ﷺ, his colour would change so he looked as though his blood had been drained from him, and his tongue would dry up in his mouth, out of his awe of the Messenger of Allah ﷺ. And I used to visit 'Āmir ibn 'Abdullāh ibn al-Zubayr, and when the Prophet ﷺ was mentioned before him he would weep until there were no more tears left in his eyes. And Zuhrī was the most light-hearted of people, but when he mentioned the Prophet ﷺ, it was like you did not know him, and he did not know you. And I used to go to Ṣafwān ibn Salīm, who was a devoted worshipper and *mujtahid*; and when he mentioned the Prophet ﷺ he would weep, and continue to weep until the people stood and left him." '

Ṭabarī and Ibn Kathīr (in his exegesis) narrated with a *mursal* chain of narration [see note 381, p. 168] on the authority of Sa'īd ibn Jubayr and Rabī' that the Mother of the Believers, 'Ā'isha said: 'A man came to the Prophet ﷺ and said: "O Messenger of Allah, you are dearer to me than myself, and dearer to me than my family, and dearer to me than my son; and oftentimes I am at home and think of you, and I cannot rest until I come and see you and look upon you." ' And Qāḍī 'Iyāḍ mentioned in *al-Shifā* that Isḥāq al-Tajīnī said: 'The Companions of the Prophet ﷺ never mentioned him after his time except that they became meek, and their skin broke out in shivers, and they wept.' Qāḍī 'Iyāḍ said: 'This was also prevalent amongst the second generation; some of them did this out of love and yearning for him, and some out of their awe and respect for him.'

And our Master Abū Bakr al-Ṣiddīq ﷺ would be moved to weep simply by thinking of being parted from the Messenger of Allah ﷺ, even when the Prophet ﷺ was still before his eyes. Muslim narrated in his *Ṣaḥīḥ* that Abū Sa'īd al-Khudrī ﷺ said: 'The Messenger of Allah ﷺ sat on the pulpit and said: "There is a slave unto whom Allah has offered the choice between this world and that which is with Him, and has chosen that which is with Him." So Abū Bakr wept and wept, and said, "We would give our mothers and fathers in ransom for you!" The Messenger of Allah ﷺ was the one given this choice, and out of us all Abu Bakr knew it.' Reflect on his words 'so he wept and wept', because he knew that this was an allusion to the passing of the Messenger of Allah ﷺ, and he had accompanied him all his life, and had stayed with him day after day from the moment the Revelation began; so what about those who had only seen him a few times, and what about those who never saw him ﷺ at all – how could they not weep?

*If your eyes are dry of tears, then seek*
*To borrow the eye of one whose tears flow;*
*But who can lend you an eye with which to weep:*
*Have you ever seen an eye being lent for weeping?*[2]

I ask myself, and those I love for Allah's sake, after mentioning these poignant and moving images, vibrant as they are with love for the Messenger of Allah ﷺ, and his remembrance, and the invocation of blessings upon him, and yearning for him: where do we stand in relation to the way of the noble Companions? What is our state compared with theirs? And does our state reflect the truth of our speech? And where is the mark of this love on us? And where is the reality behind what we claim?

---

[2] These lines were composed by 'Abbās ibn Aḥnaf.

In the hearts of the Companions رضي الله عنهم was something which our own souls fail even to consider; and they preserved in their emotions that which our own feelings are bereft of; and their vision was linked to the realm of the unseen just as it was with the material realm, whilst our own vision goes no further than our eyelids. Their insights were illuminated by the light of the Chosen Prophet ﷺ by their frequent remembrance of him, and their intense love of him, and the comfort they found in his words, and the guidance they found in his teachings ﷺ, whilst our own aspiration is defunct, and our actions are belated – and what woe there shall be when our actions are shown to us, and what shame we shall feel when we stand before Him! O you who love the Messenger of Allah ﷺ! Time has isolated us, tribulations have spread amongst us, the charlatans have spoken,[3] and many people have preoccupied themselves with that which relieves neither hunger nor thirst. We have lost the warmth of the love of the Messenger of Allah ﷺ, the warmth that those who love him feel, and which those who yearn for him desperately seek, and in the beauty of which the most knowledgeable ones in Allah lose themselves. The reality of this love is absent, whilst claims to it are many, and the way of the Companions and the model of their love have been reduced to mere stories and legends.

---

[3] Ḥākim and Ibn Mājah narrate with a rigorously authenticated chain of transmission that Abū Hurayra رضي الله عنه said: 'The Messenger of Allah ﷺ said, "The people will be visited by years of deception, when the liar will be believed and the truthful will be denied, and the traitor will be trusted and the trusted will be treacherous, and the charlatan will speak." It was asked, "Who is the charlatan?" He said: "The fool who speaks of the affairs of the people." ' The narration of Aḥmad has it: 'The iniquitous one who speaks of the affairs of the people.' That is, the one who is ignorant, iniquitous, and wicked, and makes himself appear to be a person of knowledge, whilst he possesses not knowledge, nor guidance, nor an illuminated scripture.

So let us renew our covenant with the Messenger of Allah ﷺ, and bear the banner of love to the most sincere and lasting love, and the most enduring and faithful reverence, and the brightest and most resplendent light, and the Beloved and Chosen One of Allah. Let us carry it in our hearts, so that our state expresses it before our words do, and so our spirits are borne by it to the abode of joy, and exult in the most exquisite beauty, and breathe the fragrance of the Gardens of the All-Bountiful Lord.

*And strange it is that I should pine for them,*
*And ask of them in yearning, whilst they are with me;*
*And my eye seeks them out, whilst they lie in its pupil,*
*And my heart grieves for them,*
*whilst they are in my chest.*

The root of all of this is the attachment of the heart to Allah ﷻ. If one's heart is attached to Allah, one loves everything that Allah loves, and so loves for Allah, from Allah, and by Allah. O you who love: if you love a friend for Allah's sake, Allah is the first intention of your love; and as your love for him increases, your love for Allah increases too, as do the good deeds you offer Allah. So to love someone for Allah's sake is rooted in the love of Allah and also results in the love of Allah. So what of love for the Master of masters, and the guiding light for all who dwell upon earth and in the heavens?

Ibn Mājah narrated, with a rigorously authentic chain of transmission on the authority of Abū Umāma ؓ, that the Messenger of Allah ﷺ said: 'Whoever loves for the sake of Allah and dislikes for the sake of Allah, and gives for the sake of Allah and withholds for the sake of Allah, has perfected faith.' And so strive, O lover, for the truth, and leave aside vainglorious hopes, and plunge into the ocean of Muḥammadan love, and find felicity.

*O Lover of the Chosen One, increase your love,*
*And with the fragrance of his name anoint your tongue;*
*And pay no heed to those who seek to criticise:*
*The sign of love for Allah is love for His Beloved.*

And so, O lover, here is the second volume of *Our Master Muḥammad ﷺ The Messenger of Allah*, by the lordly scholar and Gnostic, scion of the righteous and the saintly, descendant of men of nobility and guidance, Sayyid Imām Shaykh 'Abdallāh Sirājuddīn al-Ḥusaynī al-Ḥalabī, may Allah sanctify his secret and illuminate his tomb. Cast off your sins, and cleanse your heart, and plunge into the ocean of his ﷺ character and his ﷺ attributes, and fill your heart with his treasures and illuminations, and dedicate a portion of every day to the study of the attributes of the Beloved ﷺ, and make them a companion for yourself; and do not forget to supply yourself with knowledge of the lives of his Household and Companions ﵃, that Allah might place in our hearts the love for Him He placed in their hearts. It is sufficient honour for us that our tongues utter their names and so are cleansed of vain speech, and clear the path to our hearts, and are raised by their taste.

Dhahabī narrated in his *Siyar* that it was said to Ibn al-Mubārak, 'Why do you not sit with us after the prayer?' He replied, 'I sit with the Companions and the second generation, reading their books and their sayings. What will I do with you? All you do is backbite others.'

*We have Companions, whose words never bore us,*
*Wise and trusted in their presence and their absence;*
*They pass on to us their knowledge of what went before,*
*And their patience, their manners, and their sound opinions more.*

And so what of those who spend their time studying the attributes of the Chosen Prophet ﷺ, and his life and times, and his character, and his close ones and Companions, and his mission? May Allah bless him and all of his Household, Companions, and loved ones, and give them peace.

I shall stop here, and leave the esteemed reader in the hands of my master Shaykh 'Abdallāh ﵁, that he may lead you with gentleness, care and attention to the holy Prophetic presence, and the cool shade of the Prophetic tree, and the lights of the Muḥammadan essence ﷺ, so that your eyes might delight in its presence, and your soul take wing in its pastures. Pay close attention, and keep your concentration, and immerse your heart; and ask Allah for acceptance, guidance, illumination, insight, and care. May Allah shower His blessings and peace upon our Master Muḥammad and his Household, and praise be to Allah, Lord of the worlds.

– WRITTEN BY THE NEEDY SLAVE OF ALLAH, MUḤAMMAD B. YAḤYĀ B. MUḤAMMAD AL-ḤUSAYNĪ AL-NĪNOWY AL-ḤALABĪ, MAY ALLAH FORGIVE HIM AND HIS PARENTS AND ALL THE MUSLIMS, 14TH RAMAḌĀN 1429 AH

# DEDICATION

*Dear reader,*

*When you read any of my books, please recite Sūrat al-Fātiḥa, and donate the reward of your recitation to the renowned scholar and great Gnostic, carrier of the banner of the authority of the Qur'ān and Sunnah, the Qur'ānic exegete and scholar of Ḥadīth – with sound chains of transmission from many great scholars of Ḥadīth in Aleppo, Damascus, Morocco and elsewhere in the Islamic world, complete with written authorisations which I have kept with me – my Shaykh and noble father, Shaykh Muḥammad Najīb Sirājuddīn al-Ḥusaynī, may Allah ﷻ have mercy on him, and reward him well on behalf of the Muslims; Indeed, He is All-Hearing, All-Knowing.*

*Āmīn*

– 'ABDALLĀH B. MUHAMMAD NAJĪB SIRĀJUDDĪN AL-ḤUSAYNĪ

# TABLE OF CONTENTS

## PART I: THE EXEMPLARY ETHICS OF OUR MASTER MUḤAMMAD ﷺ


His Great Shyness ﷺ 21
His Great Dignity and Stateliness ﷺ 26
His Fear ﷺ of Allah ﷻ 29
His Humility ﷺ before Allah ﷻ
and the Tears He shed out of Fear of Him 32
The Ḥadīth of Hind ibn Abī Hāla 34
His Speech and His Silence ﷺ 37
His Domestic Life ﷺ 41
His Social Life ﷺ outside of the House 43
His Custom ﷺ when sitting in Gatherings 46
His Etiquette and Manners ﷺ with those He sat with 50
His Silence ﷺ 54
Some Aspects of His General Decorum
and Dignified Bearing ﷺ 55
His Favouring of the Elderly with His Conversation ﷺ 56
The Respect He ﷺ would show to the Meritorious 57
His Praise ﷺ of what was Good
and His Encouragement of Thoroughness in Work 60
His Seeking ﷺ of His Companions' Counsel 61
His Enjoining ﷺ of the Seeking of Counsel 63
He ﷺ would acknowledge Sound Ideas
and act upon them 64
His Love ﷺ of Beautiful Names
and His Dislike of Ugly Ones 65
His Love ﷺ of Good Omens and Dislike of Evil Omens 68
His Preference ﷺ for using the Right-Hand Side
at all Times 72
His Dislike ﷺ of using Certain Words because of their
Ambiguous or Negative Connotations 75

## PART II: THE DEVOUT WORSHIP OF OUR MASTER MUḤAMMAD ﷺ

His Worship ﷺ 79
The Reality of Worship 83
The Example that the Prophet ﷺ made for all Devotees 87
His Night Vigils ﷺ 97
The Time He ﷺ would Devote to the Night Vigil 100
The Litanies He ﷺ would recite upon waking for the Night Vigil 104
The Length of His Night Vigil ﷺ 106
The Invocations He ﷺ would recite during the Night Vigil 109
The Manner of His Praying at Night ﷺ 115
His Midmorning Prayers ﷺ 117
After offering the Dawn Prayer He ﷺ would make Remembrance of Allah until the Sun rose 119
The Supererogatory Prayers He ﷺ would offer between the Sunset and Evening Prayers 119
His Supplication ﷺ 121
His Manner of Supplicating ﷺ 123
Some of His ﷺ General Supplications 131
The Supplications He ﷺ made for Specific Occasions 137
How He ﷺ would glorify and praise His Lord 154
His Prayers for Forgiveness ﷺ 157

## PART III: THE NOBLE ANCESTRY OF OUR MASTER MUḤAMMAD ﷺ

His Noble Lineage and Eminent Origins ﷺ 163
The Excellence of His Noble Lineage ﷺ 168
The Purity of His Noble Lineage ﷺ 170
His Glorious Birth ﷺ 173
Celebrating and Commemorating His Birthday 179
Allah's Protection of the Prophet ﷺ

from His Youth onwards 182
Allah protected our Master Muḥammad ﷺ
from the Evils of the Pre-Islamic Time of Ignorance 200
His Journey to Syria ﷺ 204
His Marriage ﷺ to Khadīja bint Khuwaylid ibn Asad رضي الله عنها 207
His Noble Children ﷺ 210
The Beginning of His Prophetic Mission ﷺ 212
Allah ﷻ protected His Messenger ﷺ
from the Evil of the Demonic Consort 220
Allah ﷻ protected His Messenger ﷺ from Faults and
Errors and fortified Him with the Truth at all Times 221
The Story of the Captives of Badr 224
The Story of the Date-Palms 237
Ḥubāb ibn al-Mundhir and the Battle of Badr 245

## PART IV: THE TREMENDOUS BLESSINGS OF OUR MASTER MUḤAMMAD ﷺ

The Overwhelming Blessings and Treasures
that emanated from Him ﷺ 247
His Blessed Touch ﷺ 251
He ﷺ would touch the Chests of His Companions to
strengthen the Faith in their Hearts 257
The Prophet ﷺ Touched the Face of Qatāda ibn Milḥān
and it became like a Mirror 259
The Messenger of Allah ﷺ healed the Eye of
Qatāda ibn al-Nuʿmān when it was cut out 260
The Companions would kiss the Prophet's ﷺ Hand
and Body out of Reverence for Him ﷺ and as a means
of seeking Blessing and Illuminations 262
The Companions kissed the Blessed Hand and
Feet of the Prophet ﷺ 263
The Companions kissed other Parts of His Blessed Body ﷺ 265

The Companions would seek Blessings from the Relics of the Prophet ﷺ in His Lifetime and after His Passing 267
The Companions sought Blessings from the Cut Hairs of the Prophet ﷺ and were eager to collect them and preserve them 267
Khālid Ibn al-Walīd sought Victory in his Military Campaigns by Virtue of the Prophet's ﷺ Hair 269
The Companions sought Blessings from the Fingerprints of the Messenger of Allah ﷺ 270
The Companions sought Blessings from the Leftovers of the Prophet ﷺ 271
The Companions sought Blessings from Vessels which the Prophet's ﷺ Lips had touched 271
The Companions sought Blessings and Cures from the Cloths of the Messenger of Allah ﷺ 272
The Companions sought Blessings from the Prophet's Phlegm ﷺ and the Water He used for Ablutions 273
The Prophet ﷺ cured the Companions with his Blessed Saliva 274
His Blessed Saliva ﷺ made Water Pure and Sweet 276
The Companions sought Blessings from His Blessed Saliva ﷺ 277
The Companions sought Blessings from the Prophet's Blood ﷺ 279
The Companions sought Blessings from Coins touched by the Hand of the Prophet ﷺ 281
The Companions sought Blessings from the Prophet's Staff ﷺ 282
The Companions lit their way using a Staff given to them by the Messenger of Allah ﷺ 283
The Companions sought Blessings from the Shoes of the Messenger of Allah ﷺ 284
The Companions sought Blessings from the Place on the Pulpit where the Messenger of Allah ﷺ sat 285

The Followers would seek Blessings from the Hands of the Companions that had touched the Prophet's Hand ﷺ 285
The Companions' Love for the Prophet ﷺ 287
Firstly: The Way they loved Him ﷺ more than they loved themselves and put Him ﷺ before themselves 288
Secondly: How they loved Him ﷺ and yearned for Him ﷺ 290
Thirdly: Their Contentment to be in the Company of the Messenger of Allah ﷺ 292
Fourthly: Their Ardent Desire to accompany the Prophet ﷺ in this World and the next 294
Fifthly: The Tears shed by the Companions ؓ over the Pain of being Separated from Him ﷺ 296
The Secrets, Illuminations, Blessings and Treasures that emanate from the Blessed Grave of the Prophet ﷺ 305
Epilogue 307

# PART I: THE EXEMPLARY ETHICS OF OUR MASTER MUḤAMMAD ﷺ

## HIS GREAT SHYNESS ﷺ

THE Messenger of Allah ﷺ was the shyest of people, because he was the greatest of them in faith, and He ﷺ said: 'Shyness is born of faith.'[4]

Bukhārī and Muslim narrate that Abū Saʿīd al-Khudrī رضي الله عنه said: 'The Messenger of Allah ﷺ was shyer than the maiden in her chamber.'

The narration of Bukhārī adds: 'If he disliked something, it would be seen in his face.' It is well-known that a maiden (a virgin girl) who is hidden away in her chamber (her room in the house or encampment) is especially shy; yet the Messenger of Allah ﷺ was shyer even than she.

---

[4] The Ḥadīth continues: '... and faith is in Paradise; and ribaldry is born of harshness, and harshness is in Hell.' It was narrated by Aḥmad with a chain of transmission the men of whom were rigorously authenticated, and by Tirmidhī, and by Ibn Ḥibbān in his *Ṣaḥīḥ* collection. Tirmidhī declared it a sound, rigorously authentic Ḥadīth. (*Al-Targhīb wa al-Tarhīb*)

Shyness is a characteristic that leads to the avoidance of shameful matters, and prevents any negligence in allotting people their rights. For this reason, the Prophet ﷺ said: 'Be shy before Allah, as He merits.' The people said: 'We indeed are shy before Allah, praise be to Him!' He ﷺ replied: 'This is not the case; rather, shyness before Allah entails that you protect the head and that which it contains, and protect the stomach, and that which it contains…' as we mentioned before in the forty collected Ḥadīth. This narration is a clarification that shyness inspires the one who possesses it to strive for perfection, and keeps him from settling for less. The Prophet ﷺ also said: 'Shyness brings nothing but good.'[5]

**His shyness ﷺ was such that he would never confront a person with something they would dislike**. Rather, he ﷺ would hint at the problem, or tell one of his Companions to address the person directly: Abū Dāwūd, Tirmidhī and others narrate that Anas ؓ said: 'The Messenger of Allah ﷺ would never directly confront a person with someone they would dislike. Once, there visited him a man with a yellow stain on his clothes. When he stood to leave, the Prophet ﷺ said to his Companions: "You might tell this fellow to wash off this yellow stain." '

Abū Dāwūd narrated that 'Ā'isha ؓ said: 'If the Messenger of Allah ﷺ heard something about a man, he would not say: "What is wrong with so-and-so", but would say: "What is wrong with people, that they say such-and-such?" '

**Another example of his shyness** ﷺ was when the people sat with him too long after eating, and he was too shy to ask them to leave, until a verse of the Qur'ān was revealed specifically regarding this:

---

[5] Narrated by Bukhārī.

Bukhārī narrated in his *Ṣaḥīḥ* collection that Anas ﷺ said: 'When the Messenger of Allah ﷺ was to marry Zaynab, Umm Sulaym said to me: "We should give the Messenger of Allah ﷺ a gift." I agreed. She took some dates, butter and cheese, and made a *ḥays*[6] in a pot, which I took to him ﷺ.

'He ﷺ told me to put it down, and told to invite certain men, whom he named, and to invite whomever I met. I did as he bade me. When I returned, the house was crowded with his relatives, and I saw the Messenger of Allah ﷺ place his hand in the *ḥays* and speak, and then call people ten at a time to eat from it, saying to them: "Mention Allah's name, and let each man eat what is nearest to him." This continued until they had all dispersed.'

Anas[7] was asked as to how many there were present. He replied: 'Around three hundred. Some of them left, and others stayed to talk. The Prophet ﷺ was too shy (to ask them to leave). Then he ﷺ went out and made for the bed-chambers, and I went out after him, and said: "They have gone."

'The Prophet ﷺ returned, and entered the house, and let down the curtains. I was in the room, and he ﷺ recited: ﴾O you who believe! Do not enter the houses of the Prophet unless permission is granted to you for a meal; and wait not for its preparation. But if you are invited, enter, and when you have eaten, disperse, lingering not for conversation. This would trouble the Prophet, yet he is shy from you; and Allah does not shy from the truth.﴿'[8]

---

[6] A kind of stew made of these ingredients, which the Arabs used to make.

[7] What follows is from Muslim's narration.

[8] Qur'ān 33:53

This means that because of his generosity ﷺ he was too shy to tell them to leave whilst they were sitting with him; yet Allah does not shy away from proclaiming the truth that must be honoured.

This does not contradict the fact that He [Allah] ﷻ is characterised by a generous shyness that is commensurate with His Divinity, as the Prophet ﷺ said: 'Your Lord is shy, and generous; when His servant raises his hands to Him, He is shy to refuse him.'[9] Because they were sitting in his house, out of his generosity, the Prophet ﷺ was too shy to be direct with them. However, the situation required clarification, and so the Qur'ān brought clarification from Allah Himself ﷻ.

**The scholars have mentioned that there are several types of shyness, defined according to its cause:**

**Generous shyness** is that which is caused by a generous soul, such as the Prophet's ﷺ shyness when the people sat with him for too long, as we have seen.

**Reverent shyness** is that which is caused by recognition of the majesty of the Being one is shy of; and the more the servant knows of his Lord's majesty, the more shy he will be before Him ﷻ. There is no doubt that the Prophet ﷺ knew Allah's majesty ﷻ better than any of His creation: Bukhārī and Muslim narrated in their *Ṣaḥīḥ* collections that he ﷺ said: 'By Allah, I am the most knowledgeable of you concerning Allah, and the most conscious of Him.'

**Loving shyness** is the shyness of the lover for his beloved, so that whenever thoughts of the beloved cross his mind, his shyness and concern for him increases.

---

[9] Narrated by Tirmidhī and others.

**Worshipful shyness** is the shyness that combines love, fear, and the awareness that Allah's true rank is far beyond the acts of worship by means of which the servant draws near to Him.

**A person's shyness from his own self** is the shyness that a noble, righteous person possesses: shyness on account of defects, and shameful actions, and reliance on others. This person finds that he is shy of his own self, as though he has two souls, one of which is shy of the other.

**The shyness of decorum** is shyness caused by modesty, and care to conceal what should be concealed. Ibn Mājah narrated that Bilāl ibn Ḥārith ﷺ said: 'When the Prophet ﷺ wanted to answer the call of nature, he would seek a distant place (in which to do so).'[10]

Tirmidhī and Abū Dāwūd narrated that Anas ﷺ said: 'When the Prophet ﷺ wanted to answer the call of nature, he would not lift his robe until he was close to the earth.'[11]

Ibn Sa'd narrated that (the Tābi'ī) Sa'd ibn Ṣāliḥ said: 'When the Prophet ﷺ entered the place where he would relieve himself, he would wear his shoes and cover his head ﷺ.'[12]

Imām Tirmidhī narrated in *al-Shamā'il* that 'Ā'isha ﷺ said: 'I never looked at (or 'I never saw') the private parts of the Messenger of Allah ﷺ.' This was due to his shyness, and his perfect dignity ﷺ, and his desire to cover himself.

---

[10] Also narrated by Imām Aḥmad, and Nasā'ī. Its authenticity is attested to by its numerous chains of transmission. (*Al-Jāmi' al-Ṣaghīr*)

[11] Also narrated by Ṭabarānī in *al-Awsaṭ*. (*Al-Jāmi' al-Ṣaghīr*)

[12] This Ḥadīth has some weakness in its chain of transmission.

Abū al-Ṣāliḥ narrated, on the authority of Ibn 'Abbās ☙, that 'Ā'isha ☙ said: 'The Messenger of Allah ﷺ never approached any of his wives except that he was covered, with a cloth draped over his head; and I never saw the Messenger of Allah's ﷺ private parts, nor he mine.'[13]

Bazzār narrated that Ibn 'Abbās ☙ said: 'The Messenger of Allah ﷺ would bathe behind the chambers; and no one ever saw him naked.'[14] In the course of examining all of this, it becomes clear to the person of intellect that our Master Muḥammad ﷺ attained the highest ranks of shyness and modesty.

## HIS GREAT DIGNITY AND STATELINESS ﷺ

The Messenger of Allah ﷺ possessed great dignity, and Allah ﷻ endowed him with honour and nobility, and clothed him with the mantle of eminence.

Tirmidhī and others narrated that Hind ibn Abī Hāla said, describing the Prophet ﷺ: 'The Messenger of Allah ﷺ had great and stately attributes, and was honoured as such by others. His face shone like the light of the full moon.' Our master 'Alī ☙ said, describing the Prophet ﷺ: 'Whoever saw him unexpectedly would be awe-stricken. Whoever came to know him would love him.'

---

[13] Related by Ibn al-Jawzī in *al-Wafā'*, ascribed to Khaṭīb, as mentioned by Shaykh Qārī and Shaykh Muḥammad ibn Qāsim Jasūs in their commentary on *al-Shamā'il*.
[14] Its chain of transmission is sound, according to Shaykh 'Alī al-Qārī, in *Jam' al-Wasā'il*.

The Companions ﷺ were unable to bring themselves to look at him ﷺ closely, because of the power of his dignity and gravity. This is why our descriptions of him ﷺ come from the youngest of them, or those of them who had a hand in raising him before his prophetic mission, such as Hind ibn Abī Hāla, or our Master 'Alī ﷺ.

This is attested to by Muslim's narration on the authority of 'Abdullāh ibn 'Amr ﷺ, who said: 'I kept the company of the Messenger of Allah ﷺ for a long time, and heard many of his sayings, and memorised thousands of his parables. Despite all of that, Out of shyness from him and reverence for him, I never once looked directly at him; and if I were asked to describe him, I would be unable to do so.'

Because of his great dignity and gravity, those who sat with him ﷺ would be awe-stricken by him, and might even tremble violently before him. Upon this, he ﷺ would calm them down by being kind and gentle with them.

Ibn Mājah and Ḥākim narrated that Abū Mas'ūd al-Badrī ﷺ said: 'A man came and stood before the Prophet ﷺ, and was overcome with violent trembling and dread. The Prophet ﷺ said to him: "Calm down, for I am no king or tyrant; I am but the son of a woman of Quraysh, who would eat dried meat in Mecca."[15] The man then spoke of his need.[16] The Prophet ﷺ stood, and said: "O people! It has been revealed to me that you should humble yourselves; so humble yourselves, so that no one will oppress another, and no one will be proud. Servants of Allah: be brothers!" '

---

[15] The Arabs used to eat sun-dried meat, and by mentioning it the Prophet ﷺ expressed his lack of conceit and tyranny.

[16] I.e. when he saw the modesty of the Prophet ﷺ he calmed down, and spoke of the need for which he had come.

Qayla bint Makhrama said: 'When I saw the Messenger of Allah ﷺ sitting humbly on his heels, I began to shiver in fear. A man said: "O Messenger of Allah, the poor thing is trembling!" The Messenger of Allah ﷺ said, without looking round to see me: "Poor girl, be at peace!" When he said it, Allah removed the fear that had entered my heart." ' These stories of the Companions clearly show the power of his dignified composure ﷺ.

Another example of this is the story of Abū Mas'ūd al-Badrī ﷺ, who said: 'I was beating a slave-boy of mine (for some offence), when I heard a voice from behind me say: "Watch out, Abū Mas'ūd!" Out of anger I ignored him, until he was upon me, and I saw that it was the Messenger of Allah ﷺ. When I saw him ﷺ, the stick fell from my hand out of fear of him. He said to me: "By Allah, Allah has more power over you than you have over this boy!" I replied: "By Allah, O Messenger of Allah, I will never beat another of my slaves again!" ' One narration has it: 'I said: "O Messenger of Allah, he is hereby free for Allah's sake!" He replied: "If not, the Fire will surely touch you."[17]

Zaynab al-Thaqafiyya ﵁, the wife of 'Abdullāh ibn Mas'ūd ﵁, said: 'The Messenger of Allah ﷺ said: "Give charity, O women, even if it be from your own jewellery." I went back to 'Abdullāh ibn Mas'ūd and said to him: "You are a man of scant means, and the Messenger of Allah ﷺ has commanded us to give charity. Go and ask him, and if it is acceptable for me to do so, I will give you my charity; if not, I will give it to someone else." Ibn Mas'ūd said: "Go and see him yourself." I went, and there at the door of the Messenger of Allah ﷺ was a woman of the Anṣār with the very same question I had.

[17] Narrated by Muslim, Abū Dāwūd and Tirmidhī.

' "The Messenger of Allah ﷺ was an awe-inspiring figure, and so when Bilāl happened to come out, we said to him: "Go to the Messenger of Allah ﷺ and tell him that two women are at the door, asking if they might give charity to their husbands and the orphans in their care; and do not tell him who we are."

' Bilāl went in to the Messenger of Allah ﷺ and asked him. The Messenger of Allah ﷺ said to him: "Who are they?" He said: "A woman of the Anṣār, and Zaynab." "Which Zaynab is it?" asked the Prophet ﷺ. "It is the wife of 'Abdullāh", said Bilāl. The Messenger of Allah ﷺ answered: "They have two rewards: one for keeping family ties, and the other for charity." '[18]

## HIS FEAR ﷺ OF ALLAH ﷻ

The Messenger of Allah ﷺ was more fearful of Allah ﷻ than any other person, for he knew Allah better than any, and a man's fear of Allah is commensurate with his knowledge of Him. Allah ﷻ said: ﴾None fear Allah but those of His servants who know.﴿[19]

Bukhārī and Muslim narrate that 'Ā'isha رضي الله عنها said: 'The Messenger of Allah ﷺ chose the easier course in a certain matter, and some people found fault with it. When news of this reached the Prophet ﷺ, he said: "What is wrong with people that they find fault in what I do? By Allah, I am the most knowledgeable of them concerning Allah, and more fearful of Him than they!" '

Several lessons may be adduced from this Ḥadīth:

---

[18] Agreed upon by Bukhārī and Muslim.

[19] Qur'ān 35:28

1. Following the example of the Prophet ﷺ is of the utmost importance, and extremism is forbidden.

2. It is blameworthy to avoid the lawful out of doubt over its lawfulness; knowledge of Allah ﷻ necessitates great fear of Him, but not to the extent of excessive severity in actions, as we will discuss later, if Allah wills.

3. The Prophet ﷺ exceeds all humanity in knowledge of Allah ﷻ and fear of Him; and Allah placed him ﷺ in the highest station of knowledge and fear.

Those who have attained knowledge of Allah ﷻ say that if the knowledge and fear of Allah are perfected in a person, and they reach true knowledge and true fear, the affects of this can be seen upon them, and its fruits are given to them.

It is narrated that Mu'ādh ibn Jabal ﷺ said: 'If you feared Allah ﷻ as He should be feared, you would be granted knowledge in which there is no trace of ignorance; and if you knew Allah ﷻ as He should be known, the very mountains would fall at your bidding.'[20]

So what about our Master Muḥammad ﷺ, who attained the highest degree of knowledge of Allah ﷻ, and reached the loftiest station of fear of Him?

Whatever you might imagine the affects and fruits of this could be, the reality is even more immense; and this is no overstatement, when Allah ﷻ said: ﴾The grace of Allah upon thee has been great.﴿[21]

---

[20] Ascribed in *al-Jāmi' al-Ṣaghīr* to al-Ḥakīm al-Tirmidhī, with an indication of its weakness.
[21] Qur'ān 4:113

Bukhārī and Muslim narrated that Anas ﷺ said: 'The Messenger of Allah ﷺ delivered a sermon the like of which I had never heard, saying: "If you knew what I know, you would laugh little, and weep much." Upon this, the Companions of the Messenger of Allah ﷺ covered their faces, and wept.'

Another narration has it: 'The Messenger of Allah heard something about his Companions, and so gave a sermon, saying: "Paradise and Hell were shown to me, and never have I seen good and evil the like of which I saw today. If you knew what I know, you would laugh little, and weep much." There was never a day more difficult for the Companions of the Messenger of Allah ﷺ than that day; they covered their heads, and wept.' This Ḥadīth is evidence of the Prophet's intense fear of Allah ﷻ, and the tears he shed out of fear for Him.

Another indication of the severity of his fear of Allah ﷻ is the report of Umm Salama ﷺ, who said: 'The Messenger of Allah ﷺ was in my house once, and he had a tooth-stick in his hand. He called a servant-girl[22] several times, until the annoyance showed on his face.[23] I went to the chambers, and found the girl playing with a lamb. I said to her: "Do I see you playing with this lamb, whilst the Messenger of Allah ﷺ is calling you?" The girl said: "By the One who sent you with the truth, I did not hear you." The Messenger of Allah ﷺ replied: "Were it not that I feared reprisal on the Day of Resurrection, I would smack you with this tooth-stick!" '[24]

---

[22] Either his ﷺ servant-girl, or Umm Salama's.

[23] Because she was playing, and did not answer him.

[24] Narrated by Aḥmad with this wording, with several chains of transmission, one of which is good (*jayyid*); and Ṭabarānī narrated the like of it. (*Al-Targhīb wa al-Tarhīb*)

# HIS HUMILITY ﷺ BEFORE ALLAH ﷻ AND THE TEARS HE SHED OUT OF FEAR OF HIM

The Messenger of Allah ﷺ was constantly in a state of humility, contrition and lowliness before his Lord ﷻ, throughout all of the great events of his life, and in all his acts of prayer and devotion, and all of his affairs, and his teachings, sermons, and the Revelations he received, and in everything that he did ﷺ. His humility ﷺ when praying reached such an extent that a sound could be heard emanating from his chest like that of a boiling pot: Nasā'ī narrated, on the authority of Muṭarrif, that his father ﷺ said: 'I saw the Messenger of Allah ﷺ praying, and his chest was emanating a sound like the hissing of a pot.'[25]

Ibn Khuzayma's narration has it '... like the hissing of a quern.'[26] The narration of Abū Dawūd has it that Abū Muṭarrif said: 'I saw the Messenger of Allah ﷺ praying, and his chest was emanating a sound like the hissing of a quern, because of his weeping.' Ibn Khuzayma narrated in his *Ṣaḥīḥ* collection that 'Alī ﷺ said: 'There was no horseman among us on the day of Badr except al-Miqdād. You could have seen us, every one of us asleep, except for the Messenger of Allah ﷺ, who was beneath a tree, praying and weeping, until he ﷺ reached the morn.' When he ﷺ entered Mecca on the day of the conquest, he entered in a state of humility before his Lord, whilst in the midst of such a huge spectacle, and such crowds of people in attendance: Abū Ya'lā and Ḥākim narrated, with a good, strong chain of transmission, that Anas ﷺ said: 'When the Messenger of Allah ﷺ entered Mecca on the day of the conquest, the people honoured him, and so he lowered his head onto his saddle in

---

[25] Ḥāfiẓ Mundhirī said: 'This means that his chest emanated a cry like that of a pot when it is boiling.'

[26] A quern is a hand mill used for grinding.

humility.' Bayhaqī's narration, also on the authority of Anas ﷺ, has it: 'The Messenger of Allah entered Mecca on the day of the conquest, his chin resting on his camel in humility.'

Wāqidī's narration, on the authority of Abū Hurayra ﷺ, has it: 'The Messenger of Allah ﷺ entered Mecca on the day of the conquest until he arrived at Dhū Ṭuwā,[27] and stood amidst the people. His beard was touching the middle of his saddle, or thereabouts, out of humility before Allah ﷻ, upon seeing Mecca's conquest, and the multitudes of Muslims. Then, he said: "O Allah, there is no life but the life of the Hereafter!" '

This noble quality was also manifested in the humility he ﷺ would show, and the tears he would shed when turning to Allah ﷻ in prayer and supplication: Imām Muslim narrated that 'Abdullāh ibn 'Umar ﷺ said: 'The Messenger of Allah ﷺ recited: ﴿My Lord! They have led many people astray. Yet whosoever follows me is of me; and whosoever disobeys me, still You are Forgiving, Merciful,﴾[28] and Allah's word: ﴿If You punish them, they are Your servants; and if You forgive them, You are the Mighty, the Wise.﴾[29] He then raised his hands, and said, weeping: "O Allah, my community, my community!" Upon this, Allah ﷻ said: "O Jibrīl, go to Muḥammad – and your Lord knows better – and ask him why he weeps."

'Jibrīl went to him, and asked him, and then told Allah – and He knew better – what he said. Allah ﷻ then said: "O Jibrīl, go to Muḥammad and tell him: *We will please you in regard to your community; and we will not disappoint you.*" '

---

[27] A valley in Mecca.

[28] Qur'ān 14:36

[29] Qur'ān 5:118

# THE ḤADĪTH OF HIND IBN ABĪ HĀLA

Of all the many narrations that contain descriptions of the Prophet's ﷺ physical appearance and character, and his decorum and manners, both public and private, there is one narration that is particularly clear and comprehensive in expressing his ﷺ unique qualities: the Ḥadīth of Hind ibn Abī Hāla.

Tirmidhī narrated that Ḥasan ibn 'Alī ؓ said : 'I asked my uncle Hind ibn Abī Hāla – who was gifted at describing – about the beauty of the Prophet ﷺ, hoping that he would describe to me something I could hold on to and cherish.

'He replied: "The Messenger of Allah ﷺ had great and stately attributes, and was honoured as such by others. His face shone like the light of the full moon. He was taller than a man of average height, but shorter than a tall man.[30] His head was large,[31] and his hair was wavy. If it parted easily, he would part it in the centre; if not, he would not.[32] His hair would fall beyond his earlobes if he left it be.[33] His complexion was fair,[34] his forehead wide.[35] His eyebrows were long and arched,[36] and full,

---

[30] This means that he ﷺ was taller than average when observed properly, but at first glance, he appeared to be of average height, as was mentioned in connection with the Ḥadīth of 'Alī ؓ.
(*Jam' al-Wasā'il*, and elsewhere)
[31] A large head, in proportion to the body, is a sign of a powerful intellect and sensitivity.
[32] I.e. if the hair of his noble head ﷺ was long enough to be parted easily, he would part it in the centre; and if it would not part easily, he would leave it as it was.
[33] I.e. if he ﷺ did not part it.
[34] I.e. white, with a touch of redness.
[35] Both horizontally and vertically.

without connecting;[37] between them was a vein which would throb when he became angry. The bridge of his nose was high, and curved, and there was light above it; those who did not pay close attention might think that his nose was upturned. His beard was thick, and his cheeks were even.[38] His mouth was wide,[39] and his teeth were well-spaced.[40] A thin line of hair ran from his chest to his navel. His neck was like the neck of a statue, and shone like silver.[41] He was perfectly proportioned,[42] well filled-out, and well-built.[43] His stomach and chest were lined up straight,[44] and his chest was broad. His shoulders were broadly spaced, and his joints were strong and large.[45] His unclothed limbs shone brightly.[46] A thin line of hair ran

---

[36] This means they were very well defined, and full.

[37] As for Umm Ma'bad's assertion that 'his eyebrows were fine at the corners, and connected', this means that this would appear to be so when he ﷺ was viewed at a distance, at first glance. The one who saw him ﷺ clearly, and close up, would see that his eyebrows actually did not connect.

[38] I.e. they were not raised, and this is more agreeable and beautiful.

[39] A wide mouth produces eloquent speech, and clear articulation; doubtless, such perfect accord could be found throughout his whole blessed body ﷺ.

[40] I.e. his blessed teeth ﷺ were lined up, and spaced out, not pressed tightly together.

[41] I.e. his neck ﷺ was as straight, well-proportioned, and beautiful as a statue's, and as clear-coloured and resplendent as silver.

[42] I.e. Allah ﷻ created all the parts of his ﷺ body in perfect harmony and proportion.

[43] I.e. he ﷺ was fully-fleshed, neither lean nor skinny, and his noble limbs were powerful, not limp.

[44] I.e. neither of them bulged out beyond the other.

[45] This is evidence of his great strength ﷺ.

[46] I.e. those parts of his body not covered by his clothes ﷺ shone a brilliant white.

between his chest and his navel, and besides that neither his breast nor his stomach had any hair upon it; his arms, shoulders and upper chest were covered in hair. His forearms were long, his palms wide. His hands and feet were fleshy,[47] his fingers and toes long.[48] The soles of his feet were slightly arched,[49] and his feet were smooth so that water would run right off them. When he walked, he lifted his feet with vigour,[50] leaning forwards[51] and stepping lightly.[52] His stride was long,[53] and when he walked, it was as though he were descending from a height. When he looked at something, he would turn to it with his whole body.[54] He would lower his gaze,[55] and he spent more time looking at the ground than he did at the sky.[56]

---

[47] His hands and feet ﷺ were strong, not weak and scrawny.

[48] Neither crooked nor contracted.

[49] Without being abnormal or unpleasant.

[50] I.e. he would lift his feet as though he were pulling something up. He did not drag his feet along the ground, or strut like a conceited person.

[51] Inclining towards the direction in which he was facing ﷺ.

[52] When he walked ﷺ, he would lift his feet from the ground with vigour; and when he placed them on the ground, he would place them lightly, and softly. He ﷺ would walk with composure and dignity, and forbearance and deliberateness, without stamping the ground with his feet, or making loud footsteps. Allah ﷻ praised those who walk in this way, saying: ﴾And the servants of the All-Merciful are they who tread softly upon the earth, and when the foolish ones address them say: 'Peace!'﴿ (Qur'ān 25:63)

[53] Naturally, without any affectation.

[54] I.e. he ﷺ would not simply steal a glance, or turn his head right and left, as a fickle person does.

[55] I.e. when not looking at something in particular, he ﷺ would look down; and this is the custom of the deep thinker.

[56] I.e. when he was silent he ﷺ would look at the ground more than he would look at the sky. As for when he was engaged in conversation, he

' "He would usually look at things casually, without staring.[57] He would follow behind his Companions,[58] and be the first to greet those whom he met.' "

## HIS SPEECH AND HIS SILENCE ﷺ

Ḥasan ؓ continued: 'I then asked him about the Messenger of Allah's ﷺ speech.[59] He said: "The Messenger of Allah ﷺ was constantly full of sorrow,[60] and always deep in thought; he had

---

would look at the sky often, as is narrated in the *Sunan* of Abū Dāwūd, where it states that when he ﷺ sat and talked, he would often raise his gaze to the sky.

[57] 'Allāmah Munāwī said: 'This means that when not addressing someone, he ﷺ would generally look casually.' This means that he would look with the corner of his eye nearest the temple, not the inside (nearest the nose).

[58] I.e. he ﷺ would let his Companions go first, and then walk behind them, in order to watch over them, and evaluate their state, and identify those of them who were weak, leaving his back in the protection of the Angels behind him. Dārimī narrated, with a rigorously authenticated chain of transmission, that the Prophet ﷺ said: 'Leave your backs for the Angels.' Imām Aḥmad narrated that Jābir ؓ said: 'The Companions of the Prophet ﷺ would walk in front of him, leaving his back to the Angels.' (*Jam' al-Wasā'il*) Imām Nawawī said: 'He ﷺ only walked in front of them on the day of the Trench (as Jābir reported) because he had called them to him, and they followed behind him, just as the one who invites people to eat walks ahead of them.'

[59] I.e. his manner of speaking, and his manner of being silent ﷺ, as is indicated by the answer that followed.

[60] His sorrow ﷺ was not because of the affairs of this worldly life; rather, sadness would visit him because of many reasons, all of which went back to Allah's religion, and concern for Allah's creatures. For

no rest.[61] He would be silent for long periods, and would not speak without need.[62] He would begin and end his speech by

---

this reason, Qur'ānic verses would be revealed to console him ﷺ, and ease his grief. One example of this is his grief ﷺ over those who, out of stubbornness and hostility, did not believe in the guidance he brought, although the truth had been made clear to them. This was very difficult for him ﷺ, and it caused him great grief, until Allah ﷻ revealed: ﴿Perhaps thou torment thyself because they believe not. If We willed, We would send upon them a sign from the heavens, before which their necks would stay bowed﴾ (Qur'ān 26:3), and: ﴿Whosoever disbelieves, let not his disbelief sadden thee; unto Us is their return, and We will inform them of what they did﴾ (Qur'ān 31:23), and ﴿So let not thy soul be lost in despair for them; Allah knows well what they do﴾ (Qur'ān 35:8), and ﴿Grieve not for them, and be not distressed by what they devise﴾ (Qur'ān 16:127). Another cause for his sorrow ﷺ was the deception of the hypocrites, and their pretension to Islam whilst concealing their disbelief, and their easy recourse to disbelief, as Allah ﷻ said: ﴿O Messenger! Be not aggrieved by those who are quick to disbelieve, of such as say 'We believe!' with their mouths, yet their hearts believe not.﴾ (Qur'ān 5:41) Another cause for his sorrow ﷺ was the corrupt, mendacious speech of his enemies, who accused him ﷺ of being a sorcerer, or a poet, or a madman. In this regard, the word of Allah ﷻ was revealed: ﴿We know that thou art aggrieved by what they say﴾ (Qur'ān 6:33), as well as His word: ﴿Let not their speech aggrieve thee; We know what they conceal, and what they disclose﴾ (Qur'ān 36:76), and His word: ﴿ Let not their speech aggrieve thee; all power belongs to Allah﴾ (Qur'ān 10:65).

[61] This means that the Prophet ﷺ was always deep in thought about the affairs of the Muslim community, and what would benefit them and attain for them felicity in this life and the next; and because of this, he had no rest.

[62] This means that he ﷺ would spend long periods of time in silence, not speaking save for a worldly or religious need, avoiding useless speech, in accord with Allah's ﷻ word: ﴿... and those who shun vain

mentioning the name of Allah ﷻ.[63] His speech was a compendium of discourse,[64] and his words were concise and clear, with neither excess nor dearth. He was neither boorish nor feeble.[65] He magnified blessings, no matter how small, and never disparaged them; yet he would neither criticise nor praise the taste of food or drink.[66] The affairs of this worldly life would not make him angry; but if the truth was threatened, no one would recognise him, and nothing would quieten his anger until he had achieved justice.[67] He would never become angry for his own sake, nor would he seek to avenge himself. If he pointed at something, he would point with his whole hand; and if he was pleased by something, he would turn his hand over.[68]

---

speech.﴿ (Qur'ān 23:3) The Prophet ﷺ said: 'Part of the excellence of one's Islam lies in leaving aside that which does not concern one.' (Narrated by Tirmidhī)

[63] I.e. his speech ﷺ was encompassed by the remembrance of Allah, beginning and end.

[64] He would use few words, with much meaning.

[65] I.e. he ﷺ was not coarse and rude, nor did he treat Allah's creatures with contempt; and he was not feeble or obsequious, but rather was stately, and noble, and respected, and revered ﷺ.

[66] He ﷺ would magnify Allah's blessings, both great and small, and manifest and hidden, and would not disparage any of them. Likewise, he ﷺ would never criticise the taste of food or drink that Allah made permissible, because that criticism expresses ingratitude, which is the province of the high-and-mighty, and the arrogant. He would also not praise the taste of food and drink, because that is the way of the gluttonous and the greedy.

[67] I.e. if anyone threatened the truth, and crossed the line into falsehood, it would instil in him ﷺ an insurmountable anger, and nothing would quieten his anger until he had achieved justice by just means.

[68] When he ﷺ pointed at someone or something, he would indicate with his whole hand, not just one finger as is the practice of those who

' "When he spoke, he would gesture with his hand, and strike his left thumb with his right palm.[69] When he was angry, he would turn away with his whole face. When he was happy, he would lower his gaze.[70] His laughter was mostly smiles, revealing something like hailstones.[71]" '

Ḥasan ﷺ said: 'I kept this from Ḥusayn ibn 'Alī for a time, and then told him of it. I found that he had already asked him ('Alī ﷺ) about this before me, and he had also asked him about his way of entering and leaving, and his way of sitting in gatherings ﷺ; and he did not leave out anything.'[72]

---

are arrogant and who look down on others. When he ﷺ was pleased or amazed, he would turn his hand over, as people do in such circumstances.

[69] I.e. he ﷺ would gesture with his right hand when he spoke ﷺ, in order to emphasise his words, and drive his point home, and to further clarify his meaning by gestures. He would strike his left thumb with his right hand to prevent the listener from falling into heedlessness or absent-mindedness.

[70] I.e. when he was angry with someone, he would turn away from them, and he would not confront them with his anger, in accordance with Allah's word: ﴾And turn away from the ignorant ones﴿ (Qur'ān 7:199).
When something pleased him, he would lower his gaze, and would not look at it with greed and desire.

[71] I.e. his laughter was mostly composed of smiling, and his smile was pleasant, revealing his teeth, as white and pure as hailstones.

[72] 'Allāmah Bājūrī said: 'Ḥasan narrated what his brother Ḥusayn heard on their father 'Alī's authority, and so Ḥasan is deemed the direct narrator of what has preceded, on the authority of his uncle Hind; and what follows is his narration on the authority of his father 'Alī, by way of his brother Ḥusayn.'

# HIS DOMESTIC LIFE ﷺ

Ḥusayn said: 'I asked ('Alī) about how the Messenger of Allah ﷺ was when he was at home. He replied: "When he ﷺ went home, he would divide the time he spent there into three parts: one part for Allah,[73] one for his family,[74] and one for himself. He would divide this third part between himself and the people, and this would benefit the generality by means of a select few;[75] and he would keep nothing from them.[76] His custom regarding the part of his time he devoted to his community was to give preference to the people of distinction, and to divide his time according to their religious merit. Some

---

[73] I.e. for devotion to the worship of Allah by prayer, recitation, supplication, reflection, and the like.

[74] I.e. for spending time with his family, and keeping their company, and attending to their needs and requirements.

[75] This means that he ﷺ would divide the part of his time that he kept for himself between himself and the people, and the benefit of this division would reach the generality by means of the select few. The 'select few' means those who were closest to him ﷺ, and who would dedicate themselves to him, of his Companions and family. The 'generality' means those people who were not amongst the select few. The phrase 'and this would benefit the generality by means of a select few' bears several different interpretations: (1) It might mean that the select few alone visited him ﷺ at this time, and then passed on to the generality the teachings and lessons that they heard. (2) 'By means' here (*bi*) might mean 'from' (*min*), i.e. the generality benefited from the portion of time allotted to the select few. (3) It might mean that he ﷺ gave the generality the status of the select few, so that the benefit of the situation would reach the generality rather than the select few.

[76] This means that he ﷺ would not deny the people, both their generality and their elite, anything that would benefit them in their religious and worldly lives; rather, he would always be sure to share it with them.

of them had one need to ask of him, others two, others more;[77] so he would busy himself with them, and would engage them with that which would benefit them, and the whole community, answering their questions, and informing them of what was required of them, saying: 'Let he who is witness to this inform those who are absent; and let me know the need of those who are unable to let me know themselves, for he who informs a ruler of the need of those who cannot speak for themselves will have his feet made firm for him by Allah on the Day of

---

[77] This means that his ﷺ custom was to give preference to the people of distinction, meaning of learning, righteousness and nobility, to whom he ﷺ would give priority in granting his audience. It was also his custom ﷺ to divide his time amongst his community according to their religious merit in respect to righteousness and piety, and according to their religious standing. From amongst the people of distinction and the ordinary people as well, there were those who had one need to ask of him, and others who had two, and others who had more; and so he would busy himself with attending to their needs, and answering their questions. He ﷺ would also engage them with that which would benefit them, and give benefit to the whole community, either by inviting them to ask questions in order to provide them answers, or by telling them that which would benefit them before they asked, and explaining to them what they were required to know of rulings and religious counsel and advice, in order to lead them to righteousness and felicity in this life and the next. In this way, he ﷺ would not let a single moment pass without giving any benefit to the community; and he would not leave his Companions idle, but would engage them with what was good for them, and for the whole community. This is because Allah ﷻ said: ﴿So, when thou art relieved, toil on, and strive towards thy Lord﴾ (Qur'ān 93:7-8), i.e. when you finish one task, move on to the next, and let your intention and your aspiration throughout be directed towards Allah ﷻ. From this it can be seen that the religion of Islam is a religion of hard work and toil, not of idleness and lethargy.

Resurrection.' Nothing else would be mentioned in his presence, and he would not accept anything else from anyone. People would go to him searching, and would not leave except having been granted a taste;[78] they would go out as guides to the good." '

## HIS SOCIAL LIFE OUTSIDE OF THE HOUSE ﷺ

Ḥusayn ؓ said: 'I then asked my father ('Alī ؓ) about what the Prophet's ﷺ customs were when he was out of the house. He replied: "The Messenger of Allah ﷺ would hold his tongue, except in regard to matters that concerned him.[79] He ﷺ would

---

[78] This means that people would visit him in search of what would benefit their religious and worldly lives, and ameliorate their souls, and teach them their way to felicity; and they would not leave except successful, and honoured. The Messenger of Allah ﷺ would honour them by serving them food, out of his hospitality for them; and he ﷺ would honour them with abundant knowledge and teachings, and explain to them what they needed to attend to, of religious and worldly affairs, so they would leave him ﷺ as guides, leading the people to goodness and happiness.

[79] So he ﷺ would not speak unless the matter concerned him, and gave some worldly or religious benefit, as he ﷺ said: 'Part of the excellence of one's Islam lies in leaving aside that which does not concern one.' Those who make good their Islam mind their own business, and leave aside what does not concern them. 'Allāmah Ibn Rajab said, commenting on the aforementioned Ḥadīth: 'The meaning of something "concerning" one is that one's concern be connected to it, and that one need and require it. A 'concern' means an attachment of great importance to something; to say "he is concerned with something" means that he attaches importance to it, and requires it. The meaning is not that caprice and selfish whim be allowed to define what concerns one; rather, what concerns one is defined by the Scared

make people feel comfortable, and would not frighten them off.[80] He would honour the noblemen of every tribe, entrusting their people to them.[81] He would be cautious of people, and be careful around them, without denying any of them his cheery disposition and fine character.[82] He ﷺ would miss his Companions,[83] and ask people about others.[84] He would praise

---

Law of Islam.' Many people fall into the foolishness of involving themselves in what does not concern them. Tirmidhī narrates that Anas ؓ said: 'A man from the Companions of the Prophet ﷺ died, and a man said: "Rejoice in glad tidings of Paradise!" The Prophet ﷺ said: "Are you so sure? Perhaps he spoke about that which did not concern him, or stingily withheld that which he could have done without." ' Tirmidhī pronounced it a sound, singular narration (*hasan gharīb*), and Mundhirī said that its transmitters were all reliable. Several Ḥadīths with the same import have been narrated with numerous chains of transmission, as mentioned in *al-Targhīb wa al-Tarhīb*.

[80] He ﷺ would make them comfortable by his kind companionship and pleasant conversation, and would not frighten them off by being coarse, or harsh, or by using hurtful words. He ﷺ would also make people feel comfortable with one another, and spread love amongst them; and he would not alienate them from one another.

[81] It was of his fine character ﷺ that he would honour the nobleman of a tribe with the generosity and kind welcome that his rank merited; and he ﷺ would place him in a position of authority over his people, and entrust their affairs to him. This was born of his good judgment and acumen, and his appreciation for status.

[82] This indicates his great intellect and expansive mind ﷺ; for he would be cautious around those people who were new to Islam, without testing them with weighty matters; and he would be careful around them, without denying them his kind companionship and pleasant conversation, and his cheery disposition ﷺ.

[83] I.e. he ﷺ would ask about them in their absence.

[84] The meaning of this is that he ﷺ would especially miss his

what was good, and support it; and he would condemn what was vile, and deplore it.[85] He was consistent, never contradictory.[86] He was never inattentive, fearing that the people would be become heedless, or distracted.[87] He was prepared for any

---

Companions, and would also ask after the whole community in general. He would ask those people who knew about others, and about what state they were in, whether good or bad, or in comfort or poverty, or ease or hardship, or happiness or grief; and he ﷺ would be happy with them, and sad with them, and would strive to assist them with their problems. He would also ask about people's behaviour and dealings: were they conducted in an upright manner, or were they tainted with corruption and dishonesty? This was not any kind of spying, which is forbidden; rather, it was in order to distinguish the greater from the lesser, and the perfect from the imperfect, and to be aware of people's affairs in order to correct that which was crooked, and to alert the heedless, and remind the forgetful, and to advise the community how best to cure their spiritual ailments.

[85] So if someone performed a good deed, or had a good idea, he ﷺ would praise it, and support it, and support the aspiration of the one who did it, and champion their decision; and if someone did something base and vile, he ﷺ would mention the baseness of the act, and its hazards, and its bad outcomes, in order to discourage people from falling into it.

[86] This means that all of his words and deeds ﷺ were harmonious and consistent; and he was protected from ever being inconsistent or contradictory. This is evidence of his perfect intellect and meticulousness.

[87] I.e. he ﷺ would not be unmindful of what was beneficial to his followers, reminding them, guiding them, advising them, and teaching them, so that they would not become heedless and so slip up, or become distracted by relaxation and laziness, becoming sluggish in their works. He ﷺ would encourage them to be firm, and urge them on with reminders and advice.

situation.[88] He ﷺ never fell short of the truth, nor went beyond it.[89] The people who were close to him were the best of people; and the finest of them in his sight were the ones who most sincerely advised the people; and the greatest of them in his sight were the ones who were the most beneficent, and helpful."[90]

## HIS CUSTOM WHEN SITTING IN GATHERINGS ﷺ

Ḥusayn said: 'I then asked him ('Alī ﷺ) about his ﷺ gatherings. He replied: "The Messenger of Allah ﷺ would not sit or stand without making mention of Allah ﷻ.[91] He ﷺ would not reserve

---

[88] For every situation that might arise, he was well prepared; and for every eventuality, he was ready with whatever he needed for it, and whatever was required to benefit from it.

[89] So he ﷺ was perfectly upright upon the side of truth, neither negligent nor excessive, neither falling short of the truth nor going beyond it; and this was the case for all of his affairs.

[90] The people who enjoyed close companionship with him were the best of people; and the finest of them in his sight were the ones who most sincerely advised the people, and the ones who most benefited the community in their religious and worldly affairs; and the greatest of them in his sight were the most beneficent and generous to the people in offering their selves and their wealth, and the ones who helped them the most with their concerns, and lessened their burdens, and solved their problems, and met their needs.

[91] This reflects what 'Āisha ﷺ said: 'The Messenger of Allah ﷺ would remember Allah at every moment', i.e. when he stood, and when he sat, and when he lay on his side, as Allah ﷻ said: ﴿When you have performed the prayer, remember Allah standing, sitting, and reclining upon your sides...﴾ (Qur'ān 4:103) Abū Dāwūd narrated on the authority of Abū Hurayra ﷺ that the Prophet ﷺ said: 'Whoever sits

places for himself; and he forbade others from doing so. When he came to a gathering of people, he would sit wherever he found a place, and would command others to do the same.[92] He would give everyone he sat with their share of his company, so that no one he sat with would imagine that anyone was dearer to him than them.[93] If anyone sat down with him, or sought his advice in something, he would bear them patiently, until they were the ones to leave.[94] If someone asked him ﷺ for anything,

---

without making remembrance of Allah owes Allah a debt (to be paid on the Day of Resurrection); and whoever lies down without making remembrance of Allah owes Allah a debt; and no one walks without making remembrance of Allah except that they owe Allah a debt.' This all shows that a Muslim should make remembrance of Allah ﷻ at all times.

[92] According to 'Allāmah Munāwī, this means that he ﷺ would sit wherever there was an empty space; and he would not act as though he were above his Companions, because of his great modesty, and his noble character. This is because the honourable status of a space is defined by the one who occupies it; so whichever place he ﷺ sat in was the most honourable of places. He ﷺ would also tell people to sit wherever they found a space, in order to keep them from arrogance and haughtiness above the rest of the gathering. It is mentioned in *Jam' al-Wasā'il* and elsewhere that Ṭabarānī and Bayhaqī narrated, on the authority of Shayba ibn 'Uthmān, that the Prophet ﷺ said: 'When any of you arrive at a gathering, if space is made for them, let him sit; if not, let him find the widest space he can see, and sit there.'

[93] He ﷺ would give everyone he sat with their share of his company and his cheery disposition, and his hospitality and generosity, so that everyone who sat with him would feel that there was no one dearer to the Messenger of Allah ﷺ than them, because of the kindness and benevolence that they would encounter.

[94] I.e. if someone sat down with the Prophet ﷺ, or sought his counsel, he would be patient with them; rather, his patience would outlast the one who was sitting with him, or seeking his counsel, however long

they would not leave except with either what they asked, or a reassuring word.[95] He accommodated the people with his kindness and good character, and became like a father to them; and before him, they were all equal.[96] His gatherings were gatherings of knowledge,[97] modesty, patience, and security. [98]

---

they spoke for; and he ﷺ would never be the first to stand up and leave, or stop the conversation; and he would not reveal to them any sign of boredom or ennui, but would continue to pay attention to them, until they would be the ones to leave. This is evidence of his accommodating character, and his kind companionship, and his great forbearance ﷺ,

[95] I.e. with a promise from him ﷺ that their need would be fulfilled, or the like.

[96] He granted his kind bearing, and his cheery disposition, and his fine character ﷺ to all the people, and so became like a father to them, out of his loving care for them, and his compassion for them, and his concern for their well-being. Rather, he was more caring and compassionate than a father, and more devoted and loving, and kinder and gentler; for he occupies the position, as mentioned in the Qur'ān: ﴾The Prophet is closer to the believers than their own selves﴿ (Qur'ān 33:6), as we will mention later, if Allah wills.

[97] This means that his ﷺ gatherings and assemblies were filled with the light of the knowledge that the Messenger of Allah ﷺ showered upon the people, and spread amongst them. He ﷺ would teach them the Qur'ān, and clarify its meanings, and explain its rulings and wisdoms; and he would pass on to them all manner of wise words of advice, and guidance to good conduct and exemplary behaviour; and he would tell them stories of the previous communities in order that they might heed the morals thereof.

[98] In this way, his gatherings ﷺ were graced with modesty and reverence, and he ﷺ and his Companions manifested the utmost humility, decorum and serenity. His gatherings ﷺ were also occasions where the coarseness of the Bedouin was borne with patience, as was the stubbornness and importunity of the questioner, and his excessive

Voices were not raised therein,[99] nor were honours affronted,[100] nor were sins committed therein disclosed.[101] The people were

---

questioning, as we saw in the Ḥadīth of Ḍimām, when he said: 'I will ask you strong questions, so do not be angry with me,' and the Prophet ﷺ replied: 'Ask about whatever occurs to you.' His gatherings ﷺ were also gatherings of security, where secrets between those present were kept safe, or concealed for another occasion.

[99] This is because of the severe recompense from which Allah ﷻ warned the believers, saying: ❪O you who believe! Do not raise your voices above the voice of the Prophet, and do not speak loudly to him as you do to one another, lest your works come to naught without your knowing.❫ (Qur'ān 49:2) When this noble verse was revealed, the Companions feared this admonition being applied to them, and so were careful in his ﷺ gatherings to lower their voices, and observe much silence; and they would advise one another to do this, and inform those who were ignorant of it, and remind those who forgot. Tirmidhī, Ibn Ḥibbān, and others narrated, on the authority of Ṣafwān ibn 'Assāl ؓ, that a man from the countryside came to the Messenger of Allah ﷺ, and began to call him with a loud voice: 'O Muḥammad! O Muḥammad!' ﷺ. The people told him to lower his voice, because such an action was forbidden, but he said: 'No, by Allah, not until I make him hear me!' The Prophet ﷺ said to him: 'What is it?' The man replied: 'What do you say about a man who loves some people, but is unable to match them (in their good works)?' The Prophet ﷺ said: 'A person is with those whom he loves.'

[100] This means that people's honours (in such matters as their families and wives) were not disparaged in his gatherings ﷺ, nor were they exposed to defamation or slander or the like. Rather, his gatherings ﷺ were free of any ugly speech and evil act.

[101] The scholars say that this means there were no sins committed in his gatherings ﷺ to begin with, so there were no sins to disclose; rather, the gatherings were places of decorum and virtue. According to this interpretation, the negation refers to 'sins', i.e. there were no sins to be disclosed. Or, it may mean that were any of the guests at the

equal; they would compete for precedence according to their piety.[102] They were humble; revering the elderly, having mercy on the young. They would put the needy first, and take good care of the stranger." '[103]

## HIS ETIQUETTE AND MANNERS WITH THOSE HE SAT WITH ﷺ

Ḥusayn ﷺ said: 'I also asked my father ('Alī ﷺ) about the Prophet's ﷺ manners with those whom he sat with. He replied: ' "The Messenger of Allah ﷺ was always cheery of disposition, easy-going,[104] and compassionate.

---

gathering to commit a sin, it would not be disclosed outside of the gathering; rather, the one who did it would be alerted to it, and it would then be concealed, and never mentioned again.

[102] I.e. everyone was equal to one another, and so no one would hold himself better than another, or look down on another because of his wealth or lineage. Rather, they would compete for precedence in his gatherings ﷺ based on their piety, so the most pious of them would be considered the best of them. One narration reads 'they would treat one another with affection' instead of 'they would compete for precedence'. In this case, according to 'Allāmah Khafājī, it means that they would show one another affection and compassion because of their piety and awareness of Allah, not out of ostentation, or fear of some harm befalling them.

[103] They would put those with needs ahead of themselves, in a closer proximity to the Prophet ﷺ, in order that he would attend to their needs, or answer their questions. They would also put them first by meeting their needs, or helping them to meet them, even if they themselves were also in need; and they would preserve the rights and the dignity of the stranger.

[104] His custom ﷺ was to be relaxed, not severe, in his speech and actions; he ﷺ was not difficult.

' "He was not boorish, or coarse, or raucous, of vulgar, or critical,[105] or niggardly; he did not over-praise or jest,[106] and he would ignore that which he disliked.[107] He would not dash the hopes of anyone who hoped for something from him, and they would not be disappointed.[108] He withheld from himself three things: debate, excess, and that which did not concern him;[109] and he withheld from the people three things: he would never criticise or disparage anyone, and he would not seek to shame anyone,[110] and he would not speak about anything unless he

---

[105] I.e. he ﷺ would not criticise people, animals or food. It is narrated by Bukhārī and Muslim that he ﷺ never criticised any taste, or any food: if he liked it, he would eat it; if not, he would leave it.

[106] He did not over-praise the lawful enjoyments of this world, for this is evidence of a gluttonous soul, and a strong attachment to this world.

[107] Out of kindness and tenderness, he would ignore and pay no mind to any speech or behaviour that he disliked on the part of his Companions at the gathering.

[108] Or 'and he would not disappoint them.' In one narration, it reads 'and he would not answer them concerning it', i.e. concerning what he disliked (from the previous sentence), meaning that he would be silent out of compassion and kindness. (*Jam' al-Wasāil*)

[109] This means that he ﷺ distanced himself from three things: debate and argumentation, except when supporting Allah's religion, and refuting obstinate opponents; for this is the greater *jihād*, as Allah said: ﴿And argue with them in the best way…﴾ (Qur'ān 16:125), and He said: ﴿So obey not the disbelievers, but strive against them with it (the Qur'ān), with the utmost endeavour.﴾ (Qur'ān 25:52) He also refrained from excessive speech; and one narration has it 'grandiosity', i.e. he avoided grandiose speech at all times, as can be seen by considering how he behaved with the people ﷺ. (*Jam' al-Wasāil*)

[110] This means that he ﷺ would never seek to find out anything anyone was ashamed of, such as sins and faults; and he ﷺ would not reveal

hoped to be rewarded (by Allah) for it.[111] When he spoke, his Companions would bow their heads as though upon them were birds;[112] and when he fell silent, they would speak.[113] They would not talk over one another in his presence; they would give their attention to whoever was speaking until he finished,[114] and their discourse in his presence was the discourse of the first of them.[115] He would laugh at what made them laugh, and be amazed at what amazed them.[116]

---

anything about someone that they would rather conceal; and he ﷺ would not seek out people's blemishes and sins.

[111] He ﷺ would often be silent, only speaking if he expected reward from Allah ﷻ for speaking for a reason demanded by the Sacred Law. As for speech for which no reward could be expected, he would avoid it.

[112] I.e. they would put their heads down and look at their chests, and be still and silent, out of awe and respect for him ﷺ. In this they resembled someone balancing a bird on his head that he wishes to trap, careful not to move lest he frighten it away.

[113] This was a manifestation of their perfect etiquette with him ﷺ: they would not speak before him, and they would not speak over him ﷺ.

[114] This is another evidence of the perfect etiquette of the Companions ؄, and their concern for keeping good manners in gatherings. They would not argue in his presence ﷺ, nor would any of them speak over another, nor interrupt them; rather, they would listen to whoever was speaking until he finished.

[115] I.e. the first people to arrive at the gathering would be the first to speak, and then the others would follow in order. Some say that it instead means that whichever of them spoke in his presence ﷺ, they would listen attentively as though he were the first to speak; others say that 'the first of them' means 'the best of them', i.e. the most religious and pious.

[116] He ﷺ did this out of a desire to make them feel comfortable and to gratify their hearts, and out of good companionship.

' "He would bear the coarse speech and questioning of strangers, so that even his Companions would seek their coming.[117] He would say: 'If you see a person in need, help them.' He would never accept praise except that which was appropriate.[118] He would never stop anyone from speaking until they had gone on too long, in which case he would stop them either with a word, or by standing." '[119]

---

[117] I.e. the Companions would seek to bring strangers to the Prophet's gatherings ﷺ so that they could benefit from the questions the strangers would ask.

[118] It is said that this means he ﷺ would not accept praise unless it was balanced, neither exaggerated nor understated. 'Exaggerated' here means to the extent he himself ﷺ clarified in his saying: 'Do not extol me as the Christians extolled 'Isā ibn Maryam, making him the son of Allah, but say instead: "The slave and Messenger of Allah." ' It is also said to mean that he ﷺ would not accept praise except from one he knew to be a true Muslim, whose words reflected his innermost hearts, not from the hypocrites, who said with their mouths what was not in their hearts, praising openly and defaming secretly. It is also said to mean that he ﷺ would not accept praise except from those for whom he had done some good, who praised him as recompense for the favour; and if this were not the case, he would not accept the praise, but would reject it, because Allah ﷻ castigated those who love to be praised for what they have not done, saying: ﴾Think not that those who rejoice in what they have done, and love to be praised for what they have done not – think not that they are safe from chastisement…﴿ (Qur'ān 3:188) (See 'Alī al-Qarī and al-Munāwī's commentary on the *Shamā'il*, and Khafājī's commentary on *al-Shifā*).

[119] Out of his humility ﷺ, and his generosity towards those he sat with, he would not stop anyone from speaking, but would listen to them until they finished, unless they transgressed the limits that Allah prescribed, in which case he would end the conversation by telling them to stop, or by standing up from the gathering.

## HIS SILENCE ﷺ

The narrations of Ṭabarānī and others add that Ḥusayn ؓ said: 'I then asked my father 'Alī ؓ about the Prophet's ﷺ silence. He replied: "He would be silent for four reasons: forbearance, caution, appreciation, and reflection.[120] As for his appreciation ﷺ, it was in the form of looking and listening to all the people equally. As for his reflection, it was upon that which ends, and that which is eternal.

' "Forbearance and patience were embodied in him ﷺ,[121] and nothing would anger him, or agitate him. Caution was manifested in him regarding four things: he would accept what was good so that he would be followed; and he would leave aside that which was bad so that it would be avoided; and he would strive to arrive at what was good for his community; and he would work to accumulate for them this world and the next." '[122]

Any intelligent person who reflects on the perfect attributes, and exceptional characteristics, and praiseworthy qualities, and

---

[120] One narration has it 'making judgements, caution, pondering, and reflection.'

[121] One narration has it: 'forbearance was embodied in him by patience'. Khafājī explains this to mean that because of his forbearance ﷺ, he was patient, never becoming exasperated or tense.

[122] This means that he ﷺ would expend his best efforts for the good of the community, and combine for them the goodness and felicity of this world and the next. Zabīdī said in *Sharḥ al-Iḥyā* that this Ḥadīth was narrated by Tirmidhī in *al-Shamā'il* and by Baghawī, and by Ṭabarānī, and by Bayhaqī in *al-Dalā'il*, and by Ibn Mandah, with several chains of transmission. Ḥāfiẓ Dhahabī also narrated it in *Tārīkh al-Islām* with several chains of transmission; and Ḥāfiẓ Ibn Kathīr ascribed it in *al-Bidāya* to Ṭabarānī.

unquestionable merits, which were embodied in our Master Muḥammad ﷺ, and which manifested in their perfect forms, must realise with certainty that our Master Muḥammad ﷺ is not an ordinary human being like the rest of humanity: he has been specially chosen by the Lord of the worlds, who has gifted him with these extraordinary attributes, and singled him out above all others with these outstanding virtues.

He is the Prophet and Messenger of Allah ﷺ. All this is not down to the work of artisans, or the wisdom of sages, or the nobility of aristocrats; it is down to the fact that he is the Messenger of Allah, and the Seal of the Prophets, may Allah's benedictions and salutations be upon him, and upon them all!

## SOME ASPECTS OF HIS GENERAL DECORUM AND DIGNIFIED BEARING ﷺ

The Messenger of Allah ﷺ was the most dignified and refined of people, and the most eminent and noble.

Abū Dāwūd narrated in his *Marāsīl* that Khārija ibn Zayd al-Anṣārī ؓ said: 'The Messenger of Allah ﷺ was the most dignified person in any gathering he attended; he showed almost nothing of himself.'

The scholars explain this to mean that he ﷺ would not reveal any part of his noble body, out of dignity. 'Allāmah Qārī said that it means that he ﷺ would not expel anything from his nose or mouth, or cut his nails.

Ibn Mājah narrated that Ismā'īl said: 'We visited Ḥasan (al-Baṣrī) in a group so large that we filled the house. He drew his legs up, and said that he had once visited Abū Hurayra in a group so large that they filled the house, and so he too drew up his legs, saying: "We once visited the Messenger of Allah ﷺ in a group so large that we filled the house. He ﷺ was reclining on his side, but when he saw us he drew up his legs, and said: 'People will come to you after me, seeking knowledge; so welcome them, and greet them, and teach them.' " '[123]

## HIS FAVOURING OF THE ELDERLY WITH HIS CONVERSATION ﷺ

Out of respect and honour for their status, the Messenger of Allah ﷺ would give preference to the elderly who wished to converse with him and ask him questions.

Bukhārī narrated, on the authority of Sahl ibn Abī Ḥathma, that a delegation including 'Abd al-Raḥmān ibn Sahl, and Ḥuwayyiṣa and Muḥayyiṣa, the sons of Mas'ūd, came to the Prophet ﷺ, saying to him: 'O Messenger of Allah! We went to Khaybar, and found that one of our own had been killed!' 'Abd al-Raḥmān, the youngest of the group, was the first to speak, and so the Prophet ﷺ said: 'Let the eldest begin' (one narration has it that he ﷺ said: 'Honour the eldest'), i.e. 'let the one who is older than you speak'.

Aḥmad narrated in his *Musnad*, on the authority of Ibn 'Abbās, that the Prophet ﷺ said: 'The one who does not revere the elderly, nor have mercy on the young, nor command what is good, nor forbid what is evil, is not one of us.'

---

[123] See the introduction of the *Sunan* collection of Ibn Mājah on the merits of knowledge. The author of *al-Zawā'id* said that the chain of transmission of this Ḥadīth is weak (*ḍa'īf*).

# THE RESPECT HE WOULD SHOW TO THE MERITORIOUS ﷺ

Ibn ʿAbbās ؓ reported that the Messenger of Allah ﷺ said: 'Blessed increase lies with your leaders.' (Bazzār's narration has it: 'Goodness lies with your betters.')[124]

This means that blessed increase lies with those who lead the people in religion and knowledge, as is borne out by the Ḥadīth narrated by ʿUbāda ibn al-Ṣāmit ؓ in which the Messenger of Allah ﷺ said: 'The one who does not respect our elderly, nor have mercy on our young, nor acknowledge the due of our scholars, is not from my community.'[125]

One manifestation of this was the reverence and respect that he ﷺ showed his uncle ʿAbbās ؓ, and the pride that he felt for him, which he ﷺ announced to his Companions in order that they follow his example.

Ṭabarānī narrated, with a sound chain of transmission on the authority of Umm al-Faḍl, that ʿAbbās went to the Prophet ﷺ, and when he saw him, he ﷺ stood up and kissed him between the eyes, and sat him down on his right, and then said: 'This is my uncle; let he who wills be proud of his uncle!' ʿAbbās said: 'What fine speech is this, O Messenger of Allah!'

---

[124] Narrated by Ibn Ḥibbān, who declared it rigorously authentic, and by Bayhaqī, and by Ḥākim in *al-Mustadrak*, who said: 'It is rigorously authentic according to the conditions of Muslim, as was mentioned in *al-Targhīb* in the section on etiquette. It was also narrated by Bazzār and Ṭabarānī. The chain of transmission of Bazzār contains Ḥammād, who was declared reliable by many, although he has some weakness; the rest of the narrators are rigorously authenticated.'

[125] Narrated by Aḥmad and Ṭabarānī with a sound chain of transmission. (*Majmaʿ al-Zawāʾid*)

Ḥākim narrated, on the authority of Ibn ʻUmar ﷺ, that ʻUmar sought rain by means of ʻAbbās, saying: ʻO Allah, this is the uncle of Your Prophet; we turn to You through him, so send us rain!' They had not departed before they were granted rain.

ʻUmar then gave a sermon, saying: ʻO People! The Messenger of Allah ﷺ treated ʻAbbās like a son treats his father: he would revere him, and honour him, and validate his oaths. Follow the example of the Messenger of Allah ﷺ regarding his uncle, ʻAbbās, and take him as an intermediary[126] between you and Allah, in whatever befalls you.'[127]

The Companions ﷺ would treat ʻAbbās with honour and respect, following the example of the Messenger of Allah ﷺ. Ḥāfiẓ Ibn ʻAbd al-Barr narrated that Ibn Shihāb said: ʻThe Companions would acknowledge the merit of ʻAbbās, and give him precedence, and seek his advice, and follow his counsel.' He also narrated that Abū al-Zinād said: "ʻAbbās never passed by ʻUmar and ʻUthmān whilst they were riding except that – out of respect for him – they dismounted and waited until he had passed, saying: "The uncle of the Messenger of Allah ﷺ!" '

ʻAbbās, too, showed the Prophet ﷺ great respect and reverence: Ibn Abī ʻĀṣim narrated on the authority of Abū Razīn, and Baghawī narrated on the authority of Ibn ʻUmar, that ʻAbbās was asked who was older,[128] he or the Prophet ﷺ. He replied: ʻHe is older than me, and I was born before him.'[129]

---

126 *Wasīla.*

127 Part of this Ḥadīth was also narrated by Bukhārī in his *Saḥīḥ* collection.

128 ʻOlder' in Arabic (*akbar*) has many connotations other than age; it can mean ʻbigger', ʻgreater', ʻgrander', etc, which serves to explain ʻAbbās' response. [t]

129 See *al-Iṣāba*, and *Sharḥ al-Zurqānī ʻalā al-Mawāhib.*

It is mentioned in *al-Iṣāba* that al-Sha'bī reported that Zayd ibn Thābit ؓ was about to mount his horse, and so Ibn 'Abbās ؓ took hold of the stirrup for him. Zayd said: 'Stand back, O nephew of the Messenger of Allah ﷺ!' Ibn 'Abbās replied: 'Nay, such is how we treat our scholars and leaders!'[130]

Ṭabarānī narrated that Abū Umāma ؓ said: 'The Messenger of Allah ﷺ was once with a group of his Companions, including Abū Bakr, 'Umar, and Abū 'Ubayda ibn al-Jarrāḥ, when a beverage was brought for them to drink. The Messenger of Allah ﷺ offered it to Abū 'Ubayda, who said: "You should come before me, O Prophet of Allah!" The Prophet ﷺ said: "Take it", so Abū 'Ubayda took the vessel, and before he had drunk, said: "Take it, O Prophet of Allah!" "Drink", said the Prophet ﷺ, "for blessed increase lies with our leaders; and the one who does not have mercy on our young, nor revere our elderly, is not one of us." '[131]

The Prophet ﷺ wanted to honour Abū 'Ubayda, and so he gave him the vessel first, and praised him, saying: 'Blessed increase lies with our leaders.'

Abū Dāwūd narrated, on the authority of Abū Mūsā ؓ, that the Messenger of Allah ﷺ said: 'Glorifying Allah entails certain things, among them: honouring the white-haired Muslim and the one who memorises the Qur'ān, being neither excessive therein nor neglectful; and honouring the just ruler.'

---

[130] Narrated by Ṭabarānī; the transmitters are all rigorously authenticated, except for Razīn al-Ramānī, who is reliable. (*Majma' al-Zawā'id*, 9:345)

[131] Narrated by Ṭabarānī; the chain of transmission contains 'Alī ibn Yazīd al-Alhānī, who is weak. (*Majma' al-Zawā'id, Kitāb al-Adab*)

# HIS PRAISE ﷺ OF WHAT WAS GOOD AND HIS ENCOURAGEMENT OF THOROUGHNESS IN WORK

The Messenger of Allah ﷺ would always commend and praise anything good, honouring those who did good works, and inspiring them to strive further; and he would condemn and reject anything deplorable.

Yaḥyā ibn al-Jazzār reported that a group of the Companions of the Messenger of Allah ﷺ went to Umm Salama ؓ, and said: 'O Mother of the Believers, tell us about the private life of the Messenger of Allah ﷺ.' She replied: 'His private and public lives are identical.' Then, she regretted what she had said, saying: 'I have disclosed the secret of the Messenger of Allah ﷺ!' When the Messenger of Allah ﷺ came home, she told him what she had done, and he said: 'You did well!'[132]

Ibn Ḥibbān narrated in his *Ṣaḥīḥ* collection that Ṭalq ibn ʿAlī al-Ḥanafī[133] said: 'I participated in the building of the mosque with the Messenger of Allah ﷺ. I began to shovel the clay mixture, and this seemed to please him, for he said: "Leave the clay to al-Ḥanafī, for he is the most skilled of you all with it." '

Ibn Saʿd narrates in his *Ṭabaqāt* that Ṭalq said: 'I approached the Prophet ﷺ whilst he was building his mosque and the Muslims were working alongside him. I was skilled in preparing and mixing clay, and so I took up the spade and began to mix it. The Messenger of Allah ﷺ looked at me, and said: "This Ḥanafī is skilled with clay!" '[134]

---

[132] Narrated by Aḥmad and Ṭabarānī; its narrators are all rigorously authenticated. (*Majmaʿ al-Zawāʾid*)

[133] Of the tribe of Banū Ḥanīfa

[134] See *al-Tarātīb*.

The Prophet ﷺ would encourage precision and excellence in any work; 'Ā'isha ﵂ reported that he ﷺ said: 'Allah Almighty loves that, if any of you do any work, he excels therein.'[135] Bayhaqī narrated, on the authority of Shihāb, that the Prophet ﷺ said: 'Allah Almighty loves for the worker to excel in his craft.'[136]

## HIS SEEKING ﷺ OF HIS COMPANIONS' COUNSEL

Allah ﷻ said: ﴾Seek their counsel in the conduct of affairs; and when thou art resolved, put thy trust in Allah. Allah loves those who put their trust (in Him).﴿[137] By this, Allah commanded His Prophet ﷺ to seek counsel in those matters that still required consultation. The language of the verse implied that only after this consultation had led his heart to be resolved on a certain course was he to take that course, and trust in Allah. Allah ﷻ commanded His Prophet ﷺ to seek counsel from the sagacious and wise of his Companions in such matters as required it, despite the fact that their intellects compared with his ﷺ were as the light of a distant star is compared to the brightness of the midmorning sun; and there are several underlying reasons as to why He did this:

**Firstly**, it was to lift their spirits, so that if they followed a particular course (in war, for example), they would do so willingly, with high spirits. Qatāda said: 'Allah ﷻ commanded His Prophet ﷺ to consult his Companions, even though he was

---

[135] Ascribed in *al-Jāmi' al-Ṣaghīr* to Bayhaqī. 'Allāmah Munāwī said: 'It was also narrated by Abū Ya'lā, Ibn 'Asākīr, and others.'

[136] Narrated thus in *al-Jāmi' al-Ṣaghīr*, with an indication of the weakness of its chain of transmission.

[137] Qur'ān 3:159

visited by Divine Revelation, because it served better to lift the people's spirits.'

**Secondly**, it was to strengthen their opinions, for if their opinions were in agreement with his ﷺ, they would derive strength from him. Imām Aḥmad narrated, on the authority of 'Abd al-Raḥmān ibn Ghanam, that the Messenger of Allah ﷺ said to Abū Bakr and 'Umar: 'If you two were to agree with one another in your counsel, I would not disagree with you.'

**Thirdly**, it was so that such would be the practice of his community after him ﷺ. Bayhaqī narrated that Ḥasan ؓ said, commenting on this verse: 'Allah ﷻ knew that His Messenger ﷺ had no need of them, but He wanted those who came after him to follow his example.' Ibn 'Udayy and Bayhaqī[138] narrated with a sound chain of transmission that Ibn 'Abbās ؓ said: 'When the verse ❮Seek their counsel...❯ was revealed, the Messenger of Allah ﷺ said: "Indeed, Allah and His Messenger have no need for this, but Allah Almighty ordained it as a mercy to my community; whosoever seeks their counsel will not be bereft of guidance, and whosoever leaves it will not be free of error.'

**Fourthly**, the seeking of counsel shows appreciation for the one consulted, and acknowledges their position, and gives them the freedom to express their opinion. The one consulted feels that he is respected, and that he has a responsibility to live up to as a sincere advisor. In contrast, autocracy fails to recognise people of wisdom and sagacity, and makes slaves out of free men. Because of this, the Prophet ﷺ would often seek the counsel of his Companions. Shāfi'ī narrated that Abū Hurayra ؓ said: 'I never saw anyone more frequently in consultation with their Companions than the Messenger of Allah ﷺ.'

---

[138] In *al-Shu'ab*

**Fifthly**, consultation is a means of surveying different opinions, and strengthening minds and intellects; and by its means there can be ascertained the measure of a man, and the extent of his knowledge and experience.

## HIS ENJOINING ﷺ OF THE SEEKING OF COUNSEL

The Prophet ﷺ would encourage and enjoin the seeking of counsel. 'Ā'isha reported that the Messenger of Allah ﷺ said: 'The one who seeks counsel is in need, and the one from whom counsel is sought is in a position of trust; so if counsel is sought from any of you, let his advice be that which he himself would do.'[139] As the scholars have said, *counsel* means to extract the finest and purest notions from the innermost heart, just as beekeepers extract honey.[140] One tradition has it: 'Prune your intellects with conversation; and seek help in your affairs with consultation.' The scholars have stated that a person suitable to be asked for his advice and counsel must be trustworthy, respected, sincere, and self-possessed, and must not be conceited, fickle, or dishonest. Some scholars also add that he must not be overly interested in the matter concerning which his counsel is sought, lest they be swayed by his passions; and he must not be ascetical, for he who does not know of this world cannot be asked to give counsel concerning it; and he must not be infatuated with this world, for this will corrupt his opinions; and he must not be miserly.[141] Abū Mas'ūd reported

---

[139] Narrated by al-'Askarī; its essential content is in the *Sunan*.

[140] This comparison is arrived at by dint of the verbs in both cases having derived from the same root in Arabic. [t]

[141] See the fourth volume of *Sharḥ al-Mawāhib* for details of all of this; the author also mentions that counsel should be sought before the

that the Prophet ﷺ said: 'The one from whom counsel is sought is in a position of trust, and he has a choice:[142] if he wishes, he may speak; and if he wishes, he may be silent. If he should speak, he must exert great effort in reaching his opinion.'[143] Ṭabarānī narrated, on the authority of Anas ﷺ, that the Prophet ﷺ said: 'He who seeks guidance will not be disappointed; and he who seeks counsel will not regret it.'[144]

## HE ﷺ WOULD ACKNOWLEDGE SOUND IDEAS AND ACT UPON THEM

The Messenger of Allah ﷺ would acknowledge the soundness of any good idea anyone would present to him, and would let it be known to all. By doing so he would ennoble the one who had come up with the idea, and encourage them, and put value on their knowledge. This shows that he ﷺ was sensitive to the wisdom and purpose of ideas, and the potential outcomes they could have, and so he would acknowledge those of them that were sound, and reject those that were deficient. Ibn Sa'd narrated in his *Ṭabaqāt* that on the day of Qurayẓa and Naḍīr, the Prophet ﷺ sought counsel, and al-Ḥubāb ibn al-Mundhir said: 'I think that we should take up positions

---

guidance prayer of *Istikhāra* is performed, as is also mentioned in *al-Madkhal.*

[142] Except in cases where it is essential that he give counsel, such as if some harm will befall the one who seeks his counsel should he withhold it.

[143] Narrated by Imām Aḥmad; its essential content is also narrated in the four *Sunan* collections.

[144] Narrated by Ṭabarānī in *al-Awsaṭ* with a very weak (*ḍa'īf jiddan*) chain of transmissions; however the Ḥadīth has several other variant narrations that strengthen it, as mentioned in *Majma' al-Zawā'id, al-Jāmi' al-Ṣaghīr*, and *Sharḥ al-Mawāhib.*

between the fortresses, so we prevent each faction from communicating with the other.' The Prophet ﷺ acted in accordance with this advice.[145]

Ṭabarānī narrated that Nubaysha al-Khayr went to see the Messenger of Allah ﷺ whilst he was holding several prisoners of war, and said to him: 'O Messenger of Allah, either treat them kindly, or ransom them.' The Prophet ﷺ replied: 'You have enjoined what is good, O Nushayba al-Khayr!'[146] Ṭabarānī and Sa'īd ibn Manṣūr narrate, on the authority of Ṭalḥa, the Prophet ﷺ said: 'O 'Amr, you are indeed a man of sound judgement regarding Islam.'

## HIS LOVE ﷺ OF BEAUTIFUL NAMES AND HIS DISLIKE OF UGLY ONES

The Prophet ﷺ loved good and beautiful names for Muslims, and disliked for them to have bad and ugly names, desiring that Muslims be honoured above being known by ugly names, or called ugly names, or having ugly names ascribed to them, whether as a name, a title, or an agnomen. Ṭabarānī and Abū Ya'lā narrated, on the authority of Ḥanẓala ibn Hizyam ؓ, that the Prophet liked for a man to be called by whichever of his names and agnomens was most beloved to him.[147] This is because it honours people, and spreads mutual love and understanding, and makes people feel happy and at ease.

---

[145] See *al-Ṭabaqāt,* 3:567.

[146] Narrated by Ṭabarānī with a sound chain of transmission. (*Majma' al-Zawā'id*)

[147] Also narrated by Ibn Qāni' in *Mu'jam al-Ṣaḥāba*, and by al-Bāwardī; its chain of transmission is sound. Munāwī reported that al-Haythamī said: 'The narrators of Ṭabarānī are reliable.' (*al-Jāmi' al-Ṣaghīr*)

**The Prophet ﷺ enjoined the beautification of names:** Abū Dāwūd and Ibn Ḥibbān narrated, on the authority of Abū al-Dardā' ؓ, that the Messenger of Allah ﷺ said: 'You will all be called on the Day of Resurrection by your names, and the names of your fathers; so give yourselves good names.'[148] 'Allāmah Munāwī said:

> This Ḥadīth does not contradict the narration of Ṭabarānī in which it is stated that people will be called (at the Resurrection) by the names of their mothers, Allah ﷻ thereby concealing His servants from one another, because it is possible to reconcile both reports by saying that those whose lineage is sound will be called by their fathers names, and all others will be called by their mother's names. In this way, some have combined the two reports. This explanation is not sound in my opinion, however, because to call those with sound lineage by their father's names and those with unsound lineage by their mother's names would be to reveal those born illegitimately, and so the whole purpose of concealment would be lost, and shameful things would be exposed. Therefore, it is preferable to say that the tradition that states they will be called by their mother's names is weak, and so it does not constitute any contradiction to the rigorously authenticated report.

Abū Wahb al-Jushamī ؓ, who was one of the Companions, reported that the Messenger of Allah ﷺ said: 'Give yourselves the names of the Prophets; and the most beloved names to

---

[148] Also narrated by Imām Aḥmad. Nawawī said in *al-Adhkār*: 'Its chain of transmission is good (*jayyid*)'; Munāwī reported that al-Zayn al-'Irāqī concurred.

Allah are 'Abdullāh[149] and 'Abd al-Raḥmān[150], and the most sincere of them are Ḥārith[151] and Hammām[152], and the vilest of them are Ḥarb[153] and Murra[154].' Ḥāfiẓ Mundhirī said:

> It was narrated by Abū Dāwūd with this wording, and by Nasā'ī. *Ḥārith* and *Hammām* are the most sincere of names because a ploughman is one who earns by working, and someone who aspires is always intending to do something or other; and no person is bereft of these two attributes.

In other words, the meanings of these two names are manifested in everyone, because everyone first aspires – and aspiration is the beginning of desire – to do something, and then actually sets about doing it; and this concept of earning is expressed in the name *Ḥārith*, and so the two names are manifested. A noble name suggests the nobility of the one to whom the name is given, and for this reason the Messenger of Allah ﷺ would change ugly names to handsome ones. 'Ā'isha ؓ said: 'The Messenger of Allah ﷺ would change ugly names.' Ibn 'Umar ؓ related that one of 'Umar's daughters had been given the name *'Āṣiya*,[155] and so the Messenger of Allah ﷺ gave her the name *Jamīla*.[156]

---

[149] *The servant of Allah*

[150] *The servant of the All-Merciful*

[151] *Ploughman*

[152] *One who aspires*

[153] *War*

[154] *Bitter*

[155] *Rebellious*

[156] *Beautiful.* The Ḥadīth was narrated by Tirmidhī, who declared it sound; Muslim narrated it in an abridged form.

# HIS ﷺ LOVE OF GOOD OMENS AND DISLIKE OF EVIL OMENS

Bukhārī narrated, on the authority of Anas ؓ, that the Prophet ﷺ said: 'There is no contagion, and no ill omen; and the good omen that delights me is the pleasant word.' The author of *al-Nihāya* said:

> An 'ill omen' is something that inspires pessimism. The origin of the word is derived from the practice of foreboding based on the leftward or rightward movements of birds and gazelles and the like.[157] This would restrict the pagans Arabs from carrying out their intended plans. The Sacred Law prohibited and annulled this practice, and informed us that no good or ill can come from these omens. The words *ṭiyara* and *fa'l* both mean 'omen'; *fa'l* can mean either a good or bad portent, whilst *ṭiyara* generally means a bad one. It is also said that *ṭiyara* is the word for the genus as a whole, whilst *fa'l* is a particular kind of omen.[158]

This is suggested by the Ḥadīth narrated by Bukhārī, on the authority of Abū Hurayra ؓ, in which the Messenger of Allah ﷺ said: 'There are no omens (*ṭiyara*); and the best of them is the good omen (*fa'l*).' The people said: 'What is a good omen, O Messenger of Allah?' He replied: 'A good word that one of you might hear.'

---

[157] Azharī said: 'The Arabs would scare up birds, and then derive an ill omen if they flocked to the left, and a good omen if they flocked to the right.'

[158] In the above Ḥadīth, the word *ṭiyara* is used for *ill omen*, and the word *fa'l* for *good omen*. [t]

In *al-Mirqāt*, the Prophet's ﷺ statement 'and the best of them is the good omen' is explained as meaning that the best form of omen in its general linguistic sense, as derived from its original meaning, is the good omen. To summarise, we can say that the Prophet ﷺ was pleased by good omens, i.e. pleasing words that give tidings of good.

Tirmidhī narrated that Anas ؓ said: 'The Prophet ﷺ would delight, if he went out to fulfil some need, to hear the words: *O guided one, O successful one!*' So seeking good portents and glad tidings is praiseworthy according to the Sacred Law, such as for the one who is searching for something to hear *O you who has found* or the merchant to hear *O prosperous one*, or for the traveller to hear *O secure one*, or for the one in need to hear *O successful one*, or for the warrior to hear *O victorious one*, or for the pilgrim to hear *O blessed one*, or for the visitor of sacred places to hear *O accepted one*, and so on.[159]

As for the seeking of ill omens and grave portents, it is prohibited by the Sacred Law. Imām Aḥmad narrated in his *Musnad*, with a sound chain of transmission, that Ibn 'Abbās ؓ said: 'The Messenger of Allah ﷺ would seek good omens, and would not seek ill ones; and he loved beautiful names.'

Bukhārī narrated, on the authority of Abū Hurayra ؓ, that the Messenger of Allah ﷺ said: 'There is no contagion, and no ill omen, and no *hāma*, and no *ṣafar*; yet flee from the leper as you flee from the lion.' With these words, the Messenger of Allah ﷺ negated that the affects of contagion are intrinsic to its nature, and that its affects are inevitable, as they believed in the pre-Islamic times of ignorance, and explained that contagion is only a cause, whilst the true agent of causality is Allah alone.

---

[159] See *al-Mirqāt,* and elsewhere.

Bukhārī narrated that the Prophet ﷺ said: 'There is no contagion, and no *hāma*, and no *ṣafar*.' A Bedouin man said: 'O Messenger of Allah, what about the camel that runs upon the sand like a gazelle, but when it mixes with the mangy camel, it catches its mange?' The Prophet ﷺ replied: 'And who infected the first?'

Contagion is a cause, but it does not have any intrinsic affect; rather, it affects by the leave and will of Allah ﷻ, and by His power and design. For this reason, the Prophet ﷺ said: 'flee from the leper as you flee from the lion', i.e. beware lest contagion afflict you by Allah's leave and decree.

Those with deep knowledge of Allah say: 'Causes are the hosts of the Lord of Lords, who administers them according to His power, His will, and His wisdom; and He is the true cause.'

The Prophet's ﷺ statement 'there is no ill omen' means that ill omens do not in any way give us cause to fear the worst. Some say that the negation here actually represents a prohibition, and so the statement means 'do not pay heed to ill omens.'

*Hāma* is a name for a particular bird, also called a *ṣadā* (likely an owl), that people used to consider a bad omen. It is a large bird, which has poor eyesight during the day, and comes out at night, and has a distinctive cry, and lives amongst ruins; another name for it is the *bawm*. This is one of the explanations that Imām Nawawī gave for the word *hāma*.

The second explanation is that the Arabs used to believe that the bones of a dead person, or his soul, would become this kind of bird, and fly away. This is the explanation that most of the scholars give, and it is the well-known opinion.

It may be that both explanations are correct; certainly, they are both erroneous beliefs.[160]

As for *Ṣafar*, Abū Dāwūd narrated that Mālik was asked about this statement, and replied: 'the people of the pre-Islamic time of ignorance would allow fighting in the month of *Ṣafar* one year, and make it inviolable the next, and so the Prophet ﷺ said: '...and (there is) no *Ṣafar*.'[161]

The Prophet ﷺ gave guidance to a man who had a vision of something he disliked, and perhaps took a bad portent from it, telling him to say: 'O Allah, none brings forth goodness but You, and none wards off evil but You, and there is no power nor might save with You.'[162]

Imām Aḥmad narrated, on the authority of Ibn 'Amr ؓ, that the Messenger of Allah ﷺ said: 'Whoever allows an ill omen to keep him from his need has associated partners (with Allah).'

The people asked what the expiation for such an act was, and so the Prophet ﷺ replied: 'Say: "O Allah, there is no goodness but Your goodness, and no omen but Your omen, and no god but You."'[163]

---

[160] *Al-Mirqāt*.

[161] It is also said that *ṣafar* here means a disease of the stomach, which the Arabs believed to be highly contagious. (See *Fatḥ al-Bārī*) [t]

[162] Narrated by Abū Dāwūd in his *Sunan*.

[163] Narrated by Aḥmad and Ṭabarānī; its chain of transmission contains Ibn Lahība, whose narrations are sound, although he has some weakness; the rest of its narrators are reliable. The like of it was also narrated by Bazzār on the authority of Abū Hurayra ؓ and Burayda ؓ. (*Majma' al-Zawā'id*)

# HIS PREFERENCE ﷺ FOR USING THE RIGHT-HAND SIDE AT ALL TIMES

Bukhārī and Muslim narrated that 'Āisha ﵂ said: 'The Prophet ﷺ liked to use the right-hand side when putting on his shoes, and parting his hair, and making ablutions, and in all of his affairs.' The narration of Muslim has it: 'The Messenger of Allah ﷺ loved to use the right-hand side as much as he was able: when making ablutions, and putting on his shoes, and parting his hair, and in all his affairs.'

'Preferring the use of the right-hand side' means to begin all actions with the right hand where use of the hand is involved, and with the right foot where use of the feet is involved, and with the right side where the action is concerned with sides.[164]

The scholars have explained that the wisdom behind this is that it is a means of honouring the right, and seeking a good omen, for the Companions of the Right are the denizens of Paradise, who will be given their accounts in their right hands: their light shining out before them and on their right hands.

By this, the extent of his ﷺ arrangement and guidance in the matter of direct actions is manifested. In a direct action, either the left or the right hand must be used, and so the Messenger of Allah ﷺ removed any ambiguity from the matter, and established the practice of beginning with the right, and preferred it to the left for the reasons just mentioned. He ﷺ would begin with the right when making ablutions, both in the lesser and greater ablutions and in the dry ablution, and when parting his noble hair and beard ﷺ,[165] and when putting on his shoes.

---

[164] Such as sleeping or parting the hair. [t]

[165] *Jam' al-Wasā'il*

Abū Dāwūd's narration adds: '… and when he cleaned his teeth ﷺ, and in all his affairs.' Nasā'ī's narration has it: 'The Messenger of Allah ﷺ loved to use the right-hand side: he would take with his right hand, and give with his right hand, and loved to use the right-hand side in everything he did.'

The generality of his ﷺ beginning with the right hand side in all his affairs, as Imām Nawawī and others have said, is interpreted to mean all things in which there was either honour or adornment, such as giving and taking, and entering the mosque and the house, and cutting the hair and trimming the moustache, and trimming the nails, and plucking underarm hair, and applying kohl, and reclining, and eating and drinking.[166] As for that in which there was involved neither honour nor adornment, but rather removal, he ﷺ would use the left hand, which was also a means of honouring the right. This is attested to by the narration of Abū Dāwūd, on the authority of 'Ā'isha ؓ: 'The Messenger of Allah ﷺ used his right hand for performing ablutions and eating; and he used his left hand when answering the call of nature or removing any harmful thing.'

He also narrated, in his section on purity, that Ḥafṣa, the wife of the Prophet ﷺ said: 'The Prophet ﷺ would use his right hand for his food, drink, and clothes; and he would use his left hand for other things.' He also narrated, on the authority of Abū Qatāda, that the Prophet ﷺ said: 'If any of you urinates, let him not touch his private parts with his right hand; and if he answers the call of nature, let him not clean himself with his right hand; and if he drinks, let him not drink in a single gulp.' He ﷺ would enjoin the use of the right hand when eating and drinking, and giving and taking, and would prohibit the use of the left hand for those things.

---

[166] See *Jam' al-Wasā'il,* and elsewhere.

Ibn Mājah narrated, with a rigorously authenticated chain of transmission on the authority of Abū Hurayra ؓ, that the Prophet ﷺ said: 'Let each of you eat with his right hands, and drink with his right hands, and take with his right hand, and give with his right hand; for Satan eats with his left hand, and drinks with his left hand, and gives with his left hand, and takes with his left hand.'

Muslim narrated, on the authority of Ibn 'Umar ؓ, that the Messenger of Allah ﷺ said: 'Let none of you eat with his left hand, nor drink with his left hand, for Satan eats with his left hand, and drinks with it.' He ﷺ would also serve people from the right side, saying: 'The right, and then the right.' Bukhārī and Muslim narrated that Anas ؓ reported that he saw the Messenger of Allah ﷺ drinking milk in his (Anas') house. Anas said: 'And so I milked an ewe, and mixed the milk with some water from the well, and gave it to the Messenger of Allah ﷺ. He took the jug and drank. To his left was Abū Bakr, and to his right was a Bedouin man, and so the Messenger of Allah ﷺ gave to the Bedouin man first, and then said: 'The right, and then the right!' In another narration, he ﷺ said: 'Those on the right, and then those on the right'; in another: 'Prefer the right.' Ḥāfiẓ Ibn Ḥajar al-'Asqalānī said in *Fatḥ al-Bārī:*

> This means that the one who drinks should pass the drink on to the person on his right, and the next person to the one on his right, and so on. This action is recommended (*mustaḥabb*) according to all; Ibn Ḥazm deemed it obligatory.[167]

The elder of a group, or the best of them, or their leader, should be served first, and then those on his right hand side should follow.

---

[167] *Fatḥ al-Bārī* 12:188

# HIS DISLIKE ﷺ OF USING CERTAIN WORDS BECAUSE OF THEIR AMBIGUOUS OR NEGATIVE CONNOTATIONS

Bukhārī and Muslim narrate in their *Ṣaḥīḥ* collections, on the authority of 'Āisha ؓ, that the Prophet ﷺ said: 'Let none of you say: *khabuthat nafsī*, instead, say: *laqisat nafsī*.'

In Abū Dāwūd's narration, the Prophet ﷺ cautioned against the use of the phrase *ja'shat nafsī*.

These three phrases all have the same meaning according to Imām Nawawī and Imām Abū Sulaymān al-Khaṭṭābī; they mean 'I feel nauseous' or 'I feel sick'.

The reason the Prophet ﷺ disliked the use of the two terms is that they have negative connotations: the verb *khabuthat* being derived from a root with the meaning 'filthy'.

The Prophet ﷺ was teaching his Companions to use more pleasant phrases, and not to associate themselves with disagreeable phrases, for the sake of their dignity.

Another example of this is his ﷺ forbidding a slave to refer to his master as 'my lord' (*rabbī*), instead enjoining him to say 'my master' (*sayyidī*) or 'my liege' (*mawlay*).

He ﷺ also forbade the master from referring to his slaves as 'my slave' (*'abdī*), instead enjoining him to say 'my boy' or 'my girl' (*ghulāmī* or *jāriyatī*, or *fatāy*, or *fatātī*).

Muslim narrated, on the authority of Abū Hurayra ؓ, that the Prophet ﷺ said: 'Let none of you say (to another person) "my lord"; instead, say "my master" and "my liege."'

Another of Muslim's narrations has it: 'Let none of you say "my slave" or "my slave-girl"; you are all the slaves of Allah, and all of your women-folk are the slaves of Allah. Instead, say "my boy" and "my girl", and "my lad" and "my lass." '

The wisdom behind this prohibition is that it closes the door to any ambiguity, and it restrains the egos of the slave-owners from presumption, haughtiness and pride. It is also a kindness to the slaves themselves, and a means consoling them.

Another example of this is his ﷺ prohibiting one from saying: 'The people have gone to ruin', intending by this to disparage and denigrate them, whilst exonerating himself, and holding himself to be better than them.

Imām Muslim narrated in his *Ṣaḥīḥ* collection, on the authority of Abū Hurayra ؓ, that the Messenger of Allah ﷺ said: 'If a man says: "The people have gone to ruin", he is the most ruined of all of them.'

Imām Nawawī said that the Ḥadīth was also narrated as '... it is he who has ruined them'[168], and that the most well-known narration is the first ('he is the most ruined of them'). This is borne out by the narration in *al-Ḥilya*, the wording of which is: '... he is among the most ruined of them.' Ḥamīdī said that most well-known narration is 'he is the most ruined of them'.

This is the case if the man says this out of contempt for the people, intending to disparage them, and holding himself to be better than them; for he knows not the Divine wisdom in Allah's creation.

---

[168] The difference in Arabic is slight, amounting to merely the alteration of a single vowel. [t]

This means that the one who disparages others might himself be doing badly, and be destined for a bad end; and the one who he disparages might well rectify his state, and be headed for a good end.

O Allah, make good our end in all our affairs, and spare us the debasement of this world, and that of the Hereafter!

Imām Nawawī also said:

> Khaṭṭābī said this Ḥadīth means that a man who continually finds fault with the people, and mentions their failings, saying: 'The people are corrupt, and gone to ruin', and the like, is truly the most ruined of them all, i.e. he becomes worse than them because of the sin he commits in finding fault with them, and prying into their affairs. This may also lead to his becoming self-satisfied and to his seeing himself as superior to them; and in this lies his own ruin.
>
> Abū Dāwūd mentioned that Mālik said that if the person says this out of sorrow at seeing the state of the people (in their religious affairs), there is no harm in it; but if he says it out of self-satisfaction, belittling the people thereby, this is the blameworthy act that the Ḥadīth prohibits.
>
> This explanation has reached us by means of a chain of transmission of the utmost authenticity, and it is the best and most concise explanation of the Ḥadīth, particularly in light of its having come from Imām Mālik.[169]

---

[169] *Al-Adhkār.*

The Muslim must be careful not to praise himself and disparage others, or to honour himself whilst holding in contempt those Muslims who are confused; rather, he should feel sorrow and compassion for them, and beseech Allah ﷻ for their sake.

Imām Mālik narrated in the *Muwaṭṭa'* that 'Isā ibn Maryam (peace and blessings of Allah be upon him and upon our Prophet) used to say: 'Do not speak in excess without mentioning Allah, lest your hearts harden, for the hard heart is far from Allah, yet you know it not.

'And do not look at the sins of others as though you are lords; instead, look at your own sins as though you are slaves,[170] for all people dwell either in suffering or in health; therefore, have mercy on those who suffer, and praise Allah for health.'[171]

---

[170] The Muslim should not look to the sins of the people as though he is a lord, absolved of sins and faults, and as though the people are humble slaves, debased by their sins and faults. Rather, the Muslim should look to his own faults and sins as though he is a slave who fears that his master might be watching him, for no person is free of sin and fault, whether it be concealed or open, or great or small.

[171] Have mercy on those who suffer from sins by giving them sincere advice, and praise Allah for being reprieved from sin, so that the reprieve will remain. (*Sharḥ al-Zurqānī 'alā al-Muwaṭṭa'*)

# PART II: THE DEVOUT WORSHIP OF OUR MASTER MUḤAMMAD ﷺ

## HIS WORSHIP ﷺ

OUR MASTER MUḤAMMAD, the Messenger of Allah ﷺ, reached the highest station of worship, and was the closest to Allah ﷻ; he ﷺ is the Master of the servants of Allah, and the leader of all who worship Him.

Allah ﷻ said: ﴾We know well that thy breast is oft times straitened on account of what they say; but hymn the praises of thy Lord, and be of those who prostrate themselves, and worship thy Lord until the inevitable visits thee.﴿[172] With this verse, Allah charged His Messenger ﷺ with four tasks: to glorify, and to praise, and to prostrate, and to worship until death. *Glorification* is to declare Allah ﷻ exaltedly transcendent above all that does not befit Him. *Praise* is to affirm all the perfections that indeed do befit Him.

Allah ﷻ then said: ﴾And be of those who prostrate themselves﴿, that is, those who pray. The single component of prostration here used to imply the complete action of prayer.

---

[172] Qur'ān 15:97-99

This divine statement is an indication of the excellence of prostration; it is authentically narrated that the Prophet ﷺ said: 'The closest a servant ever is to his Lord ﷻ is when he prostrates; so supplicate much (therein).'[173]

These commandments came directly after Allah ﷻ mentioned the straitening of the breast that afflicted His noble Messenger ﷺ, and the sorrow that he felt because of the words of profanity, scorn and vilification that the disbelievers directed at what he had brought them from Allah ﷻ. Allah's word ﴾but hymn the praises of thy Lord, and be of those who prostrate themselves﴿ followed this as an indication that He would banish this sorrow, and remove this disquiet, and expand the breast that had been straitened; and so whenever anything saddened the Prophet ﷺ, he would seek the solace of prayer.

Allah ﷻ then said: ﴾And worship thy Lord until the inevitable visits thee﴿, meaning death, which is termed 'the inevitable' because it will assuredly visit every living creature. The meaning of this statement is: 'Be constant in your worship as long as you live, without ever forsaking it.' A proof that 'the inevitable' here refers to death is Allah's word: ﴾...Save those who will stand on the right hand: in gardens they will ask one another about the iniquitous:[174] 'What led you into perdition?' They will reply: 'We were not of those who prayed, and we fed not the poor; we used to wade (in vain discourse) with all those who waded, and we used to deny the Day of Judgement, until the inevitable visited us.'﴿[175]

---

[173] Narrated by Muslim.

[174] I.e. they will ask one another about this matter; and then the denizens of Hell will be shown to them, and they will ask them directly. (*Ḥāshiyat al-Ṣāwī 'alā Tafsīr al-Jalālayn*) [t]

[175] Qur'ān 74:39-47

Another evidence is the Ḥadīth narrated by Bukhārī, Muslim and Aḥmad, which states that when the Prophet ﷺ went to see 'Uthmān ibn Maẓ'ūn when he died, he ﷺ said: 'As for him ('Uthmān), the inevitable has come to him from his Lord; and I hope the best for him.' By 'the inevitable', he ﷺ meant death.

The meaning of Allah's word ﴾And worship thy Lord until the inevitable visits thee﴿ is 'worship your Lord for the entirety of your life, at all times.' This verse is equivalent to the words of 'Isā ibn Maryam (upon him and upon our Prophet be blessings and peace): ﴾And He has enjoined upon me prayer, and alms-giving, as long as I live.﴿[176]

Ḥāfiẓ Baghawī narrates in *Sharḥ al-Sunna*, on the authority of (the Tābi'ī) Jubayr ibn Nufayr, that the Prophet ﷺ said: 'It was not revealed to me that I should gather money and be a merchant; rather, it was revealed to me: ﴾Hymn the praises of your Lord, and be of those who prostrate themselves, and worship thy Lord until the inevitable visits thee.﴿'

No matter what station a worshipper reaches, he is never free from needing to worship his Lord ﷻ, nor is he excused from any of the responsibilities of the religion, as long as he is alive and of sound mind.

Allah ﷻ said: ﴾Lord of the heavens and the earth, and what lies between them! Therefore worship Him, and be steadfast in His worship. Know you of any who is akin to Him?﴿[177] That is, similar or equal to Him. Of course not, for He Himself said: ﴾Nothing whatsoever is as His likeness; and He is the Hearer, the Seer.﴿[178]

---

[176] Qur'ān 19:31
[177] Qur'ān 19:65
[178] Qur'ān 42:11

This means that He ﷻ has no likeness in any way, from any perspective. There are many other verses in the Holy Qur'ān with this same meaning, using different Arabic expressions; and the Qur'ān was revealed pure Arabic speech. Allah said: ﴾And there is none comparable unto Him﴿[179], that is, He has no likeness or equal.

The upshot is that Allah ﷻ charged His servants with worshipping Him, and commanded them to be steadfast in doing so, by being careful to observe the proper times of worship, and by being vigilant in its observance day and night.

This is achieved by giving every moment its due of worship, by night and by day. For this reason, the Prophet's ﷺ worship was constant and continuous, from night to day.

Abū Dāwūd narrated that 'Āisha ﵂ was asked about the devotional acts of the Messenger of Allah ﷺ, and whether he specified certain days for devotion; leaving others. She replied: 'No, his devotion was constant; and who among you is able to do the like of what the Messenger of Allah ﷺ did?'

The Messenger of Allah ﷺ never left off any of his supererogatory acts of devotion as long as he lived, as Umm Salama ﵂ said: 'The Messenger of Allah ﷺ did not die until he performed most of his (supererogatory) prayer whilst seated; the most beloved of devotional acts to him were those that a person was constant in performing, even if they (the actions) were only small.'[180]

---

[179] Qur'ān 112:4

[180] Narrated by Ibn Ḥibbān in his *Ṣaḥīḥ* collection. (*al-Targhīb wa al-Tarhīb*)

# THE REALITY OF WORSHIP

*Worship* means to draw closer to Allah ﷻ in full submission and with humility before Him, by means of those words and deeds that He established for His servants, whether they be actions of the heart, the body, or the spiritual state. Worship has a sweetness and a delight; and when a person tastes its sweetness, and samples its delectation, he becomes attached to it, and yearns for it, and so he never allows himself to be separated from it, because it becomes his source of tranquillity and repose.

The greatest of those who tasted the sweetness of worship, and experienced its delights, and bore witness to its treasures and illuminations, was our Master Muḥammad ﷺ, the leader of the devotees, the Master of the righteous, the most pious of the first and the last by the attestation of Allah's word: ﴾(Say:) My protecting friend is Allah, He who revealed the Book; and He ever befriends the righteous.﴿[181]

By this, Allah informed us that He befriends His servants according to their righteousness, and that He ﷻ befriended His Beloved ﷺ in a way that He befriended no other, which He indicated with His word: ﴾My protecting friend is Allah﴿, that is, 'My protecting friend, who takes care of all my affairs in a way unique to me, is Allah.' Divine befriending comes commensurate with righteousness, as the end of the verse indicates, and this shows that he ﷺ reached a unique station of righteousness, that was reached by no other. Because of this, the Prophet ﷺ had the most complete experience of the sweetness of worship, and he derived the most tranquillity and delight from it.

---

[181] Qur'ān 7:196

It was narrated in the *Musnad* and elsewhere that the Prophet ﷺ said: 'Arise, O Bilāl, and give us tranquillity in prayer!'[182] It is also narrated in the *Musnad* and elsewhere that the Prophet ﷺ said: 'The coolness of my eye has been placed in prayer.'

The followers of our Master Muḥammad ﷺ were also granted their share of the sweetness of worship, and the delights of devotion, according to their spiritual ranks. It is narrated that the great Shaykh and Gnostic, Ibrahim ibn Adham ؓ, said: 'If the kings knew the sweetness we have found, they would fight us with swords on its account.' Another great Shaykh and Gnostic, Abū Sulaymān al-Dārānī ؓ, said: 'The people of nightly devotion derive more delectation from their devotion than the people of idle pleasure gain from their play; were it not for nightly devotion, I would not desire to remain in this world.' Another of the saints ؓ said: 'If the denizens of Paradise are granted what we now possess, they will indeed have a fine existence!' It is for this reason that the denizens of Paradise will take it upon themselves to worship their Lord ﷻ in Paradise, without being commanded to do so; and they will worship Allah ﷻ in Paradise more than they worshipped Him in this world.

Bukhārī and Muslim narrated in their *Ṣaḥīḥ* collections, on the authority of Abū Hurayra ؓ, that Allah ﷻ says to the Angels who roam the streets seeking out the people who remember Him: 'What do My servants say?' 'They glorify You, and magnify You, and praise You, and exalt You', the Angels reply. He will say, 'Have they seen Me?'. 'No, by Allah, O Lord, they have not seen You.' He will say, 'And what if they had seen Me?' 'Had they seen You, they would worship You even more, and exalt You even more, and glorify You even more…'

---

[182] Bilāl ؓ used to perform the call to prayer for the Prophet ﷺ. [t]

The denizens of Paradise will therefore worship more than they did on earth, because they will behold their Lord ﷻ; and their worship will be voluntary, and free of difficulty. It will be their source of tranquillity and delight. Muslim narrated in his *Ṣaḥīḥ* collection, on the authority of Jābir ؓ, that the Prophet ﷺ said, about the denizens of Paradise: 'They will be inspired to speak words of glorification, praise and devotion, just as you all inspired to draw breath.'

**Acts of worship leave their mark on the soul of the worshipper**: they cleanse him from thoughtlessness and triviality, and pretension and egotism, until the worshipper's soul is purified, and he enters into the servitude of the Sovereign of Lordship. When Rabī'a ibn Ka'b al-Aslamī requested the Prophet's ﷺ companionship in Paradise, he ﷺ said to him: 'In that case, assist me for your sake by offering much prostration.'

**Acts of worship dye the heart and mind of the worshipper**, and all of his senses, with Divine light, until even his face is illuminated by it. Allah ﷻ said: ﴾(We take on) Allah's own dye; and who is better than Allah at dyeing? We are His worshippers.﴿[183] In other words, 'Keep to the dye of Allah, for He dyes with strong light, and there is no finer dye; and the means to this is adherence to the worship of your Lord as He established it for you.' The Prophet ﷺ said: 'Prayer is light, and patience is illumination.'

**Worship purifies the heart**, and cleanses and illuminates it, until the lights of the Real are manifested in it. Allah ﷻ said: ﴾Allah is the light of the heavens and the earth. The similitude of His light is as a niche…﴿[184]

---

[183] Qur'ān 2:138

[184] Qur'ān 24:35

That is, the likeness of His light in the heart of His believing servant is like a niche, wherein lies a lamp, ablaze with light. The niche refers to the breast, and the lamp means the believer's heart, resplendent with the light of faith in Allah ﷻ. One of the Gnostics said:

*When the pool lies limpid*
*And unmoved by the breeze,*
*The sky appears clear therein,*
*As do the sun and the stars;*
*Just so the hearts of the people of purity:*
*In their clarity can be seen Allah Almighty.*

All this is a case of Divine theophany, and the reflection of Divine light in the mirrors of the heart; it is not in any way a case of pantheism or Divine incarnation – Allah ﷻ is far exalted above any such thing.

**Acts of worship draw the servant closer to the Lord of Lords.** Allah ﷻ said: ﴾Prostrate thyself, and draw near﴿,[185] and in a Sacred Ḥadīth, the Prophet ﷺ reported that his Lord ﷻ said: 'My servant keeps drawing closer to Me with supererogatory acts until I love him.'[186] This is not the place to go into details about the effects and secrets of worship. We have merely mentioned a few notions; whomsoever wills might reflect upon them, and so realise that worship has a great effect on the worshipper, and contains a tremendous secret, and leads to brilliant illumination, and to a higher state, and to nearness to Allah, and His love.

---

[185] Qur'ān 96:19

[186] See our books *al-Salāt fī al-Islām* (*Prayer in Islam*) and *al-Taqarrub ilā Allāh Ta'ālā* (*Drawing Nearer to Allah Almighty*); the latter includes an examination of all the different narrations of the Ḥadīth, and an explanation of its many meanings.

What do you imagine then, O sagacious one, about the effects of the worship offered by the Master of all worshippers and devotes, and the leader of the Prophets and Messengers ﷺ? What do you estimate the strength of the illuminations of his worship might be, and its lights and treasures, and its proximity and closeness to Allah? Indeed, none can know this save Allah ﷻ, He who raised His Prophet ﷺ above all the other chosen ones.

## THE EXAMPLE THAT THE PROPHET ﷺ MADE FOR ALL DEVOTEES

The example of worship that the Prophet ﷺ left for all devotees is the best of examples, and the strongest, and the finest in the sight of Allah ﷻ, and the most just in fulfilling rights. It represents the clearest and most direct way of drawing closer to Allah ﷻ, and no matter how the devotee burdens himself with strenuous acts of worship, and tremendous works of devotion, he will never draw closer to Allah ﷻ than those who follow the Muhammadan Sunna, the example of worship and devotion that the Messenger of Allah ﷺ gave us. Bukhārī and Muslim narrated that Anas ؓ said: 'A group of three people went to the houses of the wives of the Prophet ﷺ asking about his acts of devotion. When they were told of them, it seemed that they saw them as being too few. "What is our position", they said, "when compared to that of the Messenger of Allah ﷺ whose sins, past and future, have been forgiven?"[187] One of them said: "I shall pray all night!"

---

[187] I.e. 'There is a great difference between him ﷺ and us, for we are subject to sin and a bad end, and forgiveness is by no means guaranteed for us, whilst the Prophet ﷺ is divinely protected from sin, and guaranteed forgiveness.' (Quoted in Muḥammad ibn 'Allān, *Sharḥ Riyāḍ al-Ṣāliḥīn*).

'Another said: "I shall fast every day without exception!" Another said: "I shall avoid women, and I will never marry!" The Messenger of Allah ﷺ appeared, and said: "Are you the ones who said these things? By Allah, I fear Allah more than any of you, and am more conscious of Him; but I sometimes fast, and sometimes eat; and I sometimes pray, and sometimes sleep; and I marry women – and whoever desires other than my example is not from me." '[188]

The Prophet's ﷺ custom was to perform acts of worship that were constant and regular: Abū Dāwūd narrated, on the authority of 'Ā'isha ؓ, that the Messenger of Allah ﷺ said: 'Take on whatever acts (of worship) you are able; for Allah does not lose interest when you lose interest – and the most beloved of acts to Allah is that which is most consistent, even if it is only a little.'

And so whenever he ﷺ performed an act of worship, he would establish it for himself as a regular act. Another aspect of his ﷺ spiritual guidance to all slaves and worshippers was that they be sure to take care of everything that was incumbent upon them, without allowing one duty to distract them from another, so that the performance of one responsibility would not lead to the neglect of another:

---

[188] Maṭrazī said in *Sharḥ al-Maṣābīḥ*: 'The statement "whoever desires other than my example is not from me" means, "Whoever rejects the religious affairs that I have enjoined – whether they be obligatory or Sunnah – attaching no importance to me, and ignoring me, is not from me, because he is a disbeliever"; if, however, he abandons it not out of condescension, but out of laziness, he is not a disbeliever, and "whoever desires other than my example is not from me" would in this case means "he is not one of those who follows my example and acts according to my Sunnah." ' (Ibn 'Allān, *Sharḥ Riyāḍ al-Ṣāliḥīn*).

Abū Dāwūd narrates in his *Sunan* that 'Ā'isha ﵂ said: 'The Messenger of Allah ﷺ sent a message to 'Uthmān b. Maẓ'ūn, saying: "Do you desire other than my Sunnah?" 'Uthmān replied, "No, by Allah, O Messenger of Allah! Rather, it is your Sunnah that I seek!" The Prophet ﷺ replied: "Then (know that) I sleep, and I pray; and I fast, and I eat; and I marry women. So by mindful of Allah, O 'Uthmān, for your family has a right over you, and your guests have a right over you, and your soul has a right over you: fast, and eat; pray, and sleep." '

And 'Abdullāh b. 'Amr b. al-'Āṣ ﵄ said: 'The Prophet ﷺ heard that I had been saying, "By Allah I will fast all day and pray all night as long as I live!" And so the Messenger of Allah ﷺ said: "Is it you who has been saying this?" I replied: "My father and mother be your ransom, indeed I did say it, O Messenger of Allah." He replied: "You will not be able to do this, so fast and eat, and sleep and pray. Fast three days out of every month, for good deeds are rewarded tenfold, and so this is akin to a constant fast." ' That is, since fasting one day will be rewarded as if it were ten, fasting three days a month is akin to thirty.

'Abdullāh ibn 'Amr continued: 'I then said, "I am able to do better than this." (Muslim's narration has it, "More than this.") He ﷺ replied, "Then fast one day, and eat for two days." I replied, "I can do better than that." He replied, "Then fast every other day, which was the fast of Dāwūd ﷺ, and is the most balanced fast." (In another narration, "The best of fasts", that is, non-obligatory fasts.)

I replied, "I can do better than that." The Messenger of Allah ﷺ replied: "There is nothing better than that." ' 'Abdullāh ibn 'Amr then said, 'And for me to have simply accepted the three days that the Messenger of Allah ﷺ mentioned first, seems more beloved to me now than my family and all my possessions.'

In another narration, the Messenger of Allah ﷺ said: 'Have I not been told that you fast all day and pray all night?' Ibn 'Amr replied, 'Indeed it is so, O Messenger of Allah.' He replied, 'Do not do so: fast and eat, and sleep and pray, for your body has a right over you, and your eye has a right over you, and your wife has a right over you, and your guest has a right over you. It is enough to fast three days out of every month, for your good deeds are rewarded tenfold, and so this is akin to a constant fast.' Ibn 'Amr said: 'But I was harsh on myself (that is, I did not accept the Prophet's ﷺ dispensation), and so things were made hard for me. I said: "O Messenger of A1llah, I have strength (to do more)." He ﷺ replied, "Fast as Allah's prophet Dāwūd fasted, and do no more." "What is Dāwūd's fast?" I asked. He ﷺ replied, "Half of the time.[189]" '

And when 'Abdullāh ibn 'Amr became older, and this practice became difficult for him, he would say, 'If only I had taken the dispensation of the Messenger of Allah ﷺ!' In another narration, Ibn 'Amr said: 'The Prophet ﷺ said to me: "Have I not been told that you fast every day and recite the (entire) Qur'ān every night?" I replied, "Indeed it is so, O Messenger of Allah; I mean nothing but good by it." He said, "Fast as Allah's prophet Dāwūd fasted, for he was the most devoted of people; and complete the Qur'ān once a month." I replied, "O Prophet of Allah, I can do better than that." He said, "Then complete it every ten days." I replied, "O Prophet of Allah, I can do better than that." He said, "Then complete it every seven days, and do no more than this." 'Ibn 'Amr said, 'I was harsh, and so things were made harsh for me; and the Prophet ﷺ said to me, "You know not: perhaps you will be given a long life." And indeed it was just as the Prophet ﷺ had said to me, and when I became old I wished that I had accepted his ﷺ dispensation.'

---

[189] That is, every other day. [t]

Other narrations add that the Prophet ﷺ also mentioned, 'Your child has a right over you', and that he ﷺ said, 'The one who fasts constantly has not fasted', and that he ﷺ said, 'The most beloved of fasts to Allah is the fast of Dāwūd; and the most beloved of prayers (i.e. night vigils) is the prayer of Dāwūd: he would sleep half the night, and then rise and pray one third of the night, and then sleep for the (final) sixth; and he would fast every other day; and he would never flee from an encounter (with the enemy).' Nasā'ī's narration adds, 'And when he made a promise, he would not break it.'

Another narration of this Ḥadīth has it that Ibn 'Amr said: 'My father married me to a woman of noble lineage, whom he would visit to enquire about her husband. She would say, "What a fine man is he! Neither has he entered our bed, nor drawn back our sheet!" (By this, she alluded to his not having sought conjugal relations from her.) When this went on for a long time, he ('Amr's father) mentioned it to the Prophet ﷺ, who said, "Bring him to me." When I came to him ﷺ, he said, "How much do you fast?" I replied, "Every day." He then asked, "How often do you complete (the Qur'ān)?" I said, "Every night." ' The Ḥadīth then continued as above. Imām Nawawī ﵀ said: 'All of these narrations are rigorously authentic, most of them included in both *Ṣaḥīḥ* collections of Bukhārī and Muslim, and a few in one or the other of them.' The upshot is that the Prophet ﷺ encouraged consistency in supererogatory acts of devotion, even if they were only small; and he warned against performing acts of worship so excessive that they would ultimately be abandoned, or cause the soul to resent them. He ﷺ would also enjoin the fulfilment of all duties and responsibilities in the best way possible, without any of them distracting from any others, which amounts to excessiveness on the one hand and negligence on the other. Another aspect of his ﷺ spiritual guidance is that he would encourage the performance of consistent acts of worship, even if they were small, and he would discourage copious amounts of worship if they were inconsistent: Bukhārī and Muslim narrate that 'Ā'isha ﵂ said: 'The Messenger of Allah owned a mat which he would use to pray upon at night, and spread out to sit upon during the day. People began to gather around the Prophet ﷺ and pray with him, until they numbered a great many, after which he approached them and said: "O people, take on whatever acts (of worship) you are able; for Allah does not lose interest when you lose interest – and the most beloved of acts to Allah is that which is most consistent, even if it is only a little." ' Another narration adds: '…and whenever the family of Muḥammad ﷺ took on an act of worship, they would do so consistently.' Another narration adds that the Messenger of Allah ﷺ said: 'Be moderate, and find the middle way, and know that none of you shall enter Paradise on account of his actions, and that the most beloved of acts to Allah is that which is most consistent, even if it is only a little.'[190]

**The Prophet ﷺ warned against religious extremism:** Bukhārī narrated, on the authority of Abū Hurayra ﵁, that the Messenger of Allah ﷺ said: 'Religion is ease, and no one makes the religion hard except that it defeats him;[191] so be moderate, and seek the middle way,[192] and be of good cheer, and seek the aid of the morning journey, and the evening journey, and a little of the night journey; little by little, you shall arrive.' That is, by being moderate you shall arrive at your goal, which is the blessing and good pleasure of Allah. Imām Nawawī says:

---

[190] Narrated by Bukhārī and Muslim.

[191] That is, no one becomes over-absorbed in religious acts, showing no moderation, except that he becomes unable to continue, or gives it up, and so regresses. (*Fatḥ al-Bārī*)

[192] Imām Nawawī: 'Moderation' (*al-sidād*) means uprightness and propriety, and 'seeking the middle way' (*al-muqāraba*) means to be temperate, neither extreme nor negligent.

> 'Seek the aid of the morning journey (*ghadwa*), and the evening journey (*rawḥa*), and a little of the night journey (*dujla*)' is a metaphorical expression, meaning: Seek aid in obeying Allah ﷻ by performing acts of worship at the times when you can be active, and your hearts are not occupied; you shall taste the sweetness of worship, and shall not grow tired, and you shall reach your goal, just as the intelligent traveller sets aside these times to travel, and allows himself and his mount to rest at other times, and so he reaches his destination without tiring; and Allah knows best.

Imām Aḥmad narrated with a sound chain of transmission, on the authority of Burayda ؓ, that the Messenger of Allah ﷺ said: 'Take the middle way, for whoever makes this religion hard will be defeated by it.' 'Allāmah Ibn Munīr said:

> This Ḥadīth contains one of the great prophetic teachings, because we have seen – as have those who came before us – that every religious extremist ends up burning out. The intention is not to prevent devotional perfection from being sought, for this of course is a praiseworthy thing, but rather to prevent the excess that leads to fatigue, and the immoderation in supererogatory worship that leads to the abandonment of that which is better, or the delay of the obligatory, such as someone who spends all night praying and is then overcome with sleep and so misses the congregational performance of the dawn prayer, or misses the optimal time for its performance, or sleeps until sunrise and so misses the prayer altogether. Aḥmad also narrated the Ḥadīth of Miḥjan ibn al-Adra': 'You will not obtain this matter by excess; the best of your religion is that

> which is easiest...' From this it can be inferred that to decline a valid legal dispensation (*rukhṣa*) in favour of the more difficult option (*'azīma*) is extremism, as in the case of someone who is unable to use water for ablutions for medical reasons, yet insists on using it anyway instead of performing the dry ablution (*tayammum*), and in doing so brings harm upon himself.

Another aspect of his ﷺ spiritual guidance was that he disliked that a person take on more supererogatory acts of worship than he could manage, out of fear that he would later give them up: Imām Aḥmad narrated on the authority of Anas ؓ that the Prophet ﷺ said: 'This religion is powerful, so enter it carefully.'

Bayhaqī and others narrate that the Prophet ﷺ said: 'This religion is powerful, so enter it carefully, and do not make the worship of Allah hateful to yourself; for the one who spurs his mount on too hard[193] will neither cover any land with it, nor preserve its back.'[194] Imām Ghazālī ؓ said:

> This Ḥadīth means that one should take on religious acts carefully and gradually, and not take on as much as one can all at once. This is because our nature is reticent, and can only be cleansed of moral

---

[193] The one who makes his mount travel too fast in an attempt to reach his destination quicker will end up wearing it out, so that it can go no further. He will neither cover any land, nor will he preserve his mount's back so that he can make further use of it. Likewise, the one who takes on too much worship will end up performing none at all.

[194] The Ḥadīth is narrated in full by Bayhaqī in his *Sunan*, and by Bazzār, and by Ḥākim in his *'Ulūm*, and by Abū Nu'aym, and by Qaḍā'ī, and 'Askarī, and Khaṭṭābī in *al-'Uzla*.

(Zurqānī, *Sharḥ al-Mawāhib*)

> imperfections little by little. Those who do not act gradually and who rather dive straight in, end up in an extremely difficult position, and find themselves in reversal, and that which had been beloved to them becomes hateful, and that which had been hateful to them becomes attractive – and this can only be known by firsthand experience. A parallel situation to this from our daily lives is that of a child: at first he is forced to study, and finds it hard to give up his games and be with his teacher; until one day his inner eye is opened, and he comes to love knowledge. Everything turns around, until he arrives at the point where it would be difficult for him to give up his studies.

Another aspect of his ﷺ spiritual guidance is that he advised against beginning any act of worship whilst in a state of disinclination or lethargy. Rather, one should begin one's devotional act earnestly and eagerly: Bukhārī and Muslim narrate, on the authority of Anas ؓ, that the Prophet ﷺ entered the mosque and found a rope suspended from its two pillars. 'What is this rope?' he asked. The people told him that it belonged to Zaynab, and that when she became tired she would attach herself to it. Upon hearing this, the Prophet ﷺ said: 'Untie it. Each of you should pray as much as he is able; when he tires, let him lie down.' And so if one is overcome by exhaustion or sleep whilst offering supererogatory acts of devotion, or the night vigil, one should leave off his devotion until the tiredness passes, whereupon it may be continued.

Bukhārī and Muslim also narrate, on the authority of 'Ā'isha ؓ, that the Messenger of Allah ﷺ said: 'If any of you should become drowsy whilst praying, let him recline until the drowsiness passes; for if one of you should pray whilst (heavily) drowsy, he might well begin to seek forgiveness, and wind up cursing himself.' That is, he might pray against himself without realising it because of his drowsiness.

Another aspect of his ﷺ spiritual guidance is that he warned against taking on excessive acts of worship and supererogatory devotion, and then neglecting them and falling short of the example he ﷺ himself set for such acts. The Prophet ﷺ did not approve that a man should be praised for his acts of devotion whilst he is still in the initial stage of enthusiasm and zeal that comes with embarking on new practices. Rather, some time should be allowed to pass so that he can settle down, and if after this he is in line with the Sunnah, he should be praised; otherwise, he should not:

Tirmidhī[195] narrated, on the authority of Abū Hurayra ؓ, that the Messenger of Allah ﷺ said: 'Everything has its ardour, and every ardour cools off; so if a man finds the middle way, hope the best for him; and if all fingers point to him, think nothing of him.'[196] Ibn Ḥibbān also narrated this Ḥadīth, on the authority of Abū Hurayra, with the wording: 'Every action has its ardour...' Mundhirī states in *al-Targhīb* that 'ardour' (*al-shirra*) means enthusiasm and spiritual aspiration.

Ḥāfiẓ Mundhirī also mentioned the narrations of Ibn Abī 'Āṣim and Ibn Ḥibbān (in his *Ṣaḥīḥ* collection), on the authority of 'Abdullāh ibn 'Umar ؓ, that the Messenger of Allah ﷺ said: 'Every action has its ardour, and every ardour cools off; so

---

[195] Tirmidhī declared this narration to be rigorously authentic. (*Al-Taysīr*)

[196] That is, if he avoids both excess and neglect, finding the middle way between them, rejoice in him because he will be able to continue; whilst if he performs excessive acts simply in order to become famous for his piety, do not think him to be pious, for he is actually ostentatious. (*Tuḥfat al-Aḥwadhī*) [t]

whoever stays within my Sunnah when he cools off is guided, and whoever strays outside it when he cools off is ruined.'

Ḥāfiẓ Ibn Ḥajar narrated in *al-Maṭālib al-'Āliya*, on the authority of Ibn Fākhita, that a man went to the Prophet ﷺ and said, 'O Messenger of Allah, my nephew strives to perform much worship, and works himself hard.' The Messenger of Allah ﷺ replied: 'This is the ardour of Islam; everything has its ardour, and every ardour cools off, so watch him when he cools off: if he finds the middle way, hope the best for him; if he abandons it all, woe to him.'[197]

These Ḥadīths contain advice and guidance for the Muslims on how to be constantly pious and devoted, and how to adhere consistently to their devotion, so that they do not begin acts of worship with high aspirations and zeal, and then take on more than they can handle and end up abandoning them out of lethargy, falling short of the Prophetic Sunnah.

## HIS NIGHT VIGILS ﷺ

Allah said: ﴾And part of the night, keep vigil as a free devotion from thee; perhaps thy Lord shall raise thee to a Glorious Station.﴿[198] The linguists say that *hujūd* means sleep, and *tahujjud* (night vigil) means to leave sleep in deference to prayer. So the meaning is, 'And part of the night, keep vigil by offering prayers in which the Holy Qur'ān is recited.' The morphological form of the word *tahhajud* is an example of what in Arabic is termed *al-salb*, meaning 'negation'. Other examples of this include *ta'aththum*, meaning to refrain from sin (*ithm*) and *taḥarruj*, meaning to avoid forbidden things (*ḥaraj*).

---

197 *Al-Maṭālib al-'Āliya*, vol.3, p.176.

198 Qur'ān 17:79

The meaning of ﴾as a free devotion from thee﴿ (*nāfilatan laka*) is an act of devotion offered in addition to the other obligatory prayers.

This may mean that the night vigil was also obligatory, since the *tahajjud* prayer was compulsory for the Prophet ﷺ alone, and not his community – and Ḥāfiẓ Zurqānī declared this to be the opinion of the majority of scholars, including Imām Mālik.

Or it may mean that this extra devotion was voluntary, and that the night vigil was termed a 'free devotion' for the Prophet ﷺ in view of the fact that his voluntary acts of worship were completely pure because of his exalted rank, and his abundant acts of goodness, and his high status; for he was free of sin, and therefore his night vigil was a completely free act of devotion on his part. His community, on the other hand, bear the burden of sins needing expiation, and defects needing rectification, and so they are in need of any supererogatory acts of devotion they can offer in order to expiate their sins, or rectify the defects of the obligatory acts they have offered. The Prophet ﷺ himself mentioned this when he said: '… And if his (the servant's) obligatory acts of worship are lacking in any way, Allah Almighty will say to the Angels: "Look and see if My servant has offered any supererogatory acts of worship"; and they will be used to amend what is lacking from his obligatory worship.'[199]

And so the finest and most perfect voluntary acts of worship were those offered by our Master Muḥammad ﷺ, to whom Allah gave the highest form of voluntary acts, and linked this to the Glorious Station (*al-Maqām al-Maḥmūd*) for which all creatures praise him, both the first and last, namely the station of all-encompassing intercession before Allah:

---

[199] Narrated in the *Sunan* collections.

Bukhārī narrated in his *Ṣaḥīḥ* collection[200] that Ibn 'Umar said: 'The people will go around in droves on the Day of Resurrection, every nation seeking out its Prophet and asking for his intercession, until the call for intercession comes to the Prophet ﷺ; and this will be the day Allah raises him to the Glorious Station.'

Muslim narrated that Sa'd ibn Hishām said: 'I said to 'Ā'isha "Mother of the Believers, tell me about the character of the Messenger of Allah ﷺ." She replied, "Do you not read the Qur'ān?" "Indeed I do," I said. She replied, "Indeed, the character of the Prophet of Allah ﷺ was the Qur'ān."[201]

'I understood from this that I should stand, and that I would not need to ask anyone another question until I died; and then something occurred to me, and so I said: "Then tell me of the Messenger of Allah's ﷺ night vigil." She replied, "Have you not read ❬O thou that are wrapped up in thy garment!❭[202]?" I said, "Indeed I have." She replied, "Allah ﷻ make the night vigil obligatory with the revelation of the first verses of this Sūra, and the Prophet ﷺ and his Companions offered it for a full year, whilst Allah held back in Heaven the final verse (of the Sūra) for twelve months. After this, Allah revealed the final verse of the Sūra,[203] which lightened the obligation, whereupon the night vigil became voluntary, after having been obligatory."'

---

[200] This is the Ḥadīth as it appears in *Ṣaḥīḥ al-Bukhārī*; the author relates it in a slightly different form in the original. [t]

[201] That is, his ﷺ character was the Qur'ān in that he obeyed its rulings, and followed its moral teachings, and paid heed to its stories and admonitions, and recited it correctly, and met all of its demands.

[202] Qur'ān 73:1

[203] That is, His word: ❬Recite then even so much of the Qur'ān as is easy for you…❭

Ḥāfiẓ Zurqānī declared that there is scholarly consensus (*ijmā'*) that the obligatory status of the night vigil was abrogated in the case of the Muslim community, although he mentioned that there was a minority of the Tābi'ūn who were of the opinion that it remained an obligation to offer at least a short night prayer.[204] The scholars differed as to whether or not the night vigil remained obligatory for the Prophet ﷺ alone.

## THE TIME HE ﷺ WOULD DEVOTE TO THE NIGHT VIGIL

Bukhārī and Muslim narrate that Masrūq said: 'I asked 'Ā'isha ﷺ what act (of worship) was most beloved to the Prophet ﷺ. She replied, "That which was constant." I then asked her when he would pray, and she replied, "When he heard the rooster [*al-ṣārikh*]" '

The word used for 'rooster' here is *al-ṣārikh*, literally meaning 'the crier', the bird being named after the loud cry it makes. 'Ṭayālisī said in his *Musnad,* commenting on this Ḥadīth, that it is customary for roosters to crow at midnight. Muḥammad ibn Naṣr also said this, and Ibn al-Tīn reported this to be in agreement with the statement of Ibn 'Abbās: 'At midnight, or a little before it, or a little after it.'[205]

Imām Aḥmad, Abū Dāwūd, and Ibn Mājah narrated, with a good chain of transmission on the authority of Zayd ibn Khālid al-Juhanī, that the Prophet ﷺ said: 'Abuse not the rooster, for he rouses (folk) for the prayer.' (One narration has it: '... For he calls to the prayer.')[206]

---

[204] Literally 'For at least as long as it takes to milk a goat.'

[205] *Fatḥ al-Bārī.*

[206] *Sharḥ al-Mawāhib.*

The Prophet ﷺ himself told us that to offer the night vigil at this time was the most beloved of night vigils to him, as was narrated by Bukhārī and Muslim, on the authority of Ibn 'Amr ؓ, to whom the Prophet ﷺ said: 'The most beloved of prayers (i.e. night vigils) is the prayer of Dāwūd; and the most beloved of fasts to Allah is the fast of Dāwūd: he would sleep half the night, and then rise and pray one third of the night, and then sleep for the (final) sixth; and he would fast every other day.'

This is so that one can rest after the exertion of the night vigil, and the body can relax after having stood in prayer, and the harm caused by lack of sleep and exhaustion can be averted, which would not be the case if one were to stay awake until dawn. Another wisdom of this manner of offering the night vigil is that it allows one to offer the dawn prayer and the litanies of the new day with vigour and attentiveness.

Also, this way of praying makes it easier to avoid ostentation, since if one sleeps the last sixth of the night, one will wake up looking refreshed and rested, which will make it easier to conceal the worship offered the night before, as was mentioned by 'Asqalānī in *Fatḥ al-Bārī*.

Also, this method allows the one who offers the night vigil to obtain the grace of the Lord's ﷻ manifestation in the final two thirds of the night; for Bukhārī and Muslim narrated, on the authority of Abū Hurayra ؓ, that the Messenger of Allah ﷺ said: 'Our Lord, the Blessed and Exalted, descends every night to the earth's sky, when the final third of the night remains, and says: "Who would call Me, that I might answer him? Who would ask Me, that I might give unto him? Who would seek My forgiveness, that I might forgive him?" Thus it is, until dawn breaks.'[207]

---

[207] This is the wording narrated by Muslim.

'Asqalānī mentions, in *Fatḥ al-Bārī*, that Sa'īd's narration from Abū Hurayra adds: 'Would anyone repent, that I might accept His repentance?' Abū Ja'far's narration adds: 'Who is it that seeks provision of Me, that I might provide for him? And who is it that seeks release from harm, that I might release him?' 'Aṭā's narration adds: 'Is there no sick person seeking a cure, that he might be cured?' Sa'īd ibn Marjāna's narration adds: 'Who would seek a loan from One who is neither poor, nor unjust?' 'Asqalānī also said in *Fatḥ al-Bārī*:

> Many lessons can be drawn from this Ḥadīth, among them that praying at the end of the night is superior to praying at the beginning, and that it is better to delay the *witr* pray until this time for those who are confident that they will be able to rise to pray it, and that the end of the night is the best time to supplicate and seek forgiveness, which is also alluded to by Allah's word: ﴾... And those who seek forgiveness in the watches of the night﴿[208], and that supplications at this time will be answered.

And so the Prophet ﷺ would generally rise to pray the night vigil at the beginning of the second half of the night. Bukhārī, Muslim, and Ibn Mājah narrated that 'Ā'isha ؓ said that the Prophet ﷺ would sleep for the first half of the night and keep vigil for the second. The meaning of 'the first half of the night' here is the part of the night that follows the *'ishā* prayer and the litanies and invocations that are recommended to be recited after it;[209] for it authentically narrated that the Prophet ﷺ disapproved of sleeping before the *'ishā* prayer, or holding idle conversation after it.

---

[208] Qur'ān 3:17

[209] See Zurqānī , *Sharḥ al-Mawāhib*, v. 67.

**The Prophet ﷺ would recite certain litanies and Qur'ānic verses before sleeping:** Imām Aḥmad and Tirmidhī narrated, with a rigorously authenticated chain of transmission, that 'Ā'isha ﵁ said: 'The Prophet ﷺ would not sleep until he had recited (the Qur'ānic chapters) Banī Isrā'īl[210] and al-Zumar.'

Tirmidhī and Nasā'ī narrated that Jābir ﵁ said: 'The Prophet ﷺ would no sleep until he had recited *Alif Lām Mīm, A revelation…* (al-Sajda), and *Blessed is He in whose hand is all sovereignty…* (al-Mulk).'

Imām Aḥmad and the authors of the four *Sunan* collections narrated that 'Irbāḍ ibn Sāriya ﵁ said: 'The Messenger of Allah would recite the *musabbiḥāt* before he lay down to sleep; and he said that they contain a verse equal to more than a thousand verses.'

This was also narrated by Ibn al-Ḍurays on the authority of Yaḥyā ibn Abī Kathīr, who did not mention which Companion he heard it from, and who added: 'We believe this verse to mean the closing of Sūrat al-Ḥashr'; that is, the final three verses of the chapter.

Al-Ḥāfiẓ Ibn Kathīr believed the verse to be: ﴾He is the First, and the Last, and the Outward, and the Inward; and He knows all things.﴿[211]

The six *musabbihāt* (so called because they all begin with various conjugations of the verb *sabbaḥa*, meaning 'to extol and glorify') are the chapters al-Ḥadīd, and al-Ḥashr, and al-Ṣaff, and al-Jumu'a, and al-Taghābun, and al-A'lā.

---

[210] Also known as Surat al-Isrā.

[211] Qur'ān 57:3

# THE LITANIES HE ﷺ WOULD RECITE UPON WAKING FOR THE NIGHT VIGIL

When the Messenger of Allah ﷺ woke to pray the night vigil, he would wipe his face with his hand to remove the traces of sleep, and then raise his head to the sky and say the following invocations ten times each: 'Allah is Great'; 'Praise be to Allah'; 'Glory be to Allah, I hymn His praise'; 'Glory be to Allah, the King, the All-Holy.'

Ibn Mardawayhi narrates that the Prophet ﷺ would say the preceding formulas three times each, and would then say, 'I seek forgiveness of Allah' ten times, and then 'There is no god but Allah' ten times, and then recite the final verses of Surat Āl 'Imrān, and then say: 'O Allah, I seek Your refuge from the distress of this world, and the distress of the Day of Resurrection' ten times.

Then he would supplicate by saying: 'There is no god but You! Glory be to You, Allah, whose praise I hymn! I seek Your forgiveness for my sins, and I seek Your mercy! O Allah, increase me in knowledge, and do not lead my heart astray after having guided me, and give me mercy from Your Own Self; for You are the Giver!'

We shall now mention the Ḥadīths from which these litanies are drawn: Bukhārī, Muslim, and others narrate that Ibn 'Abbās ﵄ once stayed the night at the house of his aunt, Maymūna, wife of the Prophet ﷺ, in order that he could observe the night vigil of the Messenger of Allah ﷺ. Ibn 'Abbās said of this night: 'I lay down across the width of the mattress, and the Messenger of Allah and ﷺ and his wife lay across its length.

'The Messenger of Allah ﷺ then slept until midnight, or a little before it or a little after it,[212] whereupon he ﷺ woke up, and wiped the traces of sleep from his face with his hand, and then recited the final ten verses of Sūrat Āl 'Imrān.'

Ibn Mardawayhi's has it: 'Then he sat up on his bed, and raised his head to the sky, and said: "Glory be to Allah, the King, the All-Holy" three times, and then recited the final verses of Sūrat Āl 'Imrān, and then took a water-skin than was hanging nearby and performed the lesser ritual ablution (*wuḍū*), and did so perfectly, and then began to pray.'

Muslim's narration says that the Prophet ﷺ first cleaned his teeth and then made ablutions.

Ibn 'Abbās ؓ continued: 'So I got up and did as he had done, and then I went to him and stood by his side. The Messenger of Allah ﷺ put his right hand on my head, and took my right ear and pulled it.[213] He then offered two units of prayer, and then two more, then two more, then two more, then two more, then two more, and then he finished with a single odd unit (*witr*). He then lay down until the muezzin called, whereupon he offered two short units of prayer, and then went out to pray the dawn prayer.'

Abū Dāwūd narrated that 'Ā'isha ؓ said: 'When the Messenger of Allah ﷺ awoke during the night, he would say

---

[212] Ḥāfiẓ Zurqānī said: 'Ibn 'Abbās was unsure of this because he was only ten years old of the time and so did not know of such matters, and so he left it open when telling the story; but aside from this, we know that he ﷺ would keep the night vigil in the second half of the night.'

[213] Either to wake him from his drowsiness, or to move him to the correct position for prayer. (Nawawī, *Sharḥ Ṣaḥīḥ Muslim*)

"Allah is Great" ten times, and "Praise be to Allah" ten times, and then "Glory be to Allah, I hymn His praise" ten times, and then "Glory be to Allah, the King, the All-Holy" ten times, and then he would seek Allah's forgiveness ten times,[214] and then say "There is no god but Allah" ten times, and then he would say "O Allah, I seek Your refuge from the distress of this world, and the distress of the Day of Resurrection" ten times, and then he would begin his night vigil.'[215]

## THE LENGTH OF HIS NIGHT VIGIL ﷺ

The Messenger of Allah ﷺ would lengthen his recitation when praying the night vigil, and would also lengthen his bows and prostrations, and supplicate much when prostrating.

Bukhārī and Muslim narrated that 'Ā'isha ﵂ said: 'The Messenger of Allah ﷺ would stand in prayer until his feet were swollen.' It is also narrated that she said: 'The Prophet of Allah ﷺ would stand in prayer through the night until (the skin of) his feet would crack', that is, because of his standing so long. Nasā'ī's narration on the authority of Abū Hurayra has it: '... until (the skin of) his feet would split.'

'Asqalānī says in *Fatḥ al-Bārī*: 'These narrations are not contradictory, since both swelling and cracking occurred.' The narration of Bukhārī and Muslim has it that upon seeing this, 'Ā'isha said, 'Why do you do this, Messenger of Allah, when Allah has forgiven all your past and future sins?' He ﷺ replied: 'Then should I not be a grateful servant?'

---

[214] That is, he would say 'O Allah, forgive me, and guide me, and provide for me', as one narration mentions. (*Sharḥ al-Mawāhib*)

[215] See Abū Dāwūd's *Sunan*, and Qasṭalānī's *Mawāhib*, and *Nuzul al-Abrār*.

This means, 'Should I leave my night vigil simply because I have been forgiven, and not be a grateful servant? Rather, such forgiveness warrants that I offer prayers in thanks, so how could I not do so?'

Some scholars have adduced from this Ḥadīth that it is permissible for a person to offer strenuous acts of worship which impose hardships upon his physical self.

'Asqalānī says in *Fatḥ al-Bārī*:

> All such acts are acceptable as long as they do not lead to boredom, for the Prophet's ﷺ state was the most perfect of states, and he never grew bored of worshipping his Lord, even if this imposed harms on his noble physical self ﷺ. Indeed, it is authentically reported that he ﷺ said: 'The coolness of my eye[216] has been placed in prayer.'
>
> As for others, if they fear they will grow bored they should not exhaust themselves; and this is the inference of his ﷺ word: 'Take on whatever acts (of worship) you are able; for Allah does not lose interest until you lose interest.'

Ḥāfiẓ Qasṭalānī said:

> It may be, however, that the lower self, or Satan, might steal into the heart of the one who attempts to offer such intense worship, especially if he is elderly, and say to him: 'You are weak and old, so go easy on yourself, lest your worship come to an abrupt end.'

---

[216] An Arab expression denoting intense delight and joy. [t]

> This might well be sound advice at first glance, but there is a hidden agenda within it, because if the person heeds this advice, he might well be drawn on further and end up gradually abandoning his acts of worship until there is nothing left. The Master of the Messengers, who was granted absolute forgiveness by Allah, never abandoned any of his regular acts of worship in his old age.

Muslim narrated that Ḥudhayfa ﷺ said: 'I prayed with the Prophet ﷺ one night, and he began by reciting Sūrat al-Baqara. I supposed he would bow after reaching the hundredth verse, yet he went on. I supposed he would complete it over the two halves of the prayer,[217] yet he went on. I supposed he would bow when he reached the end of it, yet he then began to recite al-Nisā. He finished it, and then began Āl 'Imrān, which he also completed. His recitation was deliberate and slow; and when he came to a verse that mentioned Allah's glory, he glorified Him; and when he came to a verse that mentioned supplication, he supplicated; and when he came a verse that mentioned seeking Allah's refuge, he sought it.' Nasā'ī's narration adds: 'Every time he came to a verse that inspired awe in Allah ﷻ or mentioned His magnificence, he would make mention of Him.'

The Ḥadīth continues: 'Then he bowed, and began to repeat, "Glory be to my Lord, the Almighty!" His bow lasted almost as long as his standing had. Then he said, "Allah hears those who praise Him", and then stood for almost as long as he had bowed, and then he prostrated, and said, "Glory be to my Lord, the Most High"; and his prostration lasted almost as long as his standing had.'

---

[217] That is, recite one half in the first unit, and one half in the second. (*Sharḥ Ṣaḥīḥ Muslim*)

# THE INVOCATIONS HE ﷺ WOULD RECITE DURING THE NIGHT VIGIL

The Messenger of Allah ﷺ would read lengthy invocations upon beginning the night vigil, using many different forms of the introductory prayer (*du'ā al-istiftāḥ*). Abū Dāwūd narrated that Ḥudhayfa ؓ once saw the Messenger of Allah pray at night, opening his prayer with the words: 'Allah is Great, Allah is Great, Allah is Great, Lord of All Sovereignty and Glory, and all Grandeur and Might!' He then recited Sūrat al-Baqara, and then bowed; and his bow was almost as long as his standing had been.

Imām Muslim and others narrated that 'Abd al-Raḥmān ibn 'Awf ؓ said: 'I asked 'Ā'isha, Mother of the Believers ؓ, what the Prophet of Allah ﷺ would say to open his prayer when he prayed the night vigil. She replied, "When he prayed the night vigil, he would open his prayer by saying: 'O Allah, Lord of Jibrīl, Mīkā'īl, and Isrāfīl,[218] Fashioner of the Heavens and the Earth, Knower of the Hidden and the Open! You pass judgement over that in which Your servants differ; guide me by Your leave to the truth which is disputed, for You guide whom You will to the straight path.' "'

Abū Dāwūd narrated that Abū Sa'īd al-Khudrī ؓ said: 'When the Messenger of Allah prayed the night vigil, he would first say "Allah is Great", and then say: "Glory be to You, Allah, I hymn Your praise! Blessed is Your name, exalted is Your splendour, and there is no god besides You." Then he would say "There is no god but Allah" three times, and then "Allah is Great Indeed" three times, and then: "I seek refuge with Allah, the All-Hearing, the All-Knowing, from the accursed Satan: from

---

[218] The Arch Angels.

his insinuations, and his pride, and his allure." Then he would begin his recitation.'

Bukhārī, Muslim and others narrated (the wording here is Muslim's), on the authority of Ibn 'Abbās ☙, that when the Messenger of Allah ﷺ would begin to pray in the watches of the night,[219] he would say: 'O Allah, all praise is Yours. You are the Light of the heavens and the earth and all that is within them. You are Truth, and Your promise is truth, and Your word is truth, and the meeting with You is true, and Paradise is true, and the Hour is true. O Allah, to You I submit, and in You I believe, and in You I trust, and for You I stand, and to Your judgement I defer. Forgive me what I have done, and what I will do, and what I have concealed, and what I have revealed; You are my God, and there is no god but You.' Imām Nawawī ☙ said:

> The explanation for his ﷺ asking for forgiveness, although he was already forgiven, is that he did so out of humility and reverence, and also to set an example of the best way to supplicate with humility and contrition. This Ḥadīth, along with others, shows the way he ﷺ persisted in prayer and remembrance of Allah throughout the night, and how he acknowledged the rights of Allah, and testified to His truth, and the truth of His promises and warnings, and the truth of the Resurrection, and Paradise and Hell, and so on.

**These are some of the invocations he ﷺ would recite whilst prostrating during the night vigil:** Muslim narrated that Abū Hurayra ☙ said: 'The Messenger of Allah ﷺ would say when

---

[219] The narration of Abū Dāwūd has it: 'In his ﷺ night vigil, after saying "Allah is great", he would say...'

prostrating: "O Allah, forgive me all my sins: the small and the great, and the first and the last, and the hidden and the open." '

Muslim and the authors of the *Sunan* collections narrate that 'Ā'isha ﷺ said: 'One night, I noticed that the Messenger of Allah ﷺ was out of bed, and so I felt around the room in search of him. My hand fell upon the soles of his feet whilst he prostrated, his feet standing on their toes. He was saying: "Glory be to you, O Allah, I hymn Your praises. There is no god but You.[220] O Allah, I seek the refuge of Your pleasure from Your wrath, and Your mercy from Your chastisement, and I seek refuge in You from You. I cannot praise You enough; You are as You have praised Yourself." '

Another of these supplications is his ﷺ prayer for increased light: Muslim narrated that Ibn 'Abbās said, when describing the night he spent at the home of his aunt Maymūna, wife of the Prophet ﷺ, in order to see him pray the night vigil: '… So the Messenger of Allah ﷺ completed thirteen units of prayer, and lay down until his chest began to heave, by which sign we knew him to be asleep. Then he went out to pray, and he began to say in his prayer (or 'his prostration'): ' "O Allah, place light in my heart, and light in my hearing, and light in my seeing, and light on my right side, and light on my left side, and light before me, and light behind me, and light above me, and light below me, and give light unto me." ' (Or, he said, 'And make me light.')

Another narration of Muslim's of this Ḥadīth adds: 'The Messenger of Allah ﷺ prayed for nineteen things that night.'[221] One of the narrators of the Ḥadīth, Salama, said: 'Kurayb told me all of them (as he heard them from Ibn 'Abbās), but I only

[220] This sentence is from the narration of Abū Ya'lā.

[221] That is, nineteen things in which he ﷺ beseeched Allah to place light. (*Sharḥ Ṣaḥīḥ Muslim*)

remembered twelve of them, and forgot the rest.' He then mentioned them (as above), and added: '… And place light in my soul, and magnify my light.' Another narration of Muslim's also on the authority of Ibn 'Abbās, has it: 'Then the muezzin called the prayer, and so the Messenger of Allah ﷺ went out to pray, saying as he went: "O Allah, place light in my heart…"'

Ḥāfiẓ Zurqānī said: 'There is no contradiction here' – that is, there is no contradiction in the different narrations stating that the Prophet ﷺ made this supplication in his prayer generally, or in his prostration specifically, or whilst going out to pray – 'because in reality he ﷺ made this supplication both in his night vigil, and when he would go out to the dawn prayer.' That is, he ﷺ recited this supplication at all of the occasions mentioned in the different narrations.

Tirmidhī narrated that Ibn 'Abbās ؓ said: 'I heard the Messenger of Allah ﷺ say one night, when he finished his prayer: "O Allah, I ask for mercy from Your own Self, by which You might guide my heart, and put right my affairs, and gather my loose ends, and rectify my inner state, and ennoble my outer state, and purify my deeds, and inspire me with guidance, and restore my repose, and protect me from all evil. O Allah, grant me faith and certitude after which there can be no disbelief, and grant me mercy by which I might gain the honour of Your grace, in this world and the next. O Allah, I ask you for victory in what is destined to be, and a place with the martyrs (in Paradise), and a joyous life, and succour against my adversaries. O Allah, I ask You to fulfil my needs, even if my reason fails and my works fall short. I am in need of Your mercy, and so I ask you, O Judge of All Things, O Healer of Hearts: as You separate the seas, separate me from the torment of Hell, and the call for annihilation,[222] and the trial of the grave. O Allah, for those things in which my reason fell short, and for which I failed to ask You, and upon which I did not fix my resolve, of all the goodness You ever Promised any of Your creatures, or gave to any of Your servants – I seek them from You now, and I ask You by Your mercy, O Lord of the Worlds!

' "O Allah, O He of the Firm Rope, and the True Guidance, I ask You for safety on the Day of Requital, and [that I might enter] Paradise on the Day of Eternity in the company of those who are brought forth to witness, and those who bow and prostrate, and those who honour their agreements; indeed, You are Merciful and Loving, and You do as You will. O Allah, make us guides for others and guided ones ourselves, not stray ones who lead others astray; make us at peace with Your friends, and at war with Your enemies; enable us to love, for sake of Your love, those who love you, and enable us to oppose, as You oppose, those who set themselves against You. O Allah, this is our prayer, and it is for You to answer; and this is all we have, and upon You we rely.

' "O Allah, place light in my heart, and light in my grave, and light before me, and light behind me, and light on my right side, and light on my left side, and light above me, and light below me, and light in my hearing, and light in my seeing, and light in my hair, and light in my skin, and light in my flesh, and light in my blood, and light in my marrow, and light in my bones; O Allah, magnify my light, and give me light, and grant me light!" '[223]

---

[222] That is, the prayer that the denizens of Hell will make, that they be utterly annihilated and so escape its torments, as in Qur'ān 25:13-14. (*Tuḥfat al-Aḥwadhī*)

[223] Ḥāfiẓ 'Irāqī said: 'It was narrated by Tirmidhī, who declared it singular (*gharīb*), and also by Ṭabarānī.' The great scholar Zabīdī

Abū ʿĀṣim's narration adds: '… And grant me light upon light.'

Ḥāfiẓ al-Zurqānī said:

> The Prophet ﷺ asked for light to be placed in all of his limbs and sides in order that his works and deeds would be increased with light upon light. That means it was a prayer that such a state would continue, for he ﷺ of course already had such a state; either that, or he intended to teach this supplication to his community. Shaykh Akmal al-Dīn said: 'The light on his ﷺ right side symbolised a means of assistance for him, and an aid to what he intended when he asked for light to be placed before him. The light on his left side symbolised the light of protection. The light behind him symbolised the light that would be cast in front of those who followed him, lying in front of them, and behind him ﷺ. This allowed them to follow him with clear sight, just as it clearly showed that he is to be followed. Allah said: ﴾Say: This is my way: I call to Allah with clear sight, I and whosoever follows me.﴿[224] The light above him symbolised the holy Divine Light that descended upon him ﷺ in the form of wondrous knowledge that had never before been disclosed or witnessed.'

This narration of Tirmidhī on the authority of Ibn ʿAbbās serves to explain the latter's statement in Muslim's abovementioned narration: 'The Messenger of Allah ﷺ prayed for nineteen things that night.'

---

said, in his *Sharḥ al-Iḥyā*: 'It was narrated by Muḥammad ibn Naṣr in *Kitāb al-Ṣalāt*, and by Bayhaqī in *Kitāb al-Daʿawāt*.

[224] Qur'ān 12:108

# THE MANNER OF HIS PRAYING AT NIGHT ﷺ

The Prophet ﷺ would pray the night vigil in three different ways, as mentioned by Qasṭalānī in *al-Mawāhib* and its commentary.

**The first way**: He ﷺ would generally pray standing, which is attested to by the rigorously authenticated Ḥadīth narrated by Aḥmad, Muslim, and Tirmidhī, which states that Ḥafṣa, the Mother of the Believers ؓ, said: 'I never saw the Messenger of Allah ﷺ pray his supererogatory prayer seated until the year before his passing, when he began to pray it seated, reciting each Sūra so slowly and deliberately that it became longer than that which was longer than it.' That is, he would recite a short chapter of the Qur'ān so slowly and deliberately that it would become longer than a long chapter recited without this deliberateness.

**The second way**: He ﷺ would pray seated, and bow seated, as narrated by Bukhārī and Muslim, on the authority of 'Ā'isha ؓ: 'The Messenger of Allah ﷺ would sometimes spend long nights standing in prayer, and sometimes spend long nights seated in prayer. If he recited standing, he would bow from a standing position; if he recited whilst sitting, he would bow from a seated position.'

**The third way**: He ﷺ would recite whilst sitting, and when he approached the end of his recitation he would stand and complete it, and then bow from a standing position. Bukhārī and Muslim narrate that 'Ā'isha ؓ said: 'The Messenger of Allah ﷺ would pray seated,[225] and recite seated, and when there were around thirty or forty verses left to recite, he would stand,

---

[225] This refers to the supererogatory prayers he ﷺ would offer during the year before his passing, as was mentioned above in the Ḥadīth of Ḥafṣa ؓ.

and recite them standing.' Ḥāfiẓ Zurqānī said: 'So the Messenger of Allah ﷺ combined sitting and standing as he was able, in order to preserve his strength and continue praying.'[226]

He ﷺ would also advise those who slept without reciting their usual nightly remembrances to make them up between the dawn and midday prayers, in order that they would be written for them as though they did them the night before:

Muslim narrated, on the authority of 'Umar ibn al-Khaṭṭāb ؓ, that the Messenger of Allah ﷺ said: 'Whoever sleeps without reciting their usual nightly litany,[227] or part of it, and so recites it between the dawn and midday prayers, will have it written for him as though he had recited it that night.' Imām Nawawī said: 'This Ḥadīth indicates the importance of being diligent in the performance of regular litanies.' That is, a Muslim should take pains to maintain performance of his regular supererogatory acts of worship, night and day, and if he ever sleeps without performing them he should make it up before the midday prayer of the next day, in order that the goodness, illumination, and reward derived from them will be continuous, without interruption.

The great scholar Qurṭubī said:

> This grace is only for those who are overcome by sleep, or have some excuse for missing their litany whilst their intention was to perform it. The apparent meaning is that they will be granted the reward for

---

[226] *Sharḥ al-Mawāhib*, vol.7, p.41.

[227] The word used here is *hizb*, whilst Ibn Mājah's narration has *juz'*. Both words, along with *wird*, signify a regular action that a Muslim undertakes to perform, such as supererogatory prayer, recitation of Qur'ān, remembrance of Allah, and so on.

> this in manifold fullness, because of their good intention and sincere eagerness to do good and their sorrow at not being able to; this is the opinion of some of our Shaykhs. Others say that the reward in such an instance will not be multiplied (as usual), because the one who offers it at night is better and closer to perfection; as we see it, the first opinion is the correct one.

It is narrated that 'Ā'isha ﵂ said: 'If the Messenger of Allah ﷺ missed the night vigil because of illness or some such thing, he would offer twelve units of prayer the next day.'

## HIS MIDMORNING PRAYERS ﷺ

Imām Muslim narrated that 'Ā'isha ﵂ said: 'The Messenger of Allah ﷺ would offer four units of prayer at midmorning, sometimes more if Allah decreed it.' Tirmidhī narrated that Anas ﵁ said: 'The Prophet ﷺ would offer six units of prayer at midmorning.' Muslim also narrated, on the authority of Umm Hāni bint Abī Ṭālib ﵂, that the Prophet ﷺ entered her house on the day of the conquest of Mecca and offered eight units of prayer. She said: 'I never saw him offer a lighter prayer; but his bows and prostrations were perfect.'[228] Muslim also narrated that Abū Hurayra ﵁ said: 'My beloved friend ﷺ advised me to do three things: to fast three days out of every month, and offer two units of prayer at midmorning, and offer the *witr* prayer before sleeping.' Ḥākim narrated that Umm Salama ﵂ said: 'The Messenger of Allah ﷺ would offer twelve units of prayer at midmorning.'[229]

---

[228] That is, although his ﷺ prayer was light, he ﷺ performed every action correctly and did not rush. [t]

[229] See *Sharḥ al-Mawāhib*.

The scholars say that these different narrations are not contradictory, since the Messenger of Allah ﷺ would sometimes offer two units of prayer at midmorning (this being the minimum), and sometimes four (this being the norm), and sometimes six, and sometimes eight, and sometimes twelve (this being the best and most complete way).[230]

The Prophet ﷺ informed us of the immense reward in store for the Muslim who prays the dawn prayer in congregation, and then remains seated where he prayed making remembrance of Allah until the sun rises, whereupon he offers the midmorning prayer: Sahl ibn Muʿādh narrated on the authority of his father ؓ that the Messenger of Allah ﷺ said: 'If someone remains seated in his place of prayer when the people leave after the dawn prayer, staying there until he offers two units of midmorning prayer, saying nothing (in between) except that which is good, his sins will be forgiven even if they were as numerous as the foam of the sea.' Ḥāfiẓ Mundhirī said: 'This was narrated by Aḥmad, Abū Dāwūd, and Abū Yaʿlā; and I think that he also said: "If someone prays the dawn prayer and then sits making remembrance of Allah Almighty until the sun rises, Paradise will be guaranteed for him." '[231]

It is narrated on the authority of Abū Umāma ؓ that the Messenger of Allah ﷺ said: 'Whoever prays the dawn prayer in congregation, and then sits making remembrance of Allah Almighty until the sun rises, and then stands and offers two units of prayer, will go with the reward of Ḥajj and ʿUmra.'[232]

---

[230] See *Sharḥ al-Bājūrī ʿalā al-Shamāʾil*.

[231] Mundhirī then said: 'All three narrated it on the authority of Zabbān ibn Fāʾid by way of Sahl; this is a sound chain, and some have declared it to be rigorously authentic.'

[232] Mundhirī said: 'It was narrated by Ṭabarānī with a sound chain of transmission.'

# AFTER OFFERING THE DAWN PRAYER HE ﷺ WOULD MAKE REMEMBRANCE OF ALLAH UNTIL THE SUN ROSE

Jābir ibn Samura ؓ said: 'After praying the dawn prayer, the Prophet ﷺ would remain in his place, sitting cross-legged, until the sun had fully risen.' That is, until it was plainly raised, filling the sky with light. Mundhirī said in *al-Targhīb* that this was narrated by Muslim, Abū Dāwūd, Tirmidhī, Nasā'ī, and Ṭabarānī; it was also narrated with the wording: 'After praying the dawn prayer, he ﷺ would sit and make remembrance of Allah Almighty until the sun rose.'

It was also narrated by Ibn Khuzayma in his *Ṣaḥīḥ* collection with the wording: Samāk reported that he asked Jabir ibn Samura what the Messenger of Allah ﷺ would do after he prayed the dawn prayer. He replied: 'After praying the dawn prayer, He would sit in his place of prayer until the sun rose.'

# THE SUPEREROGATORY PRAYERS HE ﷺ WOULD OFFER BETWEEN THE SUNSET AND EVENING PRAYERS

Muḥammad ibn 'Ammār ibn Yasir ؓ said: 'I saw 'Ammār ibn Yasir pray six units of prayer after the sunset (*maghrib*) prayer. He said, "I saw my beloved, the Messenger of Allah ﷺ, pray six units of prayer after the sunset prayer, and then say, 'Whoever prays six cycles of prayer after the sunset prayer will have all his sins forgiven, even if they are like the foam of the sea.'"' Ḥāfiẓ Mundhirī said: 'This Ḥadīth was transmitted by a single narrator. Ṭabarānī included it in his three collections, and said of it: "Only Ṣāliḥ ibn Qaṭan al-Bukhārī related it." I do not have at my disposal the means to comment on its authenticity.'

**There are other narrations which attest to the virtue of these supererogatory prayers after sunset:** Abū Hurayra ؓ reported that the Messenger of Allah ﷺ said: 'If someone offers six units of prayer after the sunset prayer, not engaging in any evil talk between them, they will be counted as the equivalent of twelve years of worship.' Mundhirī said: 'It was narrated by Ibn Mājah, Ibn Khuzayma in his *Ṣaḥīḥ*, and Tirmidhī, all by way of 'Umar ibn Abī Khath'am, from, Yaḥyā ibn Abī Kathīr, from Abū Salama. Tirmidhī declared it to be a singular (*gharīb*) narration.[233] This is also attested to by the Ḥadīth narrated by Ibn Mājah on the authority of 'Ā'isha ؓ, in which is mentioned the virtue of praying twenty units of prayer after the sunset prayer.

Furthermore, the Prophet ﷺ would sometimes offer supererogatory prayers after the sunset prayer until it was time for the evening (*'ishā*) prayer: It is narrated that Ḥudhayfa ؓ said: 'I went to the Prophet ﷺ and prayed the sunset prayer with him, after which he continued to pray until the evening prayer.' Ḥāfiẓ Mundhirī said: 'This was narrated by Nasā'ī with a sound chain of transmission.'

As for the supererogatory prayers he ﷺ would offer before and after the five obligatory prayers and the Friday prayer, we have discussed the matter in detail in our book *al-Ṣalāh fī al-Islām*. As for the details of the Prophet's ﷺ manner of fasting, giving charity, and performing the Ḥajj, these are explained in detail in the Ḥadīth literature, and were it not for our fear of overburdening the reader, we would have mentioned them here in great detail. Our book *Tilāwat al-Qur'ān al-Majīd* includes much information about the Prophet's ﷺ recitation of the Qur'ān, and his love for hearing other recite it, and so on.

---

[233] That is, transmitted by a single chain of transmission from one narrator.

# HIS SUPPLICATION ﷺ

The Messenger of Allah ﷺ would make much supplication,[234] and encourage others to do the same, and he would stress its importance for many occasions; for supplication is a form of worship.

The authors of the *Sunan* collections, including Tirmidhī, who declared it rigorously authentic, narrated on the authority of Nu'mān ibn Bashīr ؓ that the Messenger of Allah ﷺ said: 'Supplication is worship,' and then recited: ﴾And your Lord has said: Call upon Me, I will answer you; those who are too proud to worship Me[235] will enter Hell in disgrace.﴿[236]

Tirmidhī also narrated, on the authority of Anas, that the Prophet ﷺ said: 'Supplication is the core of worship,' that is, its essence, and this is because the one who supplicates calls upon Allah when he has no hope in anything besides Him – and this is the essence of pure sincere worship of Allah Alone.

Supplication is also an admission of neediness, and recognition of the overwhelming power of Almighty Allah. It is also an admission of one's utter lack of power and strength, which is the mark of servitude and the sign of humility before the Lord's might. Supplication also includes praise of Allah, and recognition of the breadth of His kindness and largess.

**Supplication is also the key to Divine Mercy:** Tirmidhī narrated, on the authority of Ibn 'Umar, that the Prophet ﷺ said:

---

[234] The word *du'ā*, literally meaning 'to call', is perhaps best translated as 'prayer', but since this will inevitably be confused with the Islamic ritual prayer (*al-ṣalāh*), the word 'supplication' has been preferred. [t]

[235] Which includes supplication.

[236] Qur'ān 40:60

'If the door of supplication is opened for someone, the door of mercy is also opened; and Allah Almighty does not love to be asked for anything more than He loves to be asked for good health.'[237]

**Supplication is also a means of deriving strength, and a mighty weapon:** Abū Ya'lā, Daylamī, and Ḥākim narrated (and Ḥākim declared it to be rigorously authentic), on the authority of 'Alī ؓ, that the Prophet ﷺ said: 'Shall I not tell you that which will save you from your enemies, and amplify for you your provision? Call upon Allah night and day, for supplication is the weapon of the believer, and the buttress of religion, and the light of the heavens and the earth.'

**Supplication is also a means of pleasing Allah:** Imām Aḥmad, Tirmidhī, Ibn Ḥibban (who declared it rigorously authentic), and Ḥākim narrate, on the authority of Abū Hurayra, that the Prophet ﷺ said: 'Whosoever does not call upon Allah incurs His wrath.' 'Allāmah Ṭībī said: 'This means that those who do not call upon Allah cause His displeasure, and thus incur His wrath; for Allah loves to be beseeched.'

**The Prophet ﷺ informed us of the different ways supplications are answered:** Aḥmad narrated in his *Musnad*, on the authority of Abū Sa'īd ؓ, that the Prophet ﷺ said: 'No Muslim makes a supplication, for anything – barring sin or the severing of family ties – except that Allah answers him in one of three ways: He gives him what he asks for immediately, or He saves it for his afterlife, or He wards off a comparable evil from him.'

---

[237] Literally, 'Allah is not asked for anything more beloved to Him than to be asked for good health.'

# HIS MANNER OF SUPPLICATING ﷺ

**The Prophet ﷺ would raise his hands to the level of his shoulders when he supplicated:** This is mentioned in the narrations of many of his supplications, which he would recite on various occasions. Imām Qasṭalānī said in *Irshād al-Sārī*: 'Nawawī collected around thirty Ḥadīths in his *Sharḥ al-Muhadhab* that mention he ﷺ would raise his hands when supplicating. He (Nawawī) took from the two Ṣaḥīḥ collections and elsewhere; and Mundhirī also devoted a volume to this matter.' Salmān al-Fārisī ؓ narrated that the Messenger of Allah ﷺ said: 'Allah is shy and generous; if a man raises his hands to Him, He is shy to turn them away empty and disappointed.'[238] He ﷺ would also supplicate whilst turning the palms of his hands to the sky if the prayer was for the obtainment of something, and would supplicate whilst turning the backs of his hands to the sky if the prayer was for the warding off of harm, as narrated in the *Sunan* of Abū Dāwūd on the authority of Anas.[239] Because of this, Imām Nawawī said: 'The scholars have said that the Sunnah when praying for the warding off of harm is to raise one's hands with their backs to the sky, and when praying for the obtainment of something to turn the palms to the sky.' Bukhārī narrates in his *Ṣaḥīḥ* that Abū Mūsā al-Ashʿarī said: 'The Prophet ﷺ supplicated, and then raised his hands until I saw the whites of his armpits.'[240]

---

[238] Narrated by Abū Dāwūd, Tirmidhī (who declared it sound), Ibn Mājah, Ibn Ḥibbān in his *Ṣaḥīḥ* collection, and Ḥākim, who declared it to be rigorously authentic according to the conditions of Bukhārī and Muslim, as is mentioned in *Jāmiʿ al-ʿUlūm*, *Nuzul al-Abrār*, and elsewhere.

[239] See *Sharḥ al-Mawāhib* and elsewhere.

[240] Ḥāfiẓ Zurqānī said: 'This is either because he ﷺ had no hair there to begin with, or because he was careful always to remove it.'

**He ﷺ would also raise his hands extra high when praying for rain**, and seeking the aid of Allah ﷻ, and praying for victory over the enemy. For example, Bukhārī and Muslim narrated that he ﷺ raised his hands on the day of Badr when praying for victory against the idolaters until his ﷺ cloak fell from his shoulders.

When he ﷺ raised his hands to supplicate, he would not lower them again without first wiping his face with them:[241] Abū Dāwūd narrated that Burayda said: 'When the Prophet ﷺ supplicated and raised his hands, he would wipe his face with them.'[242] 'Allāmah Munāwī said: 'He would do this when he finished supplicating, out of hope and optimism that his hands were filled with goodness, which he then poured onto his face; it is thus recommended for all who supplicate to do the same.'[243]

**He ﷺ would also face the Qibla when he supplicated:** Aḥmad narrated in his *Musnad*, on the authority of 'Umar ibn al-Khaṭṭāb ﷺ, that when the first ten verses of Sūrat al-Mu'minūn were revealed to the Prophet ﷺ, he faced the Qibla, raised his ﷺ hands, and said: 'O Allah, increase us, and decrease us not; and be generous with us, and slight us not; and give unto us, and deny us not; and choose us, and reject us not; and give us to delight, and delight in us…'[244] The Messenger of Allah ﷺ also faced the Qibla on the day of Badr, and supplicated the Almighty.

---

[241] Narrated by al-Tirmidhī and al-Ḥākim on the authority of Ibn 'Umar; al-Tirmidhī declared it to be rigorously authentic by a single chain of narration. (*Fayḍ al-Qadīr*)

[242] Suyūṭī indicated the soundness of this narration.

[243] This was mentioned by al-Ḥalīmī.

[244] Also narrated by al-Tirmidhī in his section on exegesis, and by al-Nasā'ī in his section on prayer.

**He ﷺ would also advise those who supplicated to begin by praising Allah, and then sending benedictions upon the Prophet ﷺ:** Nawawī said in *Kitāb al-Adhkār*:

> Our transmissions of the compilations of al-Tirmidhī and Ibn Mājah include the following Ḥadīth, on the authority of 'Abdullāh ibn Abī Awfā ؓ, who said: 'The Messenger of Allah ﷺ came out to us one day, sat down, and said, "Whoever has a need of Allah, or a need of any of the Sons of Adam, should perform the lesser ablution, and do so well, and then offer two units of prayer, and then praise Allah ﷻ and send benedictions upon the Prophet ﷺ, and then say: There is no god but Allah, the Mild, the Generous. Glory be to Allah, Lord of the mighty throne. Praise be to Allah, Lord of the worlds. I ask You for the means to Your mercy, and the ways to Your forgiveness, and the benefit[245] of every virtue, and safety from every sin. Leave me no sin save that You forgive it, nor any worry save that You relieve it, nor any need that pleases You except that you meet it; O Most Merciful of the merciful!" ' Tirmidhī said that there is some dispute regarding its chain of transmission.[246]

The virtue of beginning supplications with the praise of Allah is also indicated by the Ḥadīth narrated by Imām Aḥmad and al-Ḥākim, on the authority of Salama ibn al-Akwaʿ ؓ, who said:

---

[245] Literally 'the battle-spoils of every virtue', alluding to the battle against the lower self waged by the spirit. (*Tuḥfat al-Aḥwadhī*) [t]

[246] It was also narrated by al-Ḥākim in his *Mustadrak*; and there are many other narrations that strengthen it, as is mentioned in *Nuzul al-Abrār*, and *Sharḥ al-Adhkār*, and *Tuḥfat al-Dhākirīn*.

'The Messenger of Allah ﷺ would begin his supplications by saying "Glory be to my Lord, the Most High, the Giver." '

And so the great scholar, the Proof of Islam, Imām al-Ghazālī ؓ said: '... It is therefore recommended to begin supplicating by making remembrance of Allah Almighty, especially by way of mentioning His generosity and largess.'

**Another of the good practices of supplication that the Prophet ﷺ enjoined** is to send benedictions upon him ﷺ at the beginning of the supplication, and the middle, and the end:

Aḥmad narrated in his *Musnad*, on the authority of Jābir ؓ, that the Messenger of Allah ﷺ said: 'Do not make me like the water-bottle of the traveller.' It was said, 'And what is this water-bottle of his, O Messenger of Allah?' He ﷺ replied: 'The traveller fills his water-bottle and then stows it away, and loads his gear onto his mount; and when he needs to drink, he drinks, or (when he needs) to make ablutions, he makes ablutions – otherwise, he pours it away. Mention me at the beginning of the supplication, and the middle of it, and the end of it.'[247] This means one should send benedictions upon him ﷺ at the beginning of the supplication, and the middle of it, and the end of it. It is reported that 'Alī ؓ said: 'Every supplication is veiled until benedictions have been sent upon Muḥammad ﷺ.'[248]

Tirmidhī narrated on the authority of Sa'īd ibn al-Musayyib, that 'Umar ibn al-Khaṭṭāb ؓ said: 'Supplications are suspended between Heaven and earth, no part of them rising, until you send benedictions upon your Prophet ﷺ.'

---

[247] See al-Qasṭalānī's *Mawāhib* and its commentary.

[248] Narrated by al-Ṭabarānī in *al-Awsaṭ* as a saying of 'Alī. Its narrators are all reliable, and some of them asserted that it was a saying of the Prophet ﷺ; but it is better established that it is a saying of 'Alī ؓ. (*al-Targhīb wa al-Tarhīb*).

**Another good practice of supplication is to do so with urgency and emphasis**: Abū Dāwūd narrated that Ibn Masʿūd ؓ said: 'The Prophet ﷺ would like to repeat his supplications three times, and repeat his invocation for forgiveness three times.'

It is also narrated that the Prophet ﷺ said: 'Allah loves those who supplicate with urgency.'[249]

**Among the conditions for a supplication's fulfilment taught to us by the Prophet** ﷺ is the purity of one's food, drink, and clothing, which lies in their being permitted by the Sacred Law:

Muslim and al-Tirmidhī narrated, on the authority of Abū Hurayra ؓ, that the Messenger of Allah ﷺ said: 'Allah Almighty is pure, and He only accepts that which is pure; and Allah Almighty has enjoined upon the believers that which He enjoined upon the Messengers; for He has said ﴾O Messengers! Eat that which is pure, and do good works,﴿[250] and He has said, ﴾O you who believe! Eat of the pure things with which We have provided you, and give thanks to Allah, if indeed it is He whom you worship.﴿[251]

Abū Hurayra added: 'He ﷺ then mentioned a man on a long journey, unkempt and covered with dust, who raises his hands to the sky and calls "*O Lord*"– yet his food is unlawful, and his drink is unlawful, and his clothes are unlawful, and he is nourished by unlawful things;[252] how, then can his prayers be answered?'

---

[249] Narrated by Ibn ʿUdayy in *al-Kāmil*, and al-Bayhaqī in *Shuʿab al-Īmān*, on the authority of ʿĀʾisha ؓ, as is mentioned in *Nuzul al-Abrār* and elsewhere.
[250] Qurʾān 23:51
[251] Qurʾān 2:172
[252] Or 'and he was brought up on unlawful things.'

Another of the Prophet's ﷺ counsels was that the one who supplicates should not be impatient, by saying, 'I supplicated my Lord, but He has not answered me'; for this only serves to further diminish the likelihood of his prayer being answered. Bukhārī, Muslim, and others narrate, on the authority of Abū Hurayra ◈, that the Messenger of Allah ﷺ said: 'You will be answered as long as you do not show impatience by saying, "I supplicated, but was not answered".' One narration has it, 'I supplicated my Lord, but He did not answer me.'

Aḥmad and Abū Yaʿlā narrated, with a chain of transmission whose narrators were all rigorously authenticated, on the authority of Anas ◈, that the Messenger of Allah ﷺ said, 'The servant will be fine as long as he does not show impatience.' The people said, 'O Prophet of Allah, how does he show impatience?' He ﷺ replied, 'By saying, "I supplicated, but was not answered."'

**He ﷺ would also advise the one who supplicates to be decisive, and to be certain that he will be answered**: Bukhārī and Muslim narrate, on the authority of Anas ◈, that the Messenger of Allah ﷺ said: 'None of you should say when he supplicates, "O Allah, forgive me if You will, O Allah, have mercy on me if You will, O Allah, provide for me if You will." Rather, he should be decisive when asking; for no one can force Allah Almighty to do anything.' The Prophet ﷺ discouraged this because the only reason one would need to add 'if you will' when making a request is if the one who is asked might otherwise feel compelled to comply, which means it would be possible to compel them to do so. Allah, however, is completely above being compelled to do anything, or doing anything unwillingly; everything He does is by His own will and leave, and no one can compel Him to do anything.

---

(*Tuḥfat al-Aḥwadhī*) [t]

It is related that al-Nawawī's opinion was that this statement of the Prophet ﷺ meant that such a thing is disliked (*makrūh*), which is the soundest position; whilst Ibn 'Abd al-Barr seemed to suggest that it is outright forbidden (*ḥarām*), which is a more literal reading, as mentioned in *Fath al-Bārī*.[253] Qasṭalānī said:

> It is said that the meaning of 'being decisive' here (*'azm*) is to think well of Allah, and that He will answer one's prayer, for one is calling upon the Generous. Ibn 'Uyayna said: 'None of you should be held back on account of what he knows about himself (i.e. his deficiencies), for Allah Almighty answered the supplication of the most evil of all His creatures, Iblīs, when he said: ﴾Give me respite until the day they are resurrected.﴿[254]

**He ﷺ would also encourage the one who supplicates to end his prayer by saying 'Amīn' in order that it be answered**: Abū Dāwūd narrated that Abū Zuhayr al-Numayrī said: 'We were out walking one night with the Messenger of Allah ﷺ when we came upon a man who was making fervent supplication, and so the Prophet ﷺ stopped to listen to him, and then said, "It will be his,[255] if he completes it." One of the men present said, "And how is he to complete it?" He ﷺ replied, "With *Amīn*; if he completes it with *Amīn*, it will be his." So the one who had asked the Prophet ﷺ went over to the man and said to him, "End by saying *Amīn*, and rejoice!" '

---

[253] *Sharḥ al-Mawāhib*.

[254] Qur'ān 7:14

[255] Zurqānī said: 'Ḥāfiẓ said in his *Amālī* that this meant Paradise would be his on account of this action, whilst al-Suyūṭī said, "It seems apparent that this meant he would have ensured that his prayer would be answered." '

Ḥākim narrated that Ḥabīb ibn Maslama al-Fihrī, whose supplications were frequently answered, said: 'I heard the Messenger of Allah ﷺ say: "No group gathers, one of them supplicating and the rest saying *Amīn*, except that Allah Almighty answers them.'[256]

**He ﷺ would also advise the one who supplicates to be certain that he will be answered**, and to supplicate with presence of heart, not absent-mindedness: Imām Aḥmad narrates in his *Musnad*, on the authority of 'Abdullāh ibn 'Amr ؓ, that the Prophet ﷺ said: 'Hearts are attentive, some of them more so than others, so when you beseech Allah ﷻ, O people, do so with certainty that you will be answered; for Allah does not answer the servant who calls Him with an inattentive heart.'[257]

**Another good practice when supplicating that he ﷺ is reported to have enjoined** is to pray for generalities (*jawāmi'*) rather than specifics: Abū Dāwūd narrated that 'Ā'isha ؓ said: 'The Prophet ﷺ preferred supplicating for generalities, and would leave aside everything else.'[258] Ḥākim narrated it with the wording: 'He ﷺ would like (supplicating for) generalities.' The meaning of 'supplicating for generalities' is to use phrases that are concise, yet embody the goodness of this world and the next, such as ﴾Our Lord, give us good in this world, and good in the Hereafter, and spare us the torment of the Fire.﴿[259] This is the soundest explanation of the meaning of 'supplicating for generalities' (*jawāmi' al-du'ā'*).

---

[256] See Mundhirī's *Targhīb*.

[257] Ḥāfiẓ al-Mundhirī said: 'The chain of transmission is sound, and was also narrated by al-Tirmidhī and al-Ḥākim on the authority of Abū Hurayra ؓ.'

[258] Imām al-Nawawī said in his *Adhkār* and *Riyāḍ al-Ṣāliḥīn*: 'Its chain of transmission is good (*jayyid*).'

[259] Qur'ān 2:201

In light of this, the statement of 'Ā'isha ﵂ 'and (he) would leave aside everything else' should be understood to refer to the majority of occasions, not all of them, since Ḥāfiẓ al-Mundhirī said: 'The Prophet ﷺ would sometimes supplicate for generalities, and sometimes for specifics.'[260]

The phrase 'supplication for generalities' is also said to mean using those words that best combine sound intentions and noble aspirations. It is also said to mean words that combine the praise of Allah with the good manners of supplication.

## SOME OF HIS ﷺ GENERAL SUPPLICATIONS

Bukhārī and Muslim narrate that Anas ﵁ said: 'The supplication that the Prophet ﷺ made the most frequently was, "O Allah, ﴿Our Lord, give us good in this world, and good in the Hereafter, and spare us the torment of the Fire.﴾[261]" ' The meaning of 'good in this world', as is reported on the authority of 'Alī ﵁, is a virtuous wife. Qatāda ﵁ said that it meant health and sufficiency. Ḥasan al-Baṣrī ﵁ said that it meant knowledge and worship. Suddī ﵁ said that it meant lawfully-earned wealth. Ibn 'Umar ﵁ said that it either meant devoted children or the praise of the people. Ja'far al-Ṣādiq ﵁ said that it meant the company of the righteous.
'Allāmah Ālūsī said:

> Although the word 'good' here (*ḥasan*) is indefinite, and indefinites are generally non-comprehensive in meaning, its sense here is clearly absolute, and thus implies perfection.

---

260 See Zurqānī 's *Sharḥ al-Mawāhib*, and al-Munāwī's *Fayḍ al-Qadīr*.
261 Qur'ān 2:201

> The perfect good of this world is the sum of all its goodness, and all its success; and to explain this phrase (i.e. 'good in this world') by declaring it to refer to specific things by no means defines the full breadth of its meaning, since as a rule absolutes cannot signify specifics. Rather, these specific things are intended as mere examples. The same is the case for what has been said about ﴾good in the Hereafter﴿, which has been explained variously to mean Paradise, or safety from the terrors of the Judgement and a bad Reckoning, or the maidens of Paradise, or the glory of the Beautific Vision (of Allah ﷻ), and so on and so forth, whilst the meaning is clearly that of absoluteness and perfection, which is another way of saying Divine mercy and beneficence (i.e. in the form of all of the foregoing examples, and more besides them).

Bukhārī and Muslim also narrate, on the authority of Anas, that the Messenger of Allah ﷺ called out to a Muslim man who had become as wretched as a plucked hatchling, and then said to him: 'Did you ask Allah for something?' The man replied, 'Yes, I used to say, "O Allah, if you are to punish me in the Hereafter, bring it forth to this world instead." ' The Prophet ﷺ replied, 'Glory be to Allah! You cannot manage such a thing, and you cannot bear it! Would that you had rather said, ﴾Our Lord, give us good in this world, and good in the Hereafter, and spare us the torment of the Fire.﴿' He ﷺ then prayed for the man, and Allah cured him.

**Another of his ﷺ general supplications was**: 'O Allah, make good for me my religion, which is the safeguard of my affairs; and make good for me my worldly life, wherein is my living; and make good for me my afterlife, whereto shall be my return; and make life a means of increase for me in all that is good, and make death a means of repose for me from all that is evil.'

**Another was**: 'My Lord, assist me, and assist not (others) against me; and succour me, and succour not (others) against me; and plot for me, and plot not against me;[262] and guide me,[263] and make guidance easy for me; and give me victory over those who transgress against me. My Lord, make me remember You much, and thank You much, and fear You much; (make me) obedient to You, and humble before You, plaintive and penitent.

'My Lord, accept my repentance, and wash away my errors, and answer my prayers, and make firm my argument, and strengthen my tongue, and guide my heart, and remove rancour from my breast.' (One narration has it 'from my heart'.)[264]

**Another was**: 'O Allah, I ask of You guidance and piety, and abstinence[265] and prosperity[266].' This was narrated by Muslim on the authority of Ibn Mas'ūd.

---

[262] God's plot (*makr*) is His sending tribulations upon His adversaries and sparing His allies; it is also said to mean a person's being deceived by his own good deeds, believing them to be acceptable (to Allah) when in fact they are not. The meaning here is, 'Send Your plot against Your enemies, not against me.' (*Al-Nihāya*) 'Allāmah Zurqānī said: 'The word 'plot' cannot be ascribed to Allah Almighty except in a reciprocal sense; the reciprocity here is implied by the Prophet's ﷺ words 'plot for me', which means: requite those who plot against me.

[263] That is, guide me to sound actions and virtues.

[264] Narrated by the authors of the *Sunan* collections, as well as al-Ḥākim, who declared it rigorously authentic; all narrated it on the authority of Ibn 'Abbās.

[265] That is, abstinence from the allures of this world, and from forbidden things.

**Another of his ﷺ supplications was**: 'O Allah, to You I submit, and in You I believe, and upon You I rely, and to You I turn, and on Your side I stand. O Allah, I seek refuge in Your glory – for there is no god but You – that You should sent me astray. You are the Living, who dies not.'

One narration has it: 'You are the Living, the All-Sustaining, who dies not, whilst jinn and mankind die.' Narrated by Bukhārī and Muslim on the authority of Ibn 'Abbās.

**Another of his ﷺ supplications was**: 'O Allah, give me health in my body, and health in my hearing and my sight, and make them (as unto) my heirs.[267] There is no god but Allah, the Forbearing, the Generous. Glory be to Allah, Lord of the mighty throne. Praise be to Allah, Lord of the worlds.' Narrated by al-Tirmidhī, al-Ḥākim, and al-Bayhaqī, on the authority of 'Ā'isha ﷺ.

**The supplications he ﷺ made to seek refuge with Allah included**: 'O Allah, I seek refuge with You from incapacity, and sloth, and cowardice, and decrepitude, and meanness; and I seek refuge with You from the torment of the grave; and I seek refuge with You from the trials of life and death.'

Narrated by Bukhārī and Muslim on the authority of Anas. The narration of Bukhārī reads: 'O Allah, I seek refuge with You from woe, and sadness, and incapacity, and meanness, and cowardice, and the burden of debt, and the overpowering of men.'[268]

---

[266] That is, richness of the soul, and freedom from reliance on others.

[267] That is, preserve them for me in a sound state until I die, so that they will remain with me just as an heir remains with the one he inherits from.

[268] That is, from the unlawful domination and cruelty of men.

**They also included**: 'O Allah, I seek refuge with You from *al-judhām*,[269] leprosy, madness, and (all) grave illnesses.'

Narrated by Abū Dāwūd and al-Nasā'ī on the authority of Anas, with a rigorously authenticated chain of transmission.

**They also included**: Zayd ibn Arqam ﷺ said that the Messenger of Allah ﷺ used to say: 'O Allah, I seek refuge with You from incapacity, and sloth, and cowardice, and meanness, and decrepitude, and the torment of the grave.

'O Allah, give my soul its piety, and purify it, for You are the best one to purify it; You are its Protector, and its Master. O Allah, I seek refuge with You from knowledge that brings no benefit, and a heart without humility, and an insatiable soul, and an unanswered prayer.'[270] 'Allāmah Ṭībī said:

> Every one of these items[271] is an indication that things should be judged by their ultimate ends and intentions: Knowledge should be sought in order to benefit from it; if it brings no benefit it is useless, and a source of evil (for he who possesses it). And the heart was created to be humble before its Lord; if it is not humble, it is hard, and refuge should be sought

---

[269] A disease that corrupts the makeup of the limbs, causing them to waste away or even detach. (This word is also sometimes given in translations of this Ḥadīth as 'elephantiasis', a different ailment. It may be that two different forms of leprosy with different names in Arabic are meant here by the Arabic words *judhām* and *baraṣ*. [t])

[270] Narrated by Muslim, Aḥmad, and the authors of the *Sunan* collections. (*Sharḥ al-Mawāhib*)

[271] That is, those mentioned in the Prophet's ﷺ statement 'I seek refuge with You from knowledge that brings no benefit, and a heart without humility, and an insatiable soul, and an unanswered prayer'.

from it: ﴾Woe, then, unto those whose hearts are hardened.﴿[272] And the soul only has value if it shrinks from the abode of delusion and turns to the abode of eternal life; if it is gluttonous and insatiable, it is the most pernicious of man's foes, and it is therefore of utmost importance to seek refuge from such a soul. And a prayer's not being answered is a sign that the one who makes it has not benefitted from his knowledge, and that his heart is not humble, and that his soul in insatiable.

**He ﷺ would also say**: 'O Allah, I seek refuge with You from discord, and hypocrisy, and evil conduct.'[273] Narrated by Abū Dāwūd on the authority of Abū Hurayra. The Prophet ﷺ would also seek protection for Ḥasan and Ḥusayn by saying: 'I seek protection for you[274] in the perfect[275] words of Allah[276] from every pernicious demon, and every malicious eye.'[277] He ﷺ would say of this, 'Your forebear (namely Ibrāhīm عليه السلام) would use these words to seek protection for Ismā'īl and Isḥāq.' Narrated by Bukhārī and others.

---

[272] Qur'ān 39:22

[273] 'Discord' here means enmity and conflict; and 'hypocrisy' means hypocritical actions; and 'evil conduct' means deadly sins and shameful actions.

[274] This is the narration found in *Kitāb al-Adhkār*; al-Bukhārī's narration has it simply, 'I seek refuge'.

[275] Zurqānī said: 'The word 'perfect' here means complete, or beneficial, or healing, or blessed, or authoritative and continuous without any possibility of being turned back, and without any fault of deficiency.' In any case, these attributes serve to strengthen and clarify one another.

[276] Either all His words in general or the Noble Qur'ān in particular.

[277] Meaning that which causes harm to all it looks upon.

He ﷺ would also say: 'O Allah, I seek refuge with You from the passing of Your blessings, and the withdrawal of Your grace, and the sudden calamity of Your retribution, and all (manifestations of) Your wrath.' Narrated by Muslim and Abū Dāwūd.

He ﷺ would also say: 'O Allah, I seek refuge with You from evil manners, deeds, passions, and maladies.' Narrated by al-Tirmidhī and others.

He ﷺ would also say: 'O Allah, I seek refuge with You from evil days, and evil nights, and evil hours, and evil people, and evil company in the Final Abode.' Narrated by al-Ṭabarānī on the authority of 'Uqba ibn 'Āmir.

# THE SUPPLICATIONS HE ﷺ MADE FOR SPECIFIC OCCASIONS

**The supplications he ﷺ would recite before sleeping**: When the Messenger of Allah ﷺ would lie down to sleep, he would say: 'O Allah, I seek refuge with Your Noble Countenance, and Your perfect words, from the evil of all those whose forelocks are in Your grasp. O Allah, You (Alone) ward off debt, and sin. O Allah, Your hosts are never routed, and Your promises are never broken, and wealth avails not the wealthy against You. Glory be to You, I hymn Your praises!'[278]

When he ﷺ wanted to lie down, he would place his right hand under his cheek and say, 'O Allah, spare me Your punishment on the day You resurrect Your servants' three times.[279]

---

[278] Narrated by Abū Dāwūd, al-Nasā'ī and others on the authority of 'Alī ؓ.
[279] Narrated by Abū Dāwūd on the authority of Ḥafṣa ؓ

And as he went to bed, he ﷺ would say, 'Praise be to Allah, who has fed us, and given us to drink, and sufficed us, and given us a place to rest; for many are they who have none to suffice them, nor to give them a place of rest.'[280]

**The supplications he ﷺ would recite upon waking:** When the Prophet ﷺ went to bed, he would say, 'By Your Name I die and live'; and when he rose, he would say, 'Praise be to Allah who has revived us after having caused us to die; and to Him will be the Resurrection.'[281]

**The supplications he ﷺ would recite upon entering and leaving the lavatory:** Anas ؓ related that upon entering the lavatory, the Prophet ﷺ would say: 'In the name of Allah. O Allah, I seek refuge with You from demons, male and female.' The narration of al-Ṭabarānī has it: 'O Allah, I seek refuge with You from the filthy, impure, evil, soiled, accursed Satan.'

It is narrated that 'Ā'isha ؓ said that when the Messenger of Allah ﷺ left the lavatory, he would say, '(I seek) Your forgiveness.'[282]

Ṭabarānī narrated on the authority of Ibn 'Umar that when the Messenger of Allah ﷺ left the lavatory, he would say, 'Praise be to Allah who gave to taste its sweetness, and preserved in me its energy, and removed from me its harm.'

**The supplications he ﷺ would recite upon leaving the house:** Umm Salama ؓ related that when the Prophet ﷺ left his house, he would say: 'In the name of Allah; I trust in Allah.

---

[280] Narrated by Muslim and the authors of the *Sunan* collections.
[281] Narrated by al-Bukhārī, Muslim, and others on the authority of Ḥudhayfa ؓ.
[282] Narrated by the authors of the *Sunan* collections.

'O Allah, I seek refuge with You that I should go astray or be lead astray, or that I should stumble or be tripped, or that I should do wrong or be wronged, or that I should act ignorantly or be treated with ignorance.'[283]

**The supplications he ﷺ would recite when heading to the mosque**: Ibn 'Abbās ﵄ related that the Prophet ﷺ would say as he went to the mosque: 'O Allah, place light in my heart, and light in my seeing, and light in my hearing, and light on my right side, and light behind me, and light in my nerves, and light in my flesh, and light in my blood, and light in my hair, and light in my skin.'[284]

Our Lady Fātima, daughter of the Messenger of Allah ﷺ, related that when the Messenger of Allah ﷺ entered the mosque, he would say: 'In the name of Allah; and may benedictions and salutations be upon the Messenger of Allah.

'O Allah, forgive me my sins, and open for me the doors to Your mercy.' And upon leaving the mosque, he ﷺ would say: 'In the name of Allah; and may benedictions and salutations be upon the Messenger of Allah. O Allah, forgive me my sins, and open for me the doors to Your grace.'[285]

He ﷺ would also say upon entering the mosque: 'I seek refuge with Allah the Almighty, and with His Noble Countenance and His eternal supremacy, from the accursed Satan.'[286]

---

[283] Narrated by the authors of the *Sunan* collections.

[284] Narrated by al-Bukhārī and Muslim; we have already mentioned the narration of Muslim, which mentioned the Prophet's ﷺ supplication as he went out to pray the dawn prayer.

[285] Narrated by al-Tirmidhī and others.

[286] Narrated by Abū Dāwūd; al-Nawawī declared its chain of transmission to be good (*jayyid*).

**The supplications he ﷺ would recite at morning and evening:** When morning rose on the Messenger of Allah ﷺ, he would say: 'O Allah, by Your leave we have reached the morning, and by Your leave we did reach the day's end, and by Your leave we live, and by Your leave we die, and to You is the Resurrection.'

And when evening rose upon him ﷺ, he would say: 'O Allah, by Your leave we have reached the day's end, and by Your leave we did reach the morning, and by Your leave we live, and by Your leave we die, and to You is the Resurrection.'[287] And he ﷺ would also say when evening came: 'We have reached the day's end, and sovereignty remains with Allah, and all praise is due to Allah. There is no god but Allah, Alone with no partner. His is all sovereignty, and His is all praise, and He is able to do anything. Lord, I ask You for the good of this night, and the good of what comes after, and I seek refuge with You from the evil of this night, and the evil of what comes after. Lord, I seek refuge with You from sloth, and decrepitude, and the plagues of old age, and I seek refuge with You from torment in the Fire, and torment in the grave.'

And when morning rose upon him ﷺ he would say: 'We have reached morning, and sovereignty remains with Allah,' and then continue as above.[288] He ﷺ would also say when morning rose upon him: 'We have reached morning, and sovereignty remains with Allah, and all praise is due to Allah, and all pride and might belongs to Allah; and creation and command, and night and day and all that dwell therein, belong to Allah Almighty.

---

[287] Narrated by Abū Dāwūd and al-Tirmidhī on the authority of Abū Hurayra ؓ.

[288] Narrated by Muslim and Abū Dāwūd on the authority of Ibn Mas'ūd ؓ.

'O Allah, make the first of this day righteousness, and the middle of it prosperity, and the last of it success; O Most Merciful of the merciful!'[289]

And he ﷺ said: 'When morning rises upon any of you, let him say, "We have reached morning, and sovereignty remains with Allah, the Lord of the worlds. O Allah, I ask You for the good of this day: its success, and its succour, and its light, and its blessing, and its guidance; and I seek refuge with You from the evil of it, and the evil of what follows it." Then, when he reaches the afternoon, let him say the like of it.'[290]

**He ﷺ would also recite the following supplication at morning and evening**: 'O Allah, I ask You for wellbeing in this world and the next. O Allah, I ask You for clemency and wellbeing in my religion and my worldly life, and in my family and my possessions. O Allah, cover my blemishes, and assuage my fears. O Allah, protect me from my front, and my back, and my right, and my left, and from above me. I seek refuge with Your might that I should be snatched from below.'[291]

**He ﷺ would also recite the following supplication at morning and evening**: 'O Allah, give me health in my body; O Allah, give me health in my hearing; O Allah, give me health in my sight. There is no god but You (three times). O Allah, I see refuge

---

[289] Narrated by Ibn Abī Shayba in his *Muṣannaf*, al-Ṭabarānī, and Ibn al-Sunnī on the authority of 'Abdullāh ibn Abī Awfā ﷺ. (*Tuḥfat al-Dhākirīn* and elsewhere)

[290] Nawawī said in *al-Adhkār*: 'It is in our narration of Abū Dāwūd's *Sunan*, with a chain of narration which he did not declare to have any weakness, on the authority of Abū Mālik al-Ash'arī ﷺ.'

[291] Narrated by Abū Dāwūd, al-Nasā'ī, and Ibn Mājah, on the authority of Ibn 'Umar ﷺ. 'Snatched from below' here (*ughtāla min taḥtī*) here means for Allah to cause the earth to swallow one up.

with You from disbelief and poverty. O Allah, I seek refuge with You from the torment of the grave. There is no god but You (three times).'[292]

And he ﷺ said to his noble daughter, our Lady Fāṭima ﵂: 'What prevents you from heeding my counsel? At morning and evening, say, "O Living, O All-Sustaining, by Your mercy I seek aid! Rectify all my affairs, and leave me not to my own devices for the blink of an eye!" '[293]

**And when he ﷺ was concerned about something,** he would raise his head to the sky and say: 'Glory be to Allah, the Infinite!'

**And when he ﷺ beseeched Allah with urgency**, he would say: 'O Living, O All-Sustaining!'[294]

**And when he ﷺ needed something**, he would say: 'O Allah, inspire me with what is good, and choose for me.'[295]

**And when he ﷺ purchased new clothes**, he would name the item, whether a shirt, turban, or cloak, and then say: 'O Allah, praise be to You! You clothed me in it; I ask You for the good of it, and the good for which it might be used;[296] and I seek refuge with You from the evil of it, and the evil for which it might be used.'[297]

---

[292] Narrated by Abū Dāwūd and al-Nasā'ī.

[293] Narrated by al-Nasā'ī and al-Ḥākim in his *Ṣaḥīḥ* on the authority on Anas ﵁.

[294] Narrated by al-Tirmidhī on the authority of Abū Hurayra ﵁.

[295] Narrated by al-Tirmidhī on the authority of Abū Bakr al-Ṣiddīq ﵁. Nawawī declared its chain of transmission to be weak.

[296] Literally 'the good for which it was made', and then 'the evil for which it was made'; See *'Awn al-Ma'būd.* [t]

[297] Narrated by Aḥmad, Abū Dāwūd, and al-Tirmidhī.

**And when he ﷺ saw rain**, he would say: 'O Allah, (make it) flow gently, and kindly.'[298]

**And when he ﷺ saw the new moon**, he would say: 'O Allah, make it rise above us with blessings and faith, and safety and peace. My Lord and your Lord is Allah.'[299] And he ﷺ would say: 'O Allah, make it rise above us with security and faith, and safety and peace, and the good fortune to attain what You love and commend. My Lord and your Lord is Allah.'[300]

And he ﷺ would also say: 'Allah is Great, Allah is Great! Praise be to Allah! There is no force or power save with Allah. O Allah, I ask You the good of this month, and I seek refuge with You from the evil of fate, and the evil of the Day of Gathering.'[301]

And he ﷺ would also say: 'New moon of goodness and guidance, my faith is in Him who created you' three times, and then say: 'Praise be to Allah who has brought (the old month's name) to a close, and has inaugurated (the new month's name).'[302]

---

[298] Narrated by the authors of the *Sunan* collections (and al-Bukhārī [t]) on the authority of 'Ā'isha رضي الله عنها.

[299] Narrated by Aḥmad and al-Tirmidhī. (The last part of this – my Lord and your Lord is Allah – is addressed to the new moon. [t])

[300] The author of *al-Jāmi' al-Ṣaghīr* attributed this narration to al-Ṭabarānī, and indicated that it is sound.

[301] Narrated by Imām Aḥmad and al-Ṭabarānī on the authority of Ibn 'Umar رضي الله عنهما.

[302] Narrated by Abū Dāwūd on the authority of Qatāda, who narrated it as something he had heard the Prophet ﷺ had said without mentioning from whom he heard it (*balāghan*), and by Ibn al-Sunnī on the authority of Abū Sa'īd, as is mentioned in *al-Jāmi' al-Ṣaghīr*.

**And when the month of Rajab began**, he ﷺ would say: 'O Allah, bless us in Rajab and Shaʿbān, and grant us to reach Ramaḍān.'

**And on the night before Friday**, he ﷺ would say: 'This is a fine night and a finer day still.'[303]

**And when the wind became strong**, he ﷺ would say: 'O Allah, I ask You for the good of it, and the good of what it contains, and the good of what it has been sent with; and I seek refuge with You from the evil of it, and the evil of what it contains, and the evil of what it has been sent with.'[304]

**And when he ﷺ turned over at night whilst sleeping**, he would say: 'There is no god but Allah, the One, the Invincible, Lord of the heavens and the earth and all that lies between them, the Mighty, the Ever-Forgiving.'[305]

**And when he ﷺ entered the marketplace**, he would say: 'In the name of Allah. O Allah, I ask you for the good of this marketplace, and the good of what lies within it; and I seek refuge with You from the evil of it, and the evil of what lies within it. O Allah, I seek refuge with You that I should be subject therein to a deceitful oath, or a poor deal.'[306]

---

[303] The author of *al-Jāmiʿ al-Ṣaghīr* attributed this narration to al-Bayhaqī and Ibn ʿAsākir. In *al-Adhkār*, al-Nawawī declared its chain of transmission to be weak.

[304] Narrated by Muslim and al-Tirmidhī.

[305] Narrated by al-Nasāʾī, al-Ḥākim, and Ibn Ḥibbān, on the authority of ʿĀʾisha ؓ. Ḥāfiẓ al-ʿIrāqī declared it to be rigorously authentic in his *Amālī*. (*Fayḍ al-Qadīr*)

[306] Narrated by al-Ṭabarānī on the authority of Burayda. Ḥāfiẓ al-Haythamī said: 'Its chain of transmission contains Muḥammad ibn Abān al-Jaʿfī, who is weak.' Ḥākim also narrated it.

**And when he ﷺ was brought the first crop of a fruit**, he would place it on his eyes, and then on his lips, and then say: 'O Allah, as You have shown us the first of it, show us the last of it.' Then he would give it to any children who were present.[307]

**And when food was presented to him ﷺ**, he would say: 'In the name of Allah.' When he finished eating, he would say: 'O Allah, You have given (us) to eat and drink, and You have sufficed (us) and more besides, and You have guided (us) and chosen (us); O Allah, indeed it is right to praise You for what you have given.'[308]

**And when he ﷺ finished eating**, he would say: 'Praise be to Allah, who has fed us, and given us to drink, and made us Muslims.'[309] He would also sometimes say after eating: 'O Allah, praise be to You. You fed, and gave to drink, and satisfied, and quenched, so to You be praise; (You are) neither without thanks, nor forgotten, nor unneeded.'[310]

**And when he ﷺ ate or drank**, he would say: 'Praise be to Allah, who fed, and gave to drink, and facilitated swallowing and digestion.'[311]

---

[307] Ḥāfiẓ al-Haythamī said: 'It was narrated by al-Ṭabarānī on the authority of Ibn 'Abbās in *al-Kabīr* and *al-Ṣaghīr*; and the narrators of *al-Ṣaghīr* are rigorously authentic.' Ḥākim also narrated it on the authority of Anas.

[308] Narrated by al-Nasā'ī and Aḥmad. In *Fatḥ al-Bārī*, al-'Asqalānī declared it to be rigorously authentic.

[309] Narrated by Aḥmad and Ḍiyā' *al-Mukhtāra* on the authority of Abū Sa'īd; the author of *al-Jāmi' al-Ṣaghīr* indicated it to be a sound narration.

[310] Narrated by Imām Aḥmad with a sound chain of transmission. (*Al-Jāmi' al-Ṣaghīr*)

[311] Narrated by Abū Dāwūd and others.

**And when he ﷺ broke his fast**, he would say: 'O Allah, for You did I fast, and with Your provision did I break my fast, so accept it from me, for You are the All-Hearing, the All-Knowing.'[312]

He ﷺ would also sometimes say upon breaking his fast: 'Thirst has passed, and nerves have been moistened; and the reward has been confirmed, Allah willing.'[313] If he ﷺ broke his fast as a guest, he would pray for the hosts, saying: 'Those who fasted have broken their fast with you, and the righteous have eaten your food, and the Angels have descended upon you,' that is, with mercy and Divine grace. One narration has it: '… and the Angels have prayed for you.'[314]

**And when he ﷺ ate as a guest, he would pray for his hosts** by saying: 'The righteous have eaten your food, and the Angels have prayed for you, and those who fasted have broken their fasts with you.'[315]

**And to congratulate someone upon their marriage,** he ﷺ would say: 'Allah bless you, and send you blessings, and unite the two of you in goodness.'[316]

---

[312] Narrated by Abū Dāwūd up until 'did I break my fast'; the rest is from the narrations of al-Ṭabarānī and Ibn al-Sunnī.
(*Al-Jāmiʿ al-Ṣaghīr*)
[313] Narrated by Abū Dāwūd and al-Ḥākim on the authority of Ibn 'Umar.
[314] Narrated by Imām Aḥmad and al-Bayhaqī on the authority of Anas with a sound chain of transmission, as mentioned in *al-Jāmiʿ al-Ṣaghīr*. It was also narrated by Abū Dāwūd, as is mentioned in *Fayḍ al-Qadīr*.
[315] Narrated by Aḥmad and al-Bazzār.
[316] Narrated by the authors of the *Sunan* collections, as well as Ibn Ḥibbān. Tirmidhī declared it to be sound and rigorously authentic. (See also *Fayḍ al-Qadīr* and *Tuḥfat al-Dhākirīn*, and elsewhere.)

In the pre-Islamic time of ignorance, they would say to a man when he married, 'May you find comfort, and beget sons!' The Prophet ﷺ forbade them from saying this because it contained no expressions of praise or thanks, or even any mention of Allah ﷻ, and because it alluded to the people's hatred of daughters by its mention of sons alone, and for other reasons besides this. And so he ﷺ taught them to say instead: 'Allah bless you,' that is, in your marriage, 'and send you blessings' of children and blessed progeny, 'and unite the two of you in goodness' in the form of good companionship, compatibility, and love.

And he ﷺ would teach men to say, when they married: 'O Allah, I ask You for her goodness, and the goodness You have placed in her natural disposition; and I seek refuge with You from her evil, and the evil You have placed in her natural disposition.'[317] One narration adds that the Prophet ﷺ also advised that the groom should place his hand on the bride's forehead and pray for blessings for her.

**And at times of distress**, he ﷺ would say: 'There is no god but Allah, the Infinite, the Forbearing. There is no god but Allah, Lord of the mighty Throne. There is no god but Allah, Lord of the heavens, and Lord of the earth, and Lord of the noble Throne.'[318] One of al-Bukhārī's narrations has it: 'There is no god but Allah, the Forbearing, the Generous.' Muslim's narration states that when a serious matter befell him ﷺ, he would make this invocation. He would also say in times of distress: 'O Living, O All-Sustaining, I seek the aid of Your mercy!'[319]

---

[317] Narrated by Abū Dāwūd and Abū Ya'lā, mentioned in *al-Ḥiṣn* and its commentaries.

[318] Narrated by Bukhārī and Muslim on the authority of Ibn 'Abbās ﵄.

[319] Narrated by al-Tirmidhī.

**And when he ﷺ was concerned about people who posed danger**, he would say: 'O Allah, we invoke You against them, and we seek refuge with You from their evil.'[320]

Anas said: 'We were with the Prophet ﷺ in a battle, and he met the enemy, whereupon I heard him say, "O Master of the Day of Judgement, You do I worship, and Your aid do I seek!" Upon this, I saw the enemy flounder as the Angels smote them from their front and their rear.'[321]

**And when he ﷺ visited an ill person**, he would place his right hand upon them and say: 'O Allah, Lord of men, remove all harm. Heal, for You are the Healer, and there is no cure but Your cure, a cure that leaves no trace of sickness.'[322] Anas ؓ once said to Thābit al-Banānī ؓ, 'Would you like me to recite for you the healing prayer of the Messenger of Allah ﷺ?' He replied, 'Yes', so Anas said: 'O Allah, Lord of men, and Reliever of harm: Heal, for You are the Healer and there is no Healer but You, with a cure that leaves no trace of illness.'[323]

And when he ﷺ visited an ill person, he would sit by their head and then say seven times: 'I ask Allah, the Infinite, the Lord of the mighty Throne, to heal you.'[324]

---

[320] Narrated by Abū Dāwūd and al-Nasā'ī on the authority of Abū Mūsā al-Ash'arī ؓ.

[321] Narrated by Ibn al-Sunnī; al-Nawawī said: 'It is preferable to say the invocation we mentioned in the last section, narrated by Abū Mūsā.' (I.e. 'O Allah, we invoke You against them, and we seek refuge with You from their evil.' [t])

[322] Narrated by al-Bukhārī and Muslim on the authority of Ibn 'Abbās ؓ.

[323] Narrated by al-Bukhārī.

[324] Narrated by Ibn Ḥibbān, who declared it rigorously authentic, and by al-Nasā'ī with the wording mentioned here.

Ibn 'Abbās related that the Prophet ﷺ said: 'If someone visits a sick person whose time has not yet come, and says in his presence seven times: "I ask Allah, the Infinite, the Lord of the mighty Throne, to heal you," Allah Almighty will cure their ailment.'[325] Ibn 'Abbās ؓ also related that when the Messenger of Allah ﷺ went to visit an ill person, he would first say to them, 'No harm: it is purifying, Allah willing.'[326]

**And he ﷺ would teach those who suffered from nightmares or insomnia** to say: 'I seek refuge with the perfect words of Allah from His wrath and His requital, and the evil of His servants, and the whispers of demons and their presence near me.' Ibn 'Umar used to teach this supplication to those of his children who were old enough to learn it, and would write it down and hang it around the necks of those who were too young to learn it.[327]

And the Messenger of Allah ﷺ taught Khālid ibn Walīd to say, when the latter was unable to sleep: 'O Allah, Lord of the seven heavens and all they cover, Lord of the earths and all they bear, Lord of the demons and all they lead astray! Be for me a refuge from all Your evil creatures entire, lest any of them abuse me, or tyrannise me. Mighty is Your refuge, and great is Your glory!' One narration adds: 'And blessed is Your name, and there is no god but You.'[328]

---

[325] Narrated by Abū Dāwūd and al-Tirmidhī, who declared it sound. See also *Sharḥ Riyāḍ al-Ṣāliḥīn* and *Nuzul al-Abrār*.
[326] Narrated by al-Bukhārī.
[327] Narrated by Abū Dāwūd and al-Tirmidhī, who declared it to be a sound singular narration. Nasā'ī and al-Ḥākim narrated it without mentioning its use to aid sleep, as al-Mundhirī mentions in his *Targhīb*; it can be used by anyone who experiences fear or trauma, and should be recited three times, as is mentioned in one narration.
[328] Narrated by al-Tirmidhī and al-Ṭabarānī.

**And when he ﷺ wanted to leave a gathering**, he would say: 'Glory be to You, Allah, I hymn Your praise. I bear witness that there is no god but You, and I seek Your forgiveness, and I repent to You.'

Upon hearing this, a man said, 'O Messenger of Allah, what is this you say, that you have never said before?' The Prophet ﷺ replied, 'It is a expiation for all that took place in the gathering.'[329]

Ibn 'Umar ؓ said: 'Rarely would the Messenger of Allah ﷺ rise from a gathering without first making this supplication: "O Allah, give us enough fear of You to prevent us from disobeying You, and enough obedience of You to make us reach Your Paradise, and enough certainty to make the trials of this world seem trivial to us. O Allah, give us joy of our hearing, our sight, and our strength, as long as You keep us alive, and make them (as unto) our heirs;[330] and make our vengeance fall upon those who wrong us, and give us succour against our enemies; and let not our hardships involve our religion; and let not the life of this world be our primary goal, nor the limit of our knowledge; and place not in authority over us those who will show us no mercy."'[331]

**The manners of gatherings taught to us by the Prophet ﷺ include** the sound narration of al-Tirmidhī, on the authority of Abū Hurayra ؓ, who reported that the Prophet ﷺ said: 'No group of people sit together in a gathering in which they make no mention of Allah Almighty, nor send any benedictions upon

---

(*Al-Targhīb wa al-Tarhīb*)
[329] Narrated by Abū Dāwūd, and al-Nasā'ī in *'Amal al-Yawm wal-Nahār*, on the authority of Abū Baraza ؓ.
[330] See note 267, p.134
[331] Narrated by al-Tirmidhī, who declared it sound.

their Prophet, except that it will count against them; if He wills, He will punish them, and if He wills, He will forgive them.' Imām al-Nawawī said:

> Our narration of *Ḥilyat al-Awliyā'* includes the statement of 'Alī ؓ: He who wishes to be allotted a measure from the finest scale, let him say at the end of a gathering, or when he gets up to leave it: "Glorified be your Lord, the Lord of might, from that which they attribute (to Him), and peace be upon the Messengers, and Praise be to Allah, Lord of the worlds." '

**And when he ﷺ bade someone farewell** before they travelled, he would say: 'I invoke the protection of Allah for your religion, and your trusts, and the final outcome of your deeds, [332] and I wish you peace.'

Anas ؓ related that a man came to the Prophet ﷺ and said, 'Messenger of Allah, I wish to travel, so give me something to take with me.' The Prophet ﷺ replied, 'May Allah grant you piety.' The man asked for more, so he ﷺ said, 'And may He forgive your sins.' The man said, 'Give me more, my father and mother be ransomed for you!' He ﷺ replied, 'And may He help you to find goodness wherever you may be.'[333]

---

[332] Narrated up to this point by Abū Dāwūd on the authority of Ibn 'Umar; the rest is from the narration of al-Nasā'ī and al-Tirmidhī. Khaṭṭābī says that 'trusts' here refers to the person's family and those he would leave behind when he travelled, and the money he would leave for someone to look after; and the reason for the mention of 'religion' is that travel is a time of hardship, which might lead to some religious matters being neglected.

[333] Narrated by al-Tirmidhī, who declared it to be a sound singular narration, and also by al-Nasā'ī and al-Ḥākim.

**And when he ﷺ mounted his camel with the intention of travelling**, he would say 'Allah is Great' three times, and then say: ﴾Glory be to He who subdued this for us, which we ourselves could never have done; and unto our Lord we are returning.﴿[334] O Allah, we ask you on this our journey for righteousness and piety, and such actions as please You. O Allah, lighten for us this journey of ours, and shorten for us its distance. O Allah, You are our travelling Companion, and the One in whose care we leave our family. O Allah, I seek refuge with You from the hardships of travel, and from any disheartening sights in store, and from any harm that might befall our families and property upon our return.'

And upon returning, he ﷺ would recite the same, and add: 'We return, repentant, worshipful, hymning the praises of our Lord.'[335]

**And when he ﷺ entered a graveyard**, he would say: 'Peace be upon you, abode of believing people; we too, Allah willing, shall come to join you.'[336]

Ibn 'Abbās ؓ said: 'The Messenger of Allah ﷺ passed by the graves of Medina, and as he did he turned his face to them and said, "Peace be upon you, people of the graves.

---

[334] Qur'ān 43:13

[335] Narrated by Muslim in *Kitāb al-Ḥajj*. See also *Riyāḍ al-Ṣāliḥīn*.

[336] Narrated by Muslim. The meaning of 'Allah willing' here is 'Allah willing, we will come to join you by dying upon faith as you did,' as mentioned in *Fayḍ al-Qadīr*. Some of them say that the use of the phrase 'Allah willing' here is simply for the blessing of it, and in accordance with Allah's commandment (concerning speaking about the future); and often the phrase is used as a way of adding emphasis to what came before it, and as a way of acknowledging that the thing will surely happen, but only by Allah's will.

'May Allah forgive us and forgive you; you are our forerunners, and we shall follow."'[337]

Burayda said: 'The Prophet would teach people to say when they visited graves: "Peace be upon you, folk of the abode, believers and Muslims; we too, Allah willing, shall come to join you. I ask Allah to grant us and you strength.[338] You are our leaders, and we are your followers."'

**One of the supplications he would make when performing the pilgrimage** is that which was narrated by al-Bayhaqī in his *Sunan*, on the authority of Abū Hurayra, who said that the Messenger of Allah said: 'O Allah, forgive the pilgrims, and all those for whom the pilgrims pray.'[339]

Ibn al-Sunnī narrated that Ibn 'Umar said: 'A boy came to the Prophet and said he wanted to perform the pilgrimage, so the Messenger of Allah walked with him a while, and said, "Boy, may Allah grant you piety, and direct you to goodness, and assuage all your worries."

'When the boy returned, he greeted the Prophet, who said to him, "Boy, may Allah accept your pilgrimage, and forgive your sins, and repay you what you have spent."'

---

[337] Narrated by al-Tirmidhī, who declared it sound. This Ḥadīth is proof that it is recommended to send greetings of peace upon the dead when visiting them or passing by them.

[338] Narrated by Muslim and al-Nasā'ī up to here; the rest is from one of the narrations of Ibn Mājah.

[339] Ḥākim declared it to be rigorously authentic according to the criteria of Muslim.

# HOW HE ﷺ WOULD GLORIFY AND PRAISE HIS LORD

Allah ﷻ said: ❪So hymn the praises of thy Lord, and be of those who prostrate themselves.❫[340] The Prophet ﷺ would glorify and praise Allah much, out of his deep love and passion for doing so; indeed he ﷺ once said, 'To say "Glory be to Allah, and praise be to Allah, and there is no god but Allah, and Allah is Great" is more beloved to me than all that upon which the sun rises.'[341]

So let all those inclined to reflection reflect upon the passion and love of this noble Prophet ﷺ for glorifying his Lord, and praising Him, and extolling His oneness and magnificence, and that for him to utter a single phrase embodying all this was more beloved unto him than all the beings upon which the sun rises, be they great or small, upon land or in sea.

The Prophet ﷺ once said to Abū Dharr ؓ: 'Shall I not tell you the most beloved of words to Allah Almighty?'[342] Abū Dharr replied, 'O Messenger of Allah, indeed do tell me the most beloved of words to Allah Almighty.' The Prophet ﷺ said, 'The most beloved of words to Allah Almighty are: "Glory be to Allah, I hymn His praise." '[343] One narration has it that the Messenger of Allah ﷺ was asked what the best words were, and he replied, 'They are those which Allah chose for His Angels: [one narration has it 'for His servants'] "Glory be to Allah, I hymn His praise." '

---

[340] Qur'ān 15:98
[341] Narrated by Muslim and al-Tirmidhī on the authority of Abū Hurayra.
[342] Meaning the most beloved words to Allah after the Qur'ān, which is His own speech.
[343] Narrated by Muslim.

The Prophet ﷺ would glorify Allah much, night and day. Ṭabarānī narrates that Rabīʿa ibn Kaʿb al-Aslamī said: 'I sued to serve the Prophet ﷺ by day, and when night fell I would go to the door of the Messenger of Allah ﷺ and sleep there, and I would listen him saying, "Glory be to Allah, glory be to Allah, glory be to my Lord", until sleep overcame me.'

'One day, he ﷺ said to me, "O Rabīʿa, ask me for something, and I will give it to you." I replied, "Wait a while, O Messenger of Allah, while I think about it." Then it occurred to me that the life of this world is brief and fleeting, so I said, "Messenger of Allah, I ask you to pray to Allah that He saves me from Hell and enters me into Paradise." [Muslim's narration has it that he said, 'I ask your company in Paradise.'] The Prophet ﷺ replied, "Or perhaps (you desire) something else?" I said, "No, that is all." He ﷺ replied, "Then help me for your own sake by making much prostration." '

The Prophet ﷺ approved of concise phrases that express a great deal of glorification and praise; an example of this is the invocations we would recite at midmorning:

Imām Muslim and the authors of the *Sunan* collections narrated, on the authority of Juwayriya ﵂, wife of the Prophet ﷺ, that the Prophet ﷺ left her house one day and then returned after midmorning [al-Tirmidhī's narration states that it was close to midday] to find her sitting and glorifying Allah. He ﷺ said to her, 'You are still doing what you were when I left you?' She replied, 'Yes.' The Prophet ﷺ then said, 'I will say in my stead four phrases three times each which, if they were weighed against what you have said, would outweigh it: *Glory be to Allah, I hymn His praise* the number of His creations, and as does please His Own Self, and (as is equal to) the weight of His Throne, and (as equal to) the ink of His words.'

One of Muslim's narrations has it: '*Glory be to Allah* the number of His creations, and *Glory be to Allah* as does satisfy His Own Self, and *Glory be to Allah* the weight of His Throne, and *Glory be to Allah* the ink of His words.' Nasā'ī's narration adds, 'And praise be to Allah the same.'

Another narration has it: '*Glory be to Allah, I hymn His praise, and there is no god but Allah, and Allah is great* the number of His creatures, and as does satisfy His Own Self, and (as is equal to) the weight of His Throne, and the ink of His words.'[344]

Tirmidhī and al-Ḥākim narrate that Ṣafiyya ﷺ reported that the Prophet ﷺ came to her and found her using four thousand date stones to count her expressions of glorification. Upon seeing this, he ﷺ said: 'Shall I not teach you how to make more glorification than that which you have made?' She replied, 'Indeed, do teach me.' He said, 'Say: "*Glory be to Allah* the number of his creations." '

The narration of al-Ḥākim has it 'Say: "*Glory be to Allah* the number of everything He has created." '[345]

The Prophet ﷺ would also teach the Companions other concise phrases that expressed a great deal of glorification and praise, and would encourage them to use them.

Abū Umāma said: 'The Messenger of Allah ﷺ saw me moving my lips, and said, "With what do you move you lips, Abū Umāma?" I replied, "I am making remembrance of Allah, O Messenger of Allah." He said, "Shall I not tell you of a way that is greater and better than your remembrance by night and day?" I said, "Indeed do tell me, O Messenger of Allah."

---

[344] Mundhirī, *al-Targhīb wa al-Tarhīb.*
[345] Ibid.

'He said: "Say *Glory be to Allah* the number of all He has created, and *Glory be to Allah* the quantity of all He has created, and *Glory be to Allah* the number of everything in earth and the sky, and *Glory be to Allah* the number of all His Book contains, and *Glory be to Allah* the quantity of all His Book contains, and *Glory be to Allah* the number of everything, and *Glory be to Allah* the quantity of everything.

'"And *Praise be to Allah* the number of all He has created, and *Praise be to Allah* the quantity of all He has created, and *Praise be to Allah* the number of everything in earth and the sky, and *Praise be to Allah* the number of all His Book contains, and *Praise be to Allah* the quantity of all His Book contains, and *Praise be to Allah* the number of everything, and *Praise be to Allah* the quantity of everything." '[346]

## HIS PRAYERS FOR FORGIVENESS ﷺ

Allah said: ﴾And seek forgiveness of Allah; Allah is ever Forgiving, Merciful.﴿[347] And He said: ﴾Hymn the praises of thy Lord, and seek forgiveness of Him; He is ever Relenting.﴿[348]

**To seek forgiveness** (*al-istighfār*) means to ask Allah Almighty for forgiveness. The Prophet ﷺ would seek much forgiveness at night and day, both during the ritual prayers and after them, and indeed on all occasions.

---

[346] Ḥāfiẓ al-Mundhirī said: 'It was narrated by Aḥmad, Ibn Abī Dunyā (and the wording is his), al-Nasā'ī, Ibn Khuzayma and Ibn Ḥibbān (in their *Ṣaḥīḥ* collections in an abridged form), and al-Ḥākim, who declared it rigorously authentic according to the conditions of al-Bukhārī and Muslim.

[347] Qur'ān 4:106

[348] Qur'ān 110:3

It is reported that Makhūl, who used to seek forgiveness abundantly, said: 'Abū Hurayra used to seek forgiveness often and he said that he never saw anyone seek forgiveness more than the Messenger of Allah ﷺ would.'

Muslim narrated that Abū Hurayra ؓ said, 'The Messenger of Allah ﷺ used to say when prostrating: "O Allah, forgive me all of my sins, both the slight and the grave, and the first and the last, and the hidden and the open." '

Muslim also narrated that Thawbān ؓ said: 'When the Messenger of Allah ﷺ finished praying, he would seek forgiveness of Allah three times, and then say, "O Allah, You are Peace, and from You comes peace; blessed are You, Lord of Majesty and Bounty!" '

Bukhārī narrated, on the authority of Abū Hurayra ؓ that the Messenger of Allah ﷺ said: 'By Allah, I seek Allah's forgiveness and repent to him more than seventy times a day.'

The scholars say that the Prophet's ﷺ words 'more than seventy times' mean simply a great many times, since the Arabs would use the numbers seven, seventy, and seven hundred to mean large amounts, so a Bedouin would say to someone who gave him something, 'May Allah reward you seven-fold', i.e. a great deal.

It may also be the case that the Prophet ﷺ meant this number specifically, in which case the words 'more than' would be somewhat ambiguous, which can be explained by another narration of this Ḥadīth which states: 'Some days I seek forgiveness of Allah one hundred times.'

Muslim narrated, on the authority of Agharr al-Muzanī ﷺ, that the Messenger of Allah ﷺ said: 'My heart is at times overcast, and some days I seek forgiveness of Allah one hundred times.' The word 'overcast' here is derived from the Arabic word *ghayn*, which means a thin cloud. The meaning here is a cloud of lights, not a cloud of temporal distractions.

Bukhārī and Muslim narrate, on the authority of Ibn 'Abbās ﷺ, that the Messenger of Allah ﷺ said: 'O Allah, to You I submit, and in You I believe, and in You I trust, and to You I turn, and for You I stand, and to Your judgement I defer. Forgive me what I have done, and what I will do, and what I have concealed, and what I have revealed; You are the One who sends forth, and the One who holds back, and there is no god but You, and there is no power nor might save with Allah.'

He ﷺ would also seek Allah's forgiveness much when in the company of his Companions: Abū Dāwūd and Ibn Ḥibbān narrated that Ibn 'Umar ﷺ said: 'We would sit with the Messenger of Allah ﷺ in a single gathering and count him say, "My Lord, forgive me and relent to me, for You are the Relenting, the Merciful" one hundred times.'[349]

Tirmidhī also narrated this, declaring it to be sound and rigorously authentic with a single chain of narration, with the wording: '… for You are the Relenting, the Merciful.'

Nasā'ī narrated, with a good chain of transmission on the authority of Mujāhid, who reported that Ibn 'Umar said he heard the Prophet ﷺ say, 'I seek forgiveness of Allah, besides whom there is no god, the Living, the All-Sustaining; and I repent to Him' at a single gathering one hundred times.[350]

---

[349] Ibn Ḥibbān declared it to be rigorously authentic.

[350] See *al-Mawāhib* and its commentaries.

**If it be asked** why the Messenger of Allah ﷺ sought much forgiveness of Allah even though he ﷺ was forgiven all his past and future sins, as was made clear with the verse ﴾That Allah might forgive thee thy trespasses past and future﴿[351], the answer to this is multifaceted, as the scholars and learned ones have stated:[352]

**Firstly**, to seek forgiveness of Allah is an act of worship, and a realisation of one's slavehood, and an expression of need for Divine generosity.

**Secondly**, it was a means of teaching his ﷺ community that they should also seek much forgiveness of Allah, because of their dire need for it.

**Thirdly**, it was an expression of humility before the Lord of the worlds, and a sign of a modest soul.

There are several others answers to this issue, which we will mention later in their proper place, Allah willing.

The Prophet ﷺ would also teach the Companions comprehensive invocations for forgiveness, and would encourage them to use them because of their great merit:

Bukhārī and others narrate, on the authority of Shaddād ibn Aws ؓ, that the Messenger of Allah ﷺ said: 'The leader[353] of invocations for forgiveness is: "O Allah, You are my Lord; There is no god but You.

---

[351] Qur'ān 48:2

[352] See *Sharḥ al-Zurqānī 'alā al-Mawāhib* and elsewhere.

[353] Because this prayer embodies all aspects of repentance, it was given the name 'leader' (*sayyid*), which in essence means the one to whom all turn at times of need, and to whom all matters are referred.

' "You created me, and I am Your servant, and I shall hold to Your covenant and Your word as best I can.[354] I seek refuge with You from the evil I have done. I acknowledge to You the blessing You have granted me, and I acknowledge my sin; forgive me, then, for none can forgive sins but You."

'Whoever says this by day, believing in it with conviction, and then dies before nightfall, shall be among the denizens of Paradise; and whoever says it by night, believing in it with conviction, and then dies before daybreak, shall be among the denizens of Paradise.'

Ibn Mas'ūd related that the Messenger of Allah said: 'Whoever says "I seek forgiveness of Allah, besides whom there is no god, the Living, the All-Sustaining; and I repent to Him" will be forgiven his sins, even if he is guilty of fleeing from the enemy.'[355]

Bukhārī and Muslim narrated that 'Ā'isha said: 'In the days before his passing, the Messenger of Allah often said: "Glory be to Allah, I hymn His praises. I seek forgiveness of Allah, and repent to Him.'

The Prophet would also encourage others to seek forgiveness much, because of the servant's need for it come the Hereafter:

---

[354] That is, I will hold to the covenant I made with You when You took a covenant from all humanity, gathering them all before you like so many seeds, and calling them to testify to themselves; You said to them, ﴾Am I not your Lord?﴿ (Qur'ān 7:172) and they agreed, saying, 'Indeed You are'; and I will hold to Your word by keeping faith in You and Your Messengers, and by obeying You.

[355] Imām al-Nawawī said in *Riyāḍ al-Ṣāliḥīn*: 'It was narrated by Abū Dāwūd, al-Tirmidhī, and al-Ḥākim, who declared it to be rigorously authentic according to the conditions of Bukhārī and Muslim.

Abdullāh ibn Yusr ﷺ said: 'I heard the Messenger of Allah ﷺ say, "Happy is he whose account contains much seeking of forgiveness." '[356]

He ﷺ also taught us that seeking forgiveness is a means of polishing the heart from impurities:

Bayhaqī narrated, on the authority of Anas ﷺ, that the Prophet ﷺ said: 'Hearts become rusty just as copper does; the way to polish them is to seek forgiveness.'

He ﷺ also taught us that much seeking of forgiveness assuages worries, and saves one from difficulties, and facilitates the coming of provisions:

Abū Dāwūd, al-Nasā'ī and others narrate, on the authority of Ibn 'Abbās, that the Messenger of Allah ﷺ said: 'If someone seeks forgiveness regularly, Allah gives him deliverance from every worry, and release from every dilemma, and provides for him from whence he least suspects.'

---

[356] Narrated by Ibn Mājah with a rigorously authentic chain of transmission, and by al-Bayhaqī. (*Al-Targhīb wa al-Tarhīb*)

# PART III: THE NOBLE ANCESTRY OF OUR MASTER MUḤAMMAD ﷺ

## HIS NOBLE LINEAGE AND EMINENT ORIGINS ﷺ

ALLAH ﷻ SAID: ﴾Allah knows best where to send His Message.﴿[357] And He ﷻ said: ﴾There has come to you a Messenger from your own selves, unto whom aught that overburdens you is grievous, full of concern for you, with the believers compassionate and merciful.﴿[358]

In his *Ṣaḥīḥ* collection, Imām Bukhārī related the lineage of the Prophet ﷺ, saying: 'He is Muḥammad[359] ﷺ, son of 'Abdullāh,

---

[357] Qur'ān 6:124

[358] Qur'ān 9:128

[359] So he is our Master Muḥammad ﷺ, and this noble name is derived from the word meaning pure praise (*ḥamd*), its morphological form implying abundance, for the word *muḥammad* means someone who is praised again and again, and within whom all praiseworthy attributes are combined (*Fatḥ al-Bārī*). This is because if someone is endowed with many praiseworthy attributes in their most perfect of forms, the people will praise and laud them much; and the perfect one of Allah's ﷻ creatures, and the noblest in character, and the finest in conduct,

son of 'Abd al-Muṭṭalib,[360] son of Hāshim,[361] son of 'Abd Manāf,[362] son of Quṣayy,[363] son of Kilāb,[364] son of Murra,[365] son

---

and the most comprehensively favoured, was our Master Muḥammad ﷺ. Bayhaqī narrated in his *Dalā'il* with a *mursal* chain of transmission (i.e. one where the transmitting Companion is not named), that when the Prophet ﷺ was born, 'Abd al-Muṭṭalib held a banquet to celebrate the birth. When the people had finished eating, they asked him what he had named the child. He told them he had chosen the name Muḥammad, whereupon they asked him, 'Why have you not chosen for him a name from his own tribe?' He replied, 'I desired that he be praised by Allah from on high, and praised by His creatures here on earth.' (*Fatḥ al-Bārī*) Some of the scholars say that it was rather the Prophet's ﷺ mother who named him Muḥammad, because of a vision she had in which his ﷺ status was revealed to her. Abū Nu'aym narrated, on the authority of Ibn 'Abbās, that Āmina used to say: 'A herald came to me six months into my term as I slept, and said, "O Āmina, you carry within you the best of all the worlds; when you bear him, name him Muḥammad ﷺ." ' There is no contradiction here, as al-Zurqānī says, since when Āmina told 'Abd al-Muṭṭalib about what she had seen, he named the child Muḥammad ﷺ; so he named the child because of her, which means that it is correct to say it was she that named him Muḥammad ﷺ. See *Sharḥ al-Mawāhib* vol 1, p.111, vol.2, p.114, and *Fatḥ al-Bārī* vol 1, p.124.

360 His real name was Shayba, and people would also call him *Ḥamd* ('Praise') because everyone used to praise him, and Quraysh would all turn to him at moments of crisis, and seek his opinion regarding all their affairs, and he was truly their leader in excellence and effectiveness.

361 His real name was 'Amr; he was known as Hāshim because he was the first in Mecca to mash (Ar. *hashama*) broth for the seasonal visitors, and for his own tribe first, in a year of famine.

362 His first name was Mughīra, which literally means 'one who makes others jealous'; he was given this name in the hopeful anticipation that he would make his rivals envious.

of Ka'b,[366] son of Lu'ayy,[367] son of Ghālib,[368] son of Fihr,[369] son of Mālik,[370] son of Naḍr,[371] son of Kināna,[372] son of

---

He was an authority figure amongst Quraysh, and was nicknamed 'Moon' because of his handsome appearance.

[363] He was also known as Mujammi' ('Gatherer') because, as Tha'lab states in his *Amālī*, he used to gather his people together on Fridays and address them, commanding them to respect the holiness of the Sanctuary, and telling them that one day a Prophet would be sent to them. (*Sharḥ al-Mawāhib*)

[364] This name is derived from the verb meaning to beset the enemy and harass them. His actual name was Ḥakīm; some say it was 'Urwa.

[365] The meaning of this name is 'great power'.

[366] He was named after the word for the binding knot of a spear, according to Ibn Durayd and others, because of the high position he held over his people, and his noble standing amongst them, for which reason they were subservient to him, and chronicled his death. (*Fatḥ al-Bārī*) He was known to be an eloquent speaker, and he would command his people to respect the holiness of the Sanctuary, and he would gather them together and inform them that a Prophet would one day be sent to them, and that if they were to live to see him they must follow him, just as Quṣayy would also do after him.
(*Sharḥ al-Mawāhib*, *Fatḥ al-Bārī*, and elsewhere)

[367] Aṣma'ī said that this is a diminutive form of *Liwā'*, meaning 'flag' or 'standard'.

[368] Meaning 'Victor' or 'Conqueror'.

[369] This name literally means a small stone that could fit in one's palm; it is also said to mean a long stone. He was also known as Quraysh, and all the tribes of Quraysh traced their lineage back to him; those who trace their ancestry to his forbears, but not through him, are said to be from the tribe of Kināna, not Quraysh. Ḥāfiẓ al-Zurqānī said: 'This is the position preferred by al-Dimyāṭī, al-'Irāqī, and others, and is based on the Ḥadīth narrated by Muslim and al-Tirmidhī in which the Prophet ﷺ said: "Allah Almighty chose Kināna from the progeny of Ismā'īl, and chose Quraysh from (the progeny of) Kināna…"

Khuzayma,[373] son of Mudrika,[374] son of Ilyās,[375] son of Muḍar,[376] son of Nizār,[377] son of Ma'add,[378] son of 'Adnān.[379]

---

Others say that the origin of the tribe of Quraysh was Naḍr; and this was the position of al-Shāfi'ī, and al-'Irāqī declared it to be the majority opinion. Nawawī also declared it to be the soundest and most famous opinion, as did Ḥāfiẓ Ṣalāḥ al-'Alā'ī, who said it was the opinion of the most diligent scholars. This opinion is based on the statement of (the Companion) Ash'ath ibn Qays: "I went to the Messenger of Allah ﷺ as part of a delegation of Kinda, and said to him: 'Are you not one of us, O Messenger of Allah?' He said, 'No, we are the sons of Naḍr, son of Kināna.' " (Narrated by Ibn Mājah, Ibn 'Abd al-Barr, and Abū Nu'aym in *al-Riyāḍa*)'

[370] This means 'Owner'; his nickname was Abū al-Ḥārith.

[371] His real name was Qays; he was known as Naḍr because of the luminescence (*naḍāra*) of his face, and his bright and handsome appearance. (*Sharḥ al-Mawāhib*)

[372] This name literally means a leather quiver for arrows. Abū 'Āmir al-'Udwānī is reported to have said: 'I saw Kināna ibn Khuzayma as an old man of noble bearing. The Arabs would flock to him because of his great learning and virtuous standing amongst them.' (*Fatḥ al-Bārī*)

[373] This is a diminutive form of *khazma*, which means something firm and sound, as mentioned in *Fatḥ al-Bārī* and elsewhere.

[374] This means 'realised'; he was given this name because all the honour and pride of his forebears was realised within him, and the light of the Chosen Prophet ﷺ shone plainly from him. His real name was 'Amr according to the majority; and this is the soundest opinion. Ibn Isḥāq reported that his ream name was 'Āmir, but this is a weak opinion. (*Fatḥ al-Bārī*)

[375] The well-known position is that this was his real name; it is also said that is was a nickname, and his real name was Ḥabīb. Zurqānī said: 'It is related in *al-Muntaqā* that Ilyās used to hear, in his heart, the Prophet's ﷺ *talbiya* (greetings to Allah) at the pilgrimage; and

Ḥāfiẓ Ibn Kathīr and others have said that this lineage is agreed upon unanimously by the scholars, and indeed all the Arabs of Ḥijāz could trace their ancestry back to this line; and so Ibn 'Abbās ﷺ said, about Allah's ﷻ word: ﴿Say: I do not ask of you any reward, save loving kindness among kinsfolk﴾[380], that there was not a single household in Quraysh except that the Messenger of Allah ﷺ had some kind of tie of kinship to them. Just so, all the Arab tribes of 'Adnān could trace their ancestry back to this lineage, many of them through their mothers' line, which is why the Messenger of Allah ﷺ requested all the Arab tribes to preserve this kinship, and stand with him and defend him.

---

others would sometimes hear the echoes of this coming from his breast.

[Translator's note: the narrations of this incident from *Fayḍ al-Qadīr* and *'Umdat al-Qarī* have been consulted here to make better sense of the report in *al-Muntaqā*, which only mentioned the echoes coming from Ilyās' back.] The Arabs continue to venerate Ilyās as a Sage comparable to Luqmān and those like him. He was considered the leader of his people, and the master of his kin, and no decision was made and no verdict was passed without his approval.'

[376] He was given this name because he would move (*yamḍur*) hearts because of his radiance and beauty.

[377] This name is derived from a word meaning 'extremely rare'; he was given this name because he was unique amongst his generation and the most handsome and intelligent of them.

[378] This means 'prepared' or 'willing.'

[379] This name is derived from the verb *'adana*, meaning 'to reside'. Zurqānī said: 'It is related in *al-Khamīs* that he was given this name because the eyes of the jinn and mankind were upon him, wanting to kill him, saying: "If we leave this boy to grow, there will come from his progeny one who will lead the people"; and so Allah sent to him those who would protect him.' So he resided in security and protection.

[380] Qur'ān 42:23

Furthermore, the scholars agreed that 'Adnān was a descendent of Ismā'īl, the son of our Master Ibrāhīm, peace and blessings be upon them, and upon our Prophet.

The scholars do differ as to the names of those who came between 'Adnān and Ibrāhīm ﷺ, and those who came between Ibrāhīm ﷺ and Ādam ﷺ, details of which can be found in Muḥammad ibn Yūsuf al-Shāmī's work *al-Sīrat al-Nabawiyya*, and also in al-'Asqalānī's *Fatḥ al-Bārī.*

'Asqalānī mentioned in *Fatḥ al-Bārī* that Ibn Sa'd narrated, on the authority of Ibn 'Abbās, that when the Prophet ﷺ mentioned his lineage, he never went any further back than Ma'add son of 'Adnān.

**Any person of intelligence who considers this lineage will surely recognise its purity, nobility, honour, and eminence.**

## THE EXCELLENCE OF HIS NOBLE LINEAGE ﷺ

Bukhārī narrated on the authority of Abū Hurayra ؓ that the Messenger of Allah ﷺ said: 'I was sent forth from the finest generations of the Sons of Ādam, generation after generation, until I came from the generation from which I came.'

The narration of Ibn Sa'd on the authority of Abū Ja'far al-Bāqir[381] ؓ adds: 'Then He chose the sons of Hāshim from amongst Quraysh, and then chose the sons of 'Abd al-Muṭṭalib from amongst the sons of Hāshim.'

---

[381] This narration is *mursal*, that is, the Companion who reported it was not mentioned by name in the chain of transmission.

So he ﷺ was Allah's elect, and His choice from amongst all generations of men.

Wāthila ibn al-Asqaʿ ؓ reported that the Messenger of Allah ﷺ said: 'Allah chose Ismāʿīl from the sons of Ibrāhīm, and from the sons of Ismāʿīl He chose the sons of Kināna, and from the sons of Kināna He chose Quraysh, and from the sons of Quraysh He chose the sons of Hāshim, and He chose me from amongst the sons of Hāshim.'[382]

Bukhārī narrated in his *Ṣaḥīḥ*, on the authority of Ibn ʿAbbās ؓ, that Heraclius, the Byzantine emperor, asked Abū Sufyān about the lineage of the Prophet ﷺ, and how his standing was amongst the Arabs. Abū Sufyān replied: 'Amongst us he who is a man of fine lineage', that is, Muḥammad ﷺ was of noble lineage, and was considered of high-born pedigree compared to others. Heraclius replied, 'Such is the case of Prophets: they are called forth from the nobility of their people.'

ʿAbbās ؓ reported that the Prophet heard some things people had been saying about him, and so ascended the pulpit and said: 'Who am I?' The people replied, 'You are the Messenger of Allah.' He ﷺ then said, 'I am Muḥammad, son of ʿAbdullāh, son of ʿAbd al-Muṭṭalib. Allah created all creation, and drew me from the best of His creatures; and He made them of two branches, and made me from the best branch; and He created the tribes, and drew me from the best tribe; and He divided them into houses, and drew me from the best house, so I am from the best house amongst them, and I am the best one amongst them.'[383]

---

[382] Narrated by Muslim and Tirmidhī (and this wording is that of Tirmidhī).
[383] Narrated by Imām Aḥmad.

'Ā'isha ﷺ reported that the Messenger of Allah ﷺ said: 'Jibrīl said to me, "I searched the earth from east to west and found no man finer than Muhammad ﷺ; and I searched the earth from east to west and found no kinsmen finer than the sons of Hāshim." '[384]

The only reason the Prophet ﷺ mentioned his noble ancestors and their pure lineage was to make mention of Allah's grace, and to give thanks to Him, and acknowledge their status, and show their greatness; there was not a trace of pomp or pride in this. 'Allāmah Ḥalīmī said:

> He ﷺ intended to acknowledge the status and rank of those whom he mentioned ... It may be that he intended to recognize the grace that Allah bestowed on him in himself and his forebears, in order to give thanks to Him; this was not a matter of pomp or pride in the slightest.

Consequently, Ḥāfiẓ Ibn Ḥajar said: 'The prohibition against expressing pride in one's forebears applies to boasting that leads to arrogance and the denigration of other Muslims.'

## THE PURITY OF HIS NOBLE LINEAGE ﷺ

'Abd al-Razzāq narrated, with a chain of transmission back to Imām Ja'far al-Ṣādiq, that Muḥammad al-Bāqir ﷺ said of Allah's word ﴾There has come to you a Messenger from your own selves﴿[385]. 'This means that his family-line contained no

---

[384] Narrated by al-Bayhaqī, al-Ḥākim, al-Ṭabarānī, and Ibn 'Asākīr. Shāmī said: 'Ḥāfiẓ declared in his *Amālī* that this texts bears all the traits of authenticity.' (*Sīrah*, vol.1, p.276)

[385] Qur'ān 9:128

illegitimate births. The Messenger of Allah ﷺ himself said, "I came forth from unions of marriage, not fornication." '[386]

Bayhaqī also narrated with a chain of transmission back to Imām Ja'far al-Ṣādiq that Muḥammad al-Bāqir ؓ reported that the Messenger of Allah ﷺ said: 'Allah brought me forth from unions of marriage, and did not bring me forth from unions of fornication.' Bayhaqī also narrated that the Prophet ﷺ gave a sermon, saying: 'I am Muḥammad, son of 'Abdullāh, son of 'Abd al-Muṭṭalib, son of Hāshim, son of 'Abd Manāf, son of Quṣayy, son of Kilāb, son of Murra, son of Ka'b, son of Lu'ayy, son of Ghālib, son of Fihr, son of Mālik, son of Naḍr, son of Kināna, son of Khuzayma, son of Mudrika, son of Ilyās, son of Muḍar, son of Nizār. The people never divided into sectors save that Allah placed me in the best sector; for I was brought forth from my parents, and not a trace of the fornication of the days of ignorance touched me; and I came forth from unions of marriage, and not from unions of fornication, from Adam until my father and mother. I am the best of you in person, and the best of you in lineage.'[387]

Ṭabarānī, Ibn al-Sakan and others narrated that when the Prophet ﷺ returned to Medina from the Battle of Tabūk, 'Abbās ibn 'Abd al-Muṭṭalib said, 'O Messenger of Allah, will you give me leave to praise you?' The Prophet ﷺ replied, 'Speak on, and may Allah never spoil your mouth!'[388]

'Abbās then said:

---

[386] Ḥāfiẓ Ibn Kathīr said, 'This is a sound, *mursal* [see note 381, p.168] narration.'
[387] Ḥāfiẓ Ibn Kathīr said: 'Qudāmā alone narrated it, and he is a weak narrator; but there are other narrations that attest to it.'
[388] This was a prayer for 'Abbās that his mouth would be kept safe from all defects and afflictions, both literally and figuratively.

*Before it, you enjoyed the shade of Paradise,*
*Within the glade where first the leaves were plucked,*[389]
*And then to earth you fell,*[390] *not yet in human form,*
*Nor yet a piece of flesh within a mother's womb;*
*A drop that sailed within the Ark whilst mighty floods*
*Washed Nasr away, and put pay to his worshippers;*[391]
*From loin to womb you travelled through the ages,*[392]
*And all the while worlds passed on, each by each;*
*The fire beneath the Friend of Allah diminished:*
*With you within his loins, how could he burn?*
*Until your line, preserved from any fault, arrived*
*To Khandaf, a plateau above a wide expanse;*[393]
*Upon your birth, the earth was bathed in brightness,*
*And by your light the far horizons shone,*
*And we, beneath this brightness and this radiance,*
*Burn gladly in the glory of your guiding light.*[394]

---

[389] That is, before the Fall to earth, you enjoyed the shade of the Garden whilst in the loins of Adam, in the glade where Adam and Eve lived, and from where they first plucked the leaves to cover themselves.

[390] That is, you fell to earth when Adam fell, still in his loins.

[391] This means the Ark of Noah ﷺ; that is, you dwelt within the loins of Sam, son of Noah, when he boarded the Ark; and the flood destroyed Nasr, one of the idols worshipped by Noah's people, and destroyed all those who worshipped these idols.

[392] That is, as each world passed by, you were there, carried in the loins of your forebears; 'world' here means generation.

[393] Khandaf literally means 'to walk quickly'; it is a epithet for the wife of Ilyās ibn Muḍar, given to her because of the way she would run between her three sons; the word then became a symbol of fine lineage. The meaning of 'a plateau above a wide expanse' is that the Prophet's ﷺ nobility was above all other, just as the peak of a mountain is above all the lands below it. (*Sharḥ al-Mawāhib*)

# HIS GLORIOUS BIRTH ﷺ

The birth of the Prophet ﷺ was showered with Divine honour, and overseen by Holy providence. Upon his ﷺ birth, Allah ﷻ revealed many miracles and wonders, as a foreshadowing of his prophethood, and a preparation for his Message, and a sign of his immense rank, and an indication that he ﷺ occupied an exalted status.

**One manifestation of this** was the light that shone out at the moment of his birth ﷺ. Imām Aḥmad narrated, on the authority of 'Irbāḍ ibn Sariya رضي الله عنه, that the Messenger of Allah ﷺ said: 'Indeed, I was Allah's Seal of the Prophets whilst Adam yet lay in his mould of clay.[395] I shall tell you of this: I am the answer to Ibrāhīm 's prayer, and the good news of 'Isā, and the vision my mother saw, as indeed all the mothers of the Prophets saw.' 'Irbāḍ ibn Sariya added: 'When the mother of the Messenger of Allah ﷺ bore him, she saw a light that illuminated the palaces of the Levant.'[396] So he ﷺ was the answer to the prayer Ibrāhīm عليه السلام made when he said: ﴿Our Lord, and raise up among them a Messenger from amongst them, who shall convey unto them

---

[394] These lines can be found in Ibn Kathīr's *Tārīkh*, and in *Sharḥ al-Mawāhib*, and *Majma' al-Zawā'id*, and Dhahabi's *Tārīkh al-Islām*, and elsewhere.

[395] Qasṭalānī said: 'This means when he lay on the ground, before the spirit had been breathed into him.'

[396] Also narrated by Bazzār and Ṭabarānī. Ḥāfiẓ Ibn Ḥajar said: 'It was declared rigorously authentic by Ibn Ḥibbān and Ḥākim, and Aḥmad also narrated a similar Ḥadīth on the authority of Abū Umāma; and Ibn Isḥāq narrated the like of it on the authority of Thawr ibn Yazīd, on the authority of Khālid ibn Ma'dān, on the authority of several of the Companions of the Messenger of Allah ﷺ, who said that Bostra in the land of Syria was illuminated by this light.'

Your Revelations...⟩[397] And he ﷺ was the good news that 'Isa عليه السلام conveyed when he said: ⟨And (I am) a conveyer of the glad tidings of a Messenger who shall come after me, whose name is Aḥmad...⟩[398] And the light that appeared at the moment of his birth was seen by his mother with her own eyes, clearly and plainly, as the other narrations confirm.

Abū Nu'aym narrated, on the authority of Umm Salama ﷺ, that Āmina, mother of the Messenger of Allah ﷺ, said: 'On the night of his birth, I saw a light that illuminated the palaces of Syria so I could see them.'

Muḥammad ibn Sa'd narrated, on the authority of several transmitters including 'Aṭā ibn 'Abbās, that Āmina bint Wahb said: 'The moment he ﷺ came from me, a light emerged that illuminated everything from east to west, and then he ﷺ fell to the floor and knelt.'

'Uthmān ibn Abī al-'Āṣ narrated that his mother, the Companion Umm 'Uthmān al-Thaqafiyya, whose name was Fāṭima bint 'Abdullāh,[399] said: 'When I attended the birth of the Messenger of Allah ﷺ I saw that the room where he was born was filled with light, and I saw the stars come nearer until I thought they would fall upon me. When Āmina bore him, a light shone forth from her that illuminated the room and the whole house, until I could see nothing but light.'[400]

---

[397] Qur'ān 2:129
[398] Qur'ān 61:6
[399] Zurqānī said that Abū 'Umar [Ibn 'Abd al-Barr] and others counted her as being among the Companions.
[400] Zurqānī said: 'It was narrated by Bayhaqī, Ṭabarī, and Ibn 'Abd al-Barr, and the author of *Fatḥ al-Bārī* ascribed it to Ṭabarānī, and said that it is attested to by the Ḥadīth of 'Irbāḍ ibn Sariya (which we have just mentioned).' (vi.426)

In *al-Sīrat al-Shāmiyya*, it is reported that Shaykh Abū Shāma ﵀ said: 'The light that appeared at the moment of his ﷺ birth was famous amongst Quraysh, and oft-mentioned by them. It was to this light that 'Abbās ﵁ alluded in his poem when he said:

> *Upon your birth, the earth was bathed in brightness,*
> *And by your light the far horizons shone.*'

The appearance of this light at the moment of his ﷺ birth was a sign of what would later come, and the light that would guide the world, and put an end to the darkness of disbelief. Allah ﷻ said: ﴾There has come unto you from Allah a light and a clear Scripture, by which Allah will guide those who seek His pleasure to paths of peace, and take them out of the darkness and into the light by His leave.﴿[401] And with this light which he brought from Allah, he illuminated minds, and gave life to dead hearts, and opened blind eyes and deaf ears.

**Another of the wonders that accompanied his birth ﷺ to foreshadow his Prophethood** was that narrated by Bayhaqī and Abū Nu'aym, on the authority of Ḥassān ibn Thābit, the poet of the Prophet ﷺ: 'I was a boy of seven or eight years,[402] possessed of full reason and able to understand what I saw and heard, when one day, a Jew shouted: "O hordes of Quraysh! Was any born to you this night?" They answered that they did not know, and so he said, "Find out, because this night the Prophet of this community was born." '[403]

---

[401] Qur'ān 5:15-16

[402] Zurqānī said: 'they say that he lived until the age of one hundred and twenty, as did his father, grandfather, and great-grandfather before him; he died in the year 54 AH.'

[403] Narrated by Ḥākim, and also by Ya'qūb ibn Sufyān with a sound chain of transmission. (*Fatḥ al-Bārī*)

**Another of the wonders that accompanied his birth ﷺ to foreshadow his Prophethood** was the trembling and splitting of the palace of Khosrau, and the collapse of fourteen of its towers, in which state it has remained until the present day, as Ḥāfiẓ Zurqānī stated.

The palace did not split because of a defect in its construction, since its construction in Iraq was carried out proficiently, and it was built with large bricks and plaster, its breadth one hundred cubits and its height the same. The caliph Hārūn al-Rashīd wanted to demolish it because he had heard there was a great treasure buried beneath it, but he was unable to do so. This is because Allah ﷻ decreed that it remain a sign of His Prophet ﷺ for all the ages.

Ḥāfiẓ Ibn Kathīr devoted a special section of his *Bidāya* to the signs and wonders that appeared on the night of the Prophet's ﷺ birth, mentioning among them: the appearance of light as he ﷺ was born, and his falling to the ground, kneeling, and raising his head to the sky, and the light that was seen in the house in which he was born, and the way the stars drew near, and the splitting of the palace of Khosrau and the collapse of its towers, and the extinguishing of the fires, and the vision of the High Priest of the Zoroastrians.

He then added: 'And there were more signs besides these.' He then went on to list all the proofs for these events and their multiple chains of transmission.

Ḥāfiẓ Ibn Ḥajar also mentioned a number of signs of Prophethood that were revealed before the mission began, and then said, 'And as for the signs of his Prophethood ﷺ that appeared at his birth ﷺ,' and then mentioned the Ḥadīths that chronicle the appearance of the light.

He then said:

> There is also the Ḥadīth of Makhzūm ibn Hāni' al-Makhzūmī, who narrated from his father – who lived to the age of one hundred and fifty – that on the night when the Messenger of Allah ﷺ was born, the palace of Khosrau split twain, and fourteen of its towers fell, and the fires of Persia went out after having been lit for a thousand years,[404] and the waters of Lake Sāwa dried up, and the Zoroastrian High Priest dreamt of wild camels leading Arabian horses across the Tigris and spreading through the land. When Khosrau awoke, he was frightened by what had happened (i.e. the rupture of the palace and so on), and so he asked the scholars of his kingdom about it, and they sent a message to Saṭīḥ... (the story goes on)

Ḥāfiẓ 'Asqalānī also mentioned this, and ascribed it to Bayhaqī, Abū Nu'aym, Kharā'iṭī, Ibn 'Asākir and Ibn Jarīr. The only reason we have mentioned that this was narrated by all these great Ḥadīth masters is to provide a definitive argument against those whose hearts are diseased or astray, and to increase the certainty and strength of those who were already certain of these matters.

**One of the wonders that foreshadowed his Prophethood ﷺ and occurred even before his birth** was the story of the Owners of the Elephant, and how Allah ﷻ sent dense clouds of birds to attack them one by one, each bird finding its mark, not missing a single one of them, and how Allah ﷻ destroyed them and crushed them.

---

[404] The fires were kept burning as a religious rite of the pagan Zoroastrians. [t]

And all of this was for no reason other than to protect the Sacred House which would become the Qibla for the Messenger of Allah ﷺ and his followers, and their place of prayer and pilgrimage, standing firm for them until the Day of Resurrection.

Because of this, Allah ﷻ mentioned this story in the Noble Qur'ān, and revealed to the Messenger of Allah ﷺ to remind him of this great favour, and how He ﷻ charged Himself with defending this Sacred House, which one day would be the place of prayer and pilgrimage for the Messenger of Allah ﷺ; and so He said: ﴿Hast thou not seen how thy Lord dealt with the owners of the Elephant?﴾[405]

**The date of his birth** ﷺ: He ﷺ was born in the Year of the Elephant fifty days after the incident took place, on the twelfth day of *Rabī' al-Awwal* at the break of dawn, according to the opinion of the majority of the scholars. The day was a Monday, as is borne out by the Ḥadīth narrated by Muslim in his *Ṣaḥīḥ*, on the authority of Abū Qatāda, in which it was mentioned that the Messenger of Allah ﷺ was asked about the merits of fasting on Mondays, to which he replied, 'That is the day I was born, and the day I was sent.' (Or 'the day I received Revelation.')

Aḥmad narrated in his *Musnad* that Ibn 'Abbās said: 'The Messenger of Allah ﷺ was born on a Monday, and received the Revelation on a Monday, and left Mecca to emigrate to Medina on a Monday, and entered Medina on a Monday, and raised the Black Stone and put it in its place on a Monday.'

This refers to the day Quraysh rebuilt the Ka'aba, and argued as to which of them should be the one to lift the Black Stone, as we mentioned earlier.

---

[405] Qur'ān 105:1

# CELEBRATING AND COMMEMORATING HIS BIRTHDAY ﷺ

It is the duty of any intelligent person to rejoice on the day he ﷺ was born, and celebrate the day when the whole world was bathed in light, guidance and knowledge; for on that day was born the Messenger of mercy to the worlds, and the Prophet of guidance and light for all humanity, and the leader of the Prophets and Messengers. Magnify, then, that day, and honour it, and rejoice and exult in its coming!

Gathering to read the story of his ﷺ birth is a gathering that encompasses all manner of mercies and blessings, and goodness and righteousness; for the narration of the story of his glorious birth involves the recitation of many verses from the Noble Qur'ān; and remembrance of the honour and grace Allah extended to His Messenger ﷺ, and how He watched over him and protected him; and remembrance of the physical and moral beauty of our Master Muḥammad ﷺ; and the invocation of much benediction and salutation upon the Prophet ﷺ; and the reading of many poems expressing praise and love for the our Master the Messenger of Allah ﷺ; and much supplication and prayer to Allah ﷻ. Every one of these components is permitted and endorsed by the Sacred Law, and is a beloved means of drawing nearer to Allah, and the Lawgiver encouraged them all, and stressed their great reward and merit; and this is the way of the rightly-guided scholars, and the people of piety and righteousness. For instance, Imām Sakhāwī said:

> In every land, and every city, the Islamic people continue to celebrate the month of his birth ﷺ by holding fine gatherings involving all manner of dignified celebration, and making many charitable donations by night, and expressing their joy, and increasing their righteous acts, and reading the story

> of his glorious birth; and the all-embracing grace of this blessed time is manifested in them.[406]

And Imām Shāmī (d. 942 AH) said:

> Imām Ḥāfiẓ Abū al-Khayr al-Jazarī, the Shaykh of Qur'ān Reciters ﷺ, said: 'One of the special graces of this (celebrating the Prophet's ﷺ glorious birth and commemorating the month he ﷺ was born) is that it is a means of protection for the whole year, and a glad tiding of the attainment of hopes and needs.' And Ḥāfiẓ Ibn Kathīr ﷺ said in his *Tārīkh*: 'King Abū Sa'īd al-Muẓaffar ['the Victorious'] would commemorate the glorious birth of the Prophet ﷺ (the *Mawlid*) in the month of Rabī' al-Awwal, and mark it with a great celebration; and he was gallant, brave, heroic, wise, and just, may Allah Almighty have mercy on him. Shaykh Abū al-Khaṭṭāb al-Daḥiyya ﷺ wrote him a book on the *Mawlid* entitled *al-Tanwīr fī Mawlid al-Bashīr al-Nadhīr*,[407] for which he rewarded him to the sum of one thousand gold pieces.[408]

The grandson of Ibn al-Jawzī ﷺ narrated in *Mir'āt al-Zamān*, on the authority of someone who had attended the table of al-Muẓaffar at a *Mawlid* celebration, that he would provide a wide variety of meats and desserts in great abundance, and that his total spending on the *Mawlid* celebrations would be three hundred thousand gold pieces.

---

[406] Imām Muḥammad ibn Yūsuf al-Shāmī, *al-Sīrat al-Nabawiyya*, 1/439

[407] 'The Illumination: on the Birth of the Bearer of Glad Tidings and Warnings ﷺ.'

[408] See Shāmī's *Sīrah*, and *al-Mawāhib* and its commentary.

*PART III: HIS NOBLE ANCESTRY* ﷺ

Imām Muḥammad ibn Yūsuf al-Shāmī narrated in his *Sīrah*, on the authority of Shaykh Abū Abdullāh ibn Abī Muḥammad al-Nuʿmān, that Shaykh Abū Mūsā al-Zarhūnī said: 'I saw the Prophet ﷺ in my sleep, and told him about the practice of holding celebratory feasts on his birthday, and he ﷺ replied, "If someone rejoices in us, we rejoice in him." '

And the Shaykh of Qur'ān Reciters, Ḥāfiẓ Abū al-Khayr ibn al-Jazarī ؓ said:

> Abū Lahab was seen in a dream after his death, whereupon he was asked about his present state. He replied, 'I am in the Fire, yet it is lightened from me every Monday evening, and I lap from my two fingertips this much water (and he indicated his two fingertips). This is because of my freeing [the slave-girl] Thuwayba when she gave me the news of Muḥammad's ﷺ birth, and because she went on to nurse him.' If Abū Lahab, the disbeliever whom the Qur'ān itself chastised, could be rewarded[409] whilst in Hell for his joy on the night of Muḥammad's ﷺ birth, what about the monotheist Muslim from the community of Muḥammad ﷺ who rejoices in his birth, and does whatever he can to show his love for him? Upon my life, his reward from Allah the Generous will be nothing less than to enter Paradise by His grace.

The story of Abū Lahab and how he freed Thuwayba, and what followed, was narrated by Bukhārī, Ismāʿīlī, and ʿAbd al-Razzāq.

---

[409] Allah rewarded him by lightening his punishment whilst he remained in Hell, because of the joy he expressed upon the birth of our Master Muḥammad ﷺ.

Bukhārī narrated in his *Ṣaḥīḥ* that 'Urwa said: 'Thuwayba was the slave-girl of Abū Lahab whom he freed, and who nursed the Prophet ﷺ. When Abū Lahab died, he was shown to one of his family[410] in a dreadful state. He said to him, "What have you found?" Abū Lahab replied, "I found nothing[411] after leaving you save that I am given to drink here[412] by dint of my freeing Thuwayba." '

Ḥāfiẓ 'Asqalānī says in *Fatḥ al-Bārī* that Suhaylī reported that 'Abbās ؓ said: 'When Abū Lahab died, after a year had passed, I saw him in a dream in a terrible state. Abū Lahab said to me, "I found no respite after leaving you save that the torment is lightened from me every Monday." This is because the Prophet ﷺ was born on a Monday, and Thuwayba gave Abū Lahab the news of his ﷺ birth, so he freed her.'

## ALLAH'S PROTECTION OF THE PROPHET FROM HIS ﷺ YOUTH ONWARDS

Allah's ﷻ protection encompassed the Messenger of Allah ﷺ in every aspect of his being, and in everything he did, throughout his life from his youngest days. His father, Abdullāh, passed away two months after his conception, according to the most well-known narration. It is also said that it was seven months into the term, or that his father died when he ﷺ was a newborn.

---

[410] It was 'Abbās ؓ, as the other narrations make clear.

[411] The narration of Ismā'īlī has it, 'I found no ease', and 'Abd al-Razzāq has it, on the authority of Mu'ammar, on the authority of Zuhrī, 'I found no respite…'

[412] Abd al-Razzāq has it that he indicated the hollow beneath his thumb, and Ismā'īlī has it that he indicated the hollow between the thumb and the other fingers.

So there are narrations saying it was two months, or seven months, or nine months after his ﷺ conception, and the first narration is the strongest and most well-known, which means that his ﷺ father died whilst he was still in the womb. The evidence for this is the narration of Ḥākim in his *Mustadrak* on the authority of Qays ibn Makhzama: 'The father of the Prophet ﷺ died when his mother was still carrying him.' Ḥākim declared this to be rigorously authentic according to the criteria of Muslim, and Dhahabī concurred.[413]

So he ﷺ remained with his mother Āmina, and Allah ﷻ decreed that his grandfather Abd al-Muṭṭalib would care for him and look after his needs with warmth and generosity. So he ﷺ grew up in the shelter, protection and care of Allah ﷻ, who gave him the best of upbringings, intending one day to honour him, and raise his rank to that of a Prophet and Messenger ﷺ.

When he ﷺ reached the age of six,[414] his mother Āmina bint Wahb died at Abwā', between Mecca and Medina. It is also said that she died at the pass of Abū Dhi'b on Mount Ḥajūn, above Mecca.[415]

Ibn Sa'd narrated the story on the authority of Ibn 'Abbās, Zuhrī, and 'Āṣim ibn 'Amr ibn Qatāda, and pieced together their relations into a single narrative:[416]

---

[413] Ḥāfiẓ Ibn Kathīr mentioned this, as did Imām 'Asqalānī, and Ḥāfiẓ Zurqānī, and others.

[414] This is the soundest narration; others say he was four, others say older.

[415] See *Sharḥ al-Mawāhib*.

[416] Zurqānī said: 'All three narrations are considered *mursal* [see note 381, p.168], but any *mursal* narration of Ibn 'Abbās is considered to definitely go back to the Prophet ﷺ [that is, to be *mawṣūl*], since it is the *mursal* of a Companion.'

When the Messenger of Allah ﷺ reached the age of six, his mother took him to visit his kinsmen of the Banī 'Adī ibn Najjār in Medina, along with Umm Ayman. They arrived at the community of the tribe of Tubba', and stayed there for one month. Later, the Prophet ﷺ would tell stories about the time he spent there.

The Prophet ﷺ looked at the very same place in Medina after the Emigration, and said, 'Here it was that I stayed with my mother, and learned to swim in the pool of Banī 'Adī ibn Najjār. A group of Jews kept stealing looks at me, and Umm Ayman said, "I heard one of them say, 'There is the Prophet of this community, and this (Medina) will be his place of emigration' " – and I remembered everything that they said.' Then his mother set out with him for Mecca, and passed away when they reached Abwā'. The narration of Abū Nu'aym has it that he ﷺ said, 'A man from the Jews looked at me and said, "Boy, what is your name?" I replied, "Aḥmad." He then looked at my back, and I heard him say, "This is the Prophet of this community," and then he returned to his Jewish brethren and told them, and they told my mother, whereupon she feared for me, and we left Medina.'[417]

Umm Ayman, whose name was Baraka the Ethiopian, became the Prophet's ﷺ nursemaid after the passing of his mother. It is said that she was freed by the father of the Prophet ﷺ; others say that he himself ﷺ freed her. She embraced Islam, and performed both the Emigrations[418], and her virtues were manifold, Allah be pleased with her. Ibn Umm Ḥantama related that the Prophet ﷺ used to say, 'Umm Ayman is my second mother.'[419]

---

[417] See *al-Bidāya* vol.2, p.279, and *Sharḥ al-Mawāhib.*

[418] I.e. to Abyssinia and to Medina [t]

[419] Literally 'my mother after my mother.' [t]

Ḥāfiẓ 'Asqalānī said in *al-Iṣāba*:

> Ibn Sa'd narrated, from Abū Amāma, from Jarīr ibn Ḥāzim, on the authority of 'Uthmān ibn al-Qāsim, that when Umm Ayman emigrated (to Medina), evening fell upon her when she was halfway to her destination. She was very thirsty, having fasted, but had no water, and the thirst began to wear her out, whereupon a pail of water was lowered to her from the heavens by a white rope. She took it and drank until her thirst was quenched. After this, she used to say, 'Since that time I have never felt thirsty; I have fasted on blazing hot days, yet never have I felt thirsty since I took that drink.' Ibn al-Sakan narrates it thus: Umm Ayman set off to emigrate from Mecca to Medina on foot, having taken no provisions with her. She said, 'When the sun went down, there appeared a pail (of water) hanging before me. Since then, I have fasted on hot days and then circled the Ka'aba in the sun in an effort to become thirsty, but I have not become thirsty yet.'

Ibn Isḥāq said:

> (After the passing of his mother) the Messenger of Allah ﷺ stayed with his grandfather, 'Abd al-Muṭṭalib. There was a couch laid out for 'Abd al-Muṭṭalib in the shade of the Ka'aba, and his children used to sit around the bed until he came out to join them, none of his sons sitting on the couch itself out of respect for their father. The Messenger of Allah ﷺ, however, would sit on the couch, and whenever his uncles would bid him sit elsewhere, 'Abd al-Muṭṭalib would to them, 'Leave my son be, for by Allah great things are in store for him.'

> He would then sit with him on his couch, and stroke his back with his hand, and it pleased him to see him ﷺ do as he did.[420]

When 'Abd al-Muṭṭalib lay dying, he entrusted the care and protection of the Messenger of Allah ﷺ to Abū Ṭālib. He ﷺ was eight years old when 'Abd al-Muṭṭalib passed away. Abū Ṭālib took good care of the Messenger of Allah ﷺ and treated him with generosity and kindness. Wāqidī and others narrate that Ibn 'Abbās said: 'Abū Ṭālib loved the Messenger of Allah ﷺ more than even his own sons, and he would always sleep by his side, and if he went out he would take him along; and Abū Ṭālib loved him more than he loved anything else. He would always want him around when they ate. When the family of Abū Ṭālib ate – whether together or apart – they would not eat their fill, whilst if the Messenger of Allah ﷺ ate with them, they would. When about to feed them, he would say, "Wait until my son Muḥammad comes", and when the Messenger of Allah ﷺ came and ate with them, they would eat their fill and leave some food uneaten. If milk was served, he would drink first, and then they would all drink their fill from a single vessel. Abū Ṭālib would thus say, "You are indeed blessed!" '

Abū Nu'aym, Ibn Ishāq and others narrate that Ibn 'Abbās ﷺ said: 'The sons of Abū Ṭālib would awake in the morning dishevelled, with their eyes full of sleep, whilst Muḥammad ﷺ would rise clean, his skin oiled, his eyes darkened as if with kohl. Abū Ṭālib loved him intensely.'[421] And so he ﷺ grew up in a house of honour and nobility, and was honoured and esteemed therein, encompassed in Allah's protection and delighting in His care.

---

420 See *al-Bidāya*, vol.2, p.281

421 See *al-Bidāya*, vol.2, p.282, and *Sharḥ al-Mawāhib*, vol.1, p. 189.

Allah ﷻ reminded His Prophet ﷺ of His favour towards him, and the protection He vouchsafed him, and the care He took of him from his earliest childhood, enumerating all the favour and honour He extended to him with His word: ﴿By the midmorning, and by the night when it is still: thy Lord has not forsaken thee, nor does He hate thee, and what comes will be better for thee than what has passed, and thy Lord shall give unto thee, that thou might be content. Did He not find thee an orphan, and shelter thee? And find thee lost, and guide thee? And find thee needy, and enrich thee? Therefore the orphan oppress not, and the beggar deny not, and the bounty of thy Lord exult.﴾[422] In this chapter, He ﷻ mentioned all the ways in which He protected and watched over His Messenger ﷺ throughout his life, taking care of him and raising him in the best way; and His kindness to him ﷺ was without limit.

He ﷻ swore by the midmorning, at which time the rays on the sun shine with radiance, and its light spreads out, and then swore by the night when it is still and completely dark and black. This clearly provokes all who possess insight to consider the great difference between the brilliance of midmorning and the blackness of night. This was the object of His oath, and what He swore to was the protection and care of His Messenger ﷺ, and His further generosity towards him. All of this was a sign of His kindness and assistance, and a testimony that our Master Muḥammad was truly the Messenger of Allah.

The purpose of the object of the oath (i.e. midmorning and dark night), and its relation to the content of its promise, was to alert the wise to the huge contrast between the state of the people who lived in the pre-Islamic time of ignorance, being as they were ignorant, astray, and unjust, and the resplendent light and radiant brightness that the Messenger of Allah ﷺ brought.

---

[422] Qur'ān 93:1-11

Such a thing could not escape the notice of anyone endowed with the ability to think and reflect, just as no one endowed with their physical senses could fail to see the difference between midmorning and the night at its stillest.

And just as Allah's mercy dictated that He not leave His servants forever in the darkness of night, but rather guide them with the brightness of day to their means of life and sustenance, so too His mercy and wisdom dictated that He not leave His servants in the darkness of ignorance and misguidance, but rather guide them with the light of Prophethood and the Muhammadan Message to that which enriched their worldly and spiritual lives, and led them to felicity in this life and the next.

Allah ﷻ said: ﴾There has come unto you from Allah a light and a clear Scripture, by which Allah will guide those who seek His pleasure to paths of peace, and take them out of the darkness and into the light by His leave, and guide them to a straight road.﴿[423]

He ﷻ then said, ﴾Thy Lord has not forsaken thee, nor does He hate thee.﴿ He ﷻ rules out the possibility that He could ever forsake His Prophet, His Beloved, or that He could ever hate him. How could He forsake him, when He protected him with such intimate protection from the very beginning? And how could He hate him, when He took him as His Beloved? So he ﷺ was neither forsaken nor hated, but rather he remained in Allah's care, as He said: ﴾For thou art beneath Our Gaze.﴿[424] He ﷺ is the noblest Beloved of Allah, as he ﷺ said in the Ḥadīth narrated by Dārimī, Aḥmad and Tirmidhī: 'Indeed, I am the Beloved of Allah, and I boast not.'

---

[423] Qur'ān 5:15-16

[424] Qur'ān 52:48

He ﷻ then said, ﴾And what comes will be better for thee than what has passed﴿. This is generally true for every aspect of his ﷺ person, for he was in a constant state of increase, and every state he advanced to was better than that which preceded it, always and constantly. This also means that the Hereafter would be better for him ﷺ than what came before it.

He ﷻ then said, ﴾And thy Lord shall give unto thee, that thou might be content.﴿ This was a sure promise from Allah to him ﷺ that he would attain that which gave him delight and joy, and that He would give unto him until he was content. This is a great blessing and an immense grace of a magnitude known only to Allah ﷻ. This Divine Bestowal granted to the Prophet ﷺ included the great numbers of his followers, more than any other Prophet, and the great droves of people who entered his religion, and the elevation of his renown, and the supremacy of his word, and the victory he was given over his enemies by means of the trepidation that was cast into their hearts, and the predominance of his religion above all others, and its manifest authority, and the clarity of its proofs, and the granting to him ﷺ of the Pool, and the River of *Kawthar*, and the Praiseworthy Station and its attendant right to intercession both general and specific, and the station of mediation and grace, and all the other high ranks and stations that Allah ﷻ has prepared for him ﷺ in the Hereafter, of which none but Allah Himself has full knowledge. Allah ﷻ then mentioned the protection He afforded His Beloved ﷺ since his youngest days, and how He took care of him and watched over him, so to assure him that the One who looked after him in his youth, and showered him with His blessings, would continue to watch over him and bless him, and would always extend to him His favour and largess, and fulfil His promises to him, and shelter him within His protection for ever, saying: ﴾Did He not find thee an orphan, and shelter thee?﴿

For his ﷺ father 'Abdullāh passed away when he was still in his mother's womb, or shortly after his birth, and then his mother Āmina bin Wahb passed away when he was six years old. After this, Allah placed him in the care of his grandfather 'Abd al-Muṭṭalib until he too passed away when the Prophet ﷺ was eight, after which his uncle Abū Ṭālib took him in. From then on, he ﷺ continued to grow up in Allah's protection, in complete security and safety, until Allah ennobled him ﷺ with Prophethood and the Divine Message.

﴾And (did He not) find thee lost, and guide thee?﴿ Know that the word 'error' [*ḍalāl*, from which is derived the word here *ḍāll*, 'lost'] can mean the misguidance of sin, in which case it means to be lost to the truth and to goodness and righteousness; yet it can also mean many other things according to the context in which it is used, as we will make clear shortly if Allah wills. As for the notion of being lost to truth and to guidance, it is certainly not the meaning of this verse, because Allah ﷻ unequivocally ruled this out in the case of the Prophet ﷺ when He said: ﴾By the star when it wanes, your companion did not err, nor did he stray.﴿[425] So He ﷻ ruled out that the Messenger of Allah ﷺ could have fallen into error, the opposite of guidance, or fallen into straying, the opposite of moral integrity; and He absolved him ﷺ of all of this after first emphasising it by swearing an oath. This is Allah's testimony to the guidance and integrity of His Prophet in word, knowledge and deed. He ﷺ was not misguided, but rather was upon complete guidance and certainty; and he was not astray, but rather was completely righteous in his thoughts and intentions, and he sought nothing but guidance and truth. The real misguided one is the ignorant one who walks without knowledge and so loses the way, and the real stray one is he who knows the truth but ignores it and seeks something else.

---

[425] Qur'ān 53:1-2

Guidance and moral integrity are the sources of perfection in a human being. Allah ﷻ honoured His Friend Ibrāhīm ﷺ by giving him moral integrity before his prophetic mission began, as He said: ⟪And We gave Ibrāhīm his integrity a foretime, and We were Well-Aware of him.⟫[426] If this was the case with Ibrāhīm, the Friend of Allah, it is all the more fitting that it should also have been so for His Beloved ﷺ. Allah gave him his integrity before his prophetic mission, and He ﷻ made this clear to those of his people who opposed him, saying: ⟪Your companion did not err⟫, meaning: Muḥammad ﷺ was raised amongst you, and grew up amongst you, so you know him better than any other; and you know of no past misguidance or error on his part, but rather his whole life has been marked by integrity and righteousness.

So the meaning of the word 'lost' in Allah's words ⟪And (did He not) find thee lost, and guide thee⟫ is not 'lost to the truth and inclined to corruption and evil', because such a thing is scripturally negated on his ﷺ part by His words ⟪Your companion did not err, nor did he stray⟫, which is why Ibn 'Abbās ؓ said, 'He never erred to sin.'

Someone might ask, then, what the meaning of ⟪And (did He not) find thee lost, and guide thee⟫ actually is. In answer, we say: The rightly-guided scholars who came before us have offered several different explanations for Allah's words ⟪And (did He not) find thee lost, and guide thee⟫.

**The first explanation** is that the meaning of ⟪And (did He not) find thee lost, and guide thee⟫ is: He found you unaware of the prophetic mission and its teachings, and the Clear Scripture and its details, and so He guided you to this, and taught you all that there was to know.

---

[426] Qur'ān 21:51

This explanation is attested to by Allah's words: ﴾*Alif Lām Rā'*. These are the signs of the Clear Scripture. We have revealed it as discourse in Arabic, that ye might comprehend. We narrate unto thee the best of narratives in this Qur'ān we reveal unto thee, although before it thou was of the unaware.﴿[427] The unawareness (*ghafla*) alluded to here is not complete unawareness, nor the heedlessness of misguidance and error, but rather it means simply the lack of knowledge of the details and teachings of the Scripture. Allah also said: ﴾And thus have We inspired in thee a Spirit of Our command, when thou knew not what Scripture was, nor Faith...﴿[428] That is, you were unaware of the details and demands of faith in practice, until We taught them to you, o Messenger of Allah ﷺ. Allah ﷻ also said: ﴾And Allah revealed unto thee Scripture and Wisdom, and taught thee what thou knew not; and the grace of Allah towards thee has been tremendous.﴿[429]

**The second explanation** was offered by Ibn 'Abbās ؓ,[430] which is that when the Prophet ﷺ was young, in the care of his grandfather 'Abd al-Muṭṭalib, he got lost in one of the ravines around Mecca. Abū Jahl came upon him whilst out herding his sheep, and returned him to 'Abd al-Muṭṭalib, who was clinging to the hangings of the Ka'aba, imploring Allah ﷻ to return his grandson ﷺ to him.[431] Some of them say that the Prophet's ﷺ return to his grandfather at the hand of Abū Jahl, the Pharaoh of this nation, is akin to the return of Moses to his mother at the hand of Pharaoh.

---

[427] Qur'ān 12:1-3

[428] Qur'ān 42:52

[429] Qur'ān 4:113

[430] Narrated by Bayhaqī, Ibn 'Asākir, and Ibn Isḥāq, as mentioned in *Sharḥ al-Mawāhib* and elsewhere.

[431] See the Qur'ānic exegeses of Rāzī and Ibn Kathīr, and Qasṭalānī's *Mawāhib*, and elsewhere.

It is said that he ﷺ also got lost on another occasion; again in the ravines around Mecca, and that they looked for him but could not find him. 'Abd al-Muṭṭalib circled the Ka'aba seven times and implored Allah ﷻ, and then they heard a voice say: *O People, fret not, for Muḥammad has a Lord who shall not forsake him or allow him to be lost – Muḥammad is in the valley of Tihāma, under the acacia tree.* 'Abd al-Muṭṭalib went there and found him ﷺ standing under the tree.

And so in this case the word *ḍāll* (lost) in the verse means to lose one's way or follow the wrong road in a literal sense; the word is certainly used in this sense in the words of the Prophet ﷺ explaining the duties we owe to the road: '… And that you give assistance to the troubled and offer guidance to the lost (*ḍāll*)…' This explanation of the verse also fits with the preceding verse, that says ﴾Did He not find thee an orphan and shelter thee?﴿; Allah ﷻ is listing the favours He extended to His Messenger ﷺ, and the protection He gave him from the time on his youngest days onwards.

**The third explanation** is that Allah's word ﴾And (did He not) find thee lost, and guide thee﴿ alludes to an occasion in his ﷺ youth, before the prophetic mission began, when he had a desire to stay up late at night chatting as young people do, but Allah protected him from doing so, and caused him to fall asleep.[432] The Commander of the Faithful 'Alī ؓ related that the Messenger of Allah ﷺ said: 'I never desired to do anything that the people of ignorance used to do except on two occasions, and both times, Allah prevented me from doing so; and I never desired anything of the kind again until Allah honoured me with the Message.'

---

[432] According to Qasṭalānī, this was the opinion of the Commander of the Faithful, Imām 'Alī ؓ, and Qāḍī 'Iyāḍ also mentioned it in *al-Shifā*; see also the commentaries of Qārī and Khafājī.

Ḥāfiẓ al-Haythamī said that it was narrated by Bazzār, and its narrators are all rigorously authentic. This Ḥadīth will be explained in greater detail shortly when we examine how Allah protected the Prophet ﷺ from falsehood before his mission began.

**The fourth explanation** is that ﴾And (did He not) find thee lost, and guide thee﴿ means: He found you beside yourself with love for Him, and so guided you to Prophethood, and gave you the Message. In this case, the meaning of 'lost' is to be overwhelmed with ardour and lost in Divine Love.

Allah informs us that the sons of Ya'qūb ﷺ said to their father: ﴾They said, 'By Allah, you remain in your delusion (*ḍalāl*) of old!'﴿[433] By 'delusion', they meant his deep love for Yūsuf, and his infatuation with him. They certainly did not mean the delusion or error of sin, which is clear from the context; not to mention that if they indeed had meant this they would have been guilty of disbelief, because it would have amounted to accusing Ya'qūb, a Prophetic Messenger of Allah, of sin and disobedience, which is an act of disbelief. There are other explanations for the meaning of ﴾And (did He not) find thee lost, and guide thee?﴿, all of which can be found in the books of exegesis, and in *Sharḥ al-Mawāhib* and *Sharḥ al-Shifā*.

As for ﴾And (did He not) find thee needy, and enrich thee?﴿, this means: He found you impoverished, or in need, and so freed you of the need of any but Him, and opened for you the doors to provision and abundant goodness. Imām Qasṭalānī related in *al-Mawāhib* that al-Ḥalīmī said in his *Shu'ab al-Īmān*: 'Part of honouring the Prophet ﷺ is not to describe him using the imperfect attributes people have, so it should not be said that he was "poor".'

---

[433] Qur'ān 12:95

This is because such a word suggests an imperfection, and that he ﷺ was poor by necessity, not choice.

Qasṭalānī said:

> Qāḍī 'Iyāḍ said in his *Shifā*, and Shaykh Taqī al-Dīn al-Subkī quoted it in *al-Sayf al-Maslūl*, that the scholars of Andalusia passed a sentence of death by crucifixion on Ḥātim al-Mutafaqqih al-Ṭalīṭilī for disparaging the Prophet ﷺ and constantly referring to him as 'the Orphan', and alleging that his ﷺ asceticism was not of his own volition, and alleging that if he ﷺ had been able to afford fine foods he would have eaten them.

Commenting on this, Zurqānī said: 'Any of one these three would be sufficient grounds for an irrevocable death sentence according to the view of Mālik ؓ.'

Qasṭalānī also said:

> Taqī al-Dīn al-Subkī said: 'The Prophet ﷺ was not short of money in the slightest, and his way of living was not that of a pauper. Rather, he ﷺ was the wealthiest of people, and his worldly affairs were sufficient for him and for his dependents.' Regarding the Ḥadīth narrated by Ibn Mājah and Tirmidhī, 'O Allah, make me needy in life, and needy in death, and raise me to life in the ranks of the needy', Shaykh Subkī ؓ said, 'This means neediness of the heart.'

Zurqānī said, 'That is, humility of the heart, and contrition before Allah ﷻ, not the neediness that leaves one unable to provide for oneself.' Qasṭalānī continued: 'And he (Subkī) would firmly criticise anyone thought the contrary.'

Zurqānī said, 'And this is a fine opinion. The upshot is that the neediness denied here (by Subkī) is that which means poverty and a lack of material sufficiency.' Before Subkī, Bayhaqī also made this point, saying: 'He ﷺ did not ask for neediness that implies dearth, but rather the neediness of contrition and humility.' Zurqānī also said:

> Ghazālī ﵀ said something similar: 'The Prophet's ﷺ seeking refuge from poverty does not deny his neediness, because poverty has two meanings:
>
> **Firstly**, there is poverty before Allah, and the recognition of one's own humility, and need for Him. **Secondly**, there is the poverty of material need, which means to be lacking the means necessary to live, like a hungry person who is in need of bread. This is the poverty that he ﷺ sought refuge from, whilst the other kind (i.e. to be in need of Allah) is the one he ﷺ sought.[434]

'Abdullāh said: 'How could he ﷺ have been poor and short of money, when Allah ﷻ offered to give him gold that would fill the hollow of Mecca and he refused? And He bade him choose whether to be a Prophet-King or a Prophet-Slave, and he said, "Rather, I will be a Prophet-Slave?" ' Abū Umāma ﵁ related that the Prophet ﷺ said: 'My Lord offered to turn the hollow of Mecca to gold for me, and so I said, "My Lord, I would rather eat my fill one day and go hungry the next, that when I am hungry I may implore You and make mention of You, and when I am full may thank You and praise You." '[435]

---

[434] All of these quotations can be found in Zurqānī's *Sharḥ al-Mawāhib*.

[435] Narrated by Tirmidhī, who declared it sound and rigorously authentic, and by Imām Aḥmad.

Our section on his ﷺ humility[436] mentioned the Ḥadīth narrated by Ṭabarānī with a sound chain of transmission on the authority of Ibn ʿAbbās, which included:

'Isrāfīl came to him, and said: "Allah ﷻ heard what you said, and He sent me to you with the keys of the earth's treasures, and commanded me to propose to you that I send with you the like of the mountains of Tihāma in emeralds, sapphires, gold and silver. If you wish it, you will be a Prophet-King; and if you wish it, you will be a Prophet-Slave." Jibrīl gestured to him to humble himself, so he said: "Rather, I will be a Prophet-Slave," repeating it three times.'

Jābir ibn ʿAbdullāh ؓ related that the Messenger of Allah ﷺ said: 'The keys to the world were brought to me by Jibrīl, riding on a piebald horse.'[437]

So the Messenger of Allah ﷺ raised himself above the vainglories of this world, and its riches, and its gold and silver, and did not concern himself with its finery and its luxuries, although it would have been easy for him to do so. His aspirations were higher and nobler than that.

ʿAbdullāh ibn Masʿūd ؓ said: 'The Messenger of Allah ﷺ used to sleep on a reed mat, which would leave marks on his side. We said, "Messenger of Allah, we could get you a soft bed." He replied, "What do I want with this world? My place in this world is merely that of a traveller who seeks shade under a tree, and rests, then leaves it behind."'[438]

---

[436] Volume 1, p. 260.
[437] Ibn Ḥibbān declared it to be rigorously authentic.
[438] Narrated by Ibn Mājah and Tirmidhī, who declared it rigorously authentic.

It is narrated that 'Ā'isha said: 'A woman from the Medinan Helpers came to visit me, and saw that the bed of the Messenger of Allah ﷺ was a single folded cloth, and so she sent me a couch filled with wool. When the Messenger of Allah ﷺ came to me and saw it, he said, "What is this, 'Ā'isha?" I replied, "Messenger of Allah, a woman from the Helpers came to see me and saw your bed, and so went and sent this one to me." He ﷺ said, "Return it, 'Ā'isha, for by Allah, if I willed, Allah would send me mountains of gold and silver." '[439]

Abū al-Shaykh narrated it with the wording: A woman said, 'I went to see 'Ā'isha and touched the bed of the Messenger of Allah ﷺ and found it to be rough, so I said, "Mother of the Believers, I have a bed which is better and softer than this…" ' (The story then continued as before) So his poverty was not involuntary, but was rather a voluntary expression of humility.[440] And his ﷺ wealth was not about gathering, hoarding and withholding, but rather it was marked by great generosity and selflessness. Beggars would come to him, and the needy would seek him out, and he would give them their due, and then more would ask, and he would give them, and then more would ask, and he would give them, until he had no more money, or even enough food for a single person, whereupon he ﷺ and his family would go hungry!

He ﷺ used to say to them: 'Whatever good I possess, I would not keep it from you', as we mentioned in the section on his ﷺ great generosity.[441]

---

[439] Narrated by Bayhaqī.

[440] That is, it was an expression of neediness before Allah, and the choice which gave the best reward and the highest status in Allah's sight.

[441] Volume 1, p. 273.

Then Allah ﷻ told His Prophet ﷺ to honour the blessings mentioned in these verses by giving thanks to Him as they merited, saying: ﴾Therefore the orphan oppress not, and the beggar deny not, and the bounty of thy Lord exult.﴿ These verses mirror those that came before them.

So as for the orphan, do not degrade him and look down on him, but rather treat him with kindness and generosity. And as for the beggar – literally 'the asker' (*al-sā'il*), meaning anyone who makes a request, whether for knowledge or money – do not turn him away, but rather grant him what he asks, or if you cannot, at least turn him down with pleasant words.

﴾And the bounty of thy Lord exult﴿, because to make mention of Allah's blessings is an expression of thanks to He who gave them. This is why the Messenger of Allah ﷺ would make much mention of the blessings Allah gave him, and speak of the status to which He raised him, and the special favours that He granted him; and he ﷺ did so out of gratitude, not pride. An example of this is his ﷺ saying, 'I shall be the Master of the Sons of Adam on the Day of Resurrection, and I say this without pride.' That is, he ﷺ said it out of gratitude, not conceit. Another example is his ﷺ saying, 'Indeed I am the Beloved of Allah, and I say this without pride; Adam and all who came after him are under my banner, and I say this without pride.'

And he ﷺ said, 'When the Day of Resurrection comes, I shall be the leader of the Prophets, and their speaker, and their intercessor; and I say this without pride.' The same is the case for all similar statements he ﷺ made. So this chapter of the Qur'ān shows the many ways Allah protected His Messenger ﷺ, and that He ﷻ watched over His Messenger ﷺ and took care of him at all times, throughout his life.

# ALLAH PROTECTED OUR MASTER MUḤAMMAD ﷺ FROM THE EVILS OF THE PRE-ISLAMIC TIME OF IGNORANCE

Allah ﷻ watched over His noble Messenger ﷺ while he was growing up, and so our Master Muḥammad ﷺ spent his youth in the best and noblest of ways. Allah ﷻ guarded him from the foul and nefarious practices of the time of ignorance, preparing him and strengthening him for the Message with which He wished to honour him. And so he ﷺ became a man of greatness and virtue, the most chivalrous of his people, and the best mannered, and the most highly regarded, and the most amiable, and the most forbearing, and the most truthful, and the most trustworthy, and the furthest from immorality and low manners, gracious and dignified. His people called him ﷺ 'The Honest and Trustworthy One' (*al-Ṣādiq al-Amīn*), and they all agreed that it was so, and acknowledged him as much both in private and in public.

Bukhārī and Muslim narrate, on the authority of Ibn 'Abbās ؓ, that when the verse ﴾And warn thy tribe of near kin﴿[442] was revealed, the Prophet ﷺ climbed Mount Ṣafā and began to cry, 'Sons of Fihr! Sons of 'Adī!', calling all the tribes of Quraysh until they were all assembled. He then ﷺ said, 'Tell me, if I were to inform you that a cavalry lay in the valley preparing to attack you, would you believe me?' They replied, 'Yes, for we have only ever known you to be honest'... So they declared that all they had seen from him since his youth was honesty!

Another sign of this was the statement made by Naḍr ibn al-Ḥārith, as narrated by Ibn Isḥāq: 'Hordes of Quraysh! By Allah, there has come unto you something you never dreamed of before. Muḥammad was a young boy amongst you, and pleasing

---

[442] Qur'ān 26:214

to you, and the most honest of you, and the most trustworthy of you. And then, when grey hairs appeared on his temples, he came to you with this thing he has brought. You called him a sorcerer, but by Allah he is no sorcerer, for we are familiar with sorcerers, and their blowing, and their knot-tying. You called him a soothsayer, but by Allah he is no soothsayer, for we are familiar with soothsayers and their convulsions, and we have heard their rhymed speech. You called him a poet, but by Allah he is no poet, for we are familiar with poetry, and we have heard all its devices and its meters. You called him a madman, but by Allah he is no madman, for we are familiar with madmen, and he does not choke, or whisper, or display delirium. Hordes of Quraysh, mark yourselves well; for by Allah something extraordinary has come upon you.' Ibn Isḥāq added: 'Naḍr ibn al-Ḥārith was a evil man of Quraysh, and one of those who abused the Messenger of Allah ﷺ.'[443]

Another sign of this was Ibn Isḥāq's narration on the authority of al-Miswar ibn Makhzama: 'I said to Abū Jahl, who was my maternal uncle, "Uncle, did you ever accuse Muḥammad of lying before he made his claim?" Abū Jahl replied, "By Allah, my nephew, when Muḥammad was young, he was known to us as 'the Trustworthy', and when his grey hairs approached (i.e. when he turned forty), he was no liar." "Uncle," I said, "then why do you not follow him?" He replied, "Nephew, we contended with Bānī Hāshim for honour, and so when they fed, we fed, and when they gave drink, we gave drink, and when they took in guests, we took in guests; then, when we knelt like two race horses,[444] they said, 'One of us is a Prophet!' How could we compete with that?" ' That is, how could we bring our own prophet so we could be equal in merit with Banī Hāshim.

---

[443] *Sīrat Ibn Hishām*, vol.1,p.32.

[444] I.e. in equal positions before the race.

And when Quraysh rebuilt the Ka'aba, and disagreed as to who should lift the Black Stone, and decided to let the next one to enter the door of Banī Shayba decide, and the Messenger of Allah ﷺ was that person, they all said, 'This is the Trustworthy One, and we all accept him.' This Ḥadīth was mentioned in full in the section on the superiority of his ﷺ intellect.[445] So from the time of his youth he ﷺ was known for his honesty and trustworthiness, and of being far removed from any traces of deceit or falseness, or any iniquity or vice.

He ﷺ would also keep well away from idols and graven images, and from honouring them, or swearing oaths by them, avoiding the practices of the idolaters. Imām Aḥmad narrated that 'Urwa ibn al-Zubayr said: 'A neighbour of Khadīja bint Khuwaylid told me that she once heard the Messenger of Allah ﷺ say to Khadīja:[446] "Indeed, Khadīja, I shall never worship *Allāt*, and I shall never worship *'Uzzā*!" '[447]

Bazzār and others narrated that the Prophet ﷺ said: 'I have nothing to do with imbeciles, and they have nothing to do with me.' One narration has it, 'I am not from falsehood, and falsehood is not from me.'[448]

It is related that Zayd ibn Ḥāritha said: 'I was circling the Ka'aba with the Messenger of Allah one day, when I came into contact with one of the idols there. The Messenger of Allah ﷺ said to me, "Do not touch them." '[449]

---

[445] Volume 1, p. 128.

[446] That is, before the Revelation began. [t]

[447] Ḥāfiẓ Haythamī said: 'Its narrators are all rigorously authentic.'

[448] This Ḥadīth was discussed in Volume 1 (p. 230).

[449] Ḥāfiẓ Haythamī said: 'It was narrated by Ṭabarānī, and its narrators are rigorously authentic.' Ḥāfiẓ Ibn Kathīr mentioned it in *al-Bidāya*, and ascribed it to Bayhaqī.

'Alī Ibn Abī Ṭālib ؓ related that the Messenger of Allah ﷺ said: 'I never desired to partake in any of the base practices of the people of ignorance except on two occasions, and both times, Allah ﷻ protected me from doing so. I told a boy of Quraysh who was with me in the hills above Mecca tending sheep to watch the herd for me so I could spend the night in Mecca, as the other lads did. He agreed, and so I left. When I came to the first house in Mecca, I heard the music of drums and flutes. I asked what it was, and they told me that a couple were getting married. I sat to watch, but then Allah made me sleep, [450] and by Allah nothing woke me but the touch of sunlight.

'I returned to my companion, and he asked me what I did. I said I had done nothing, and then told him what had happened. Another night, I again asked him to watch the herd so I could spend the night out, and he agreed. When I arrived in Mecca, I heard the same thing I had that night, and so I asked about it, and I was told that a couple were getting married. I sat down to watch, and Allah made me sleep, and nothing woke me but the touch of sunlight.

'I returned to my companion, and he asked me what I did. I said I had done nothing, and told him what had happened. By Allah, I never desired, or went back, for anything of that kind again until Allah ﷻ honoured me with His Message.'[451]

---

[450] Literally 'covered over my ears', an idiom. [t]

[451] See *Mawārid al-Ẓam'ān*, p. 515, in the chapter on the Prophet's ﷺ infallibility; and Ibn Kathīr's *Bidāya* vol.2, p.387, where the Ḥadīth is ascribed to Bayhaqī; and Dhahabī's *Tārīkh* vol.1, p.50; and *Majma' al-Zawā'id* in the section on the Prophet's ﷺ infallibility from falsehood, where it is ascribed to Bazzār with a chain of transmission whose narrators are all reliable.

# HIS JOURNEY TO SYRIA ﷺ

When the Messenger of Allah ﷺ was twelve years old, he went with his uncle Abū Ṭālib to Syria. When they reached Bostra, a city in the region of Ḥawrān, Baḥīrā the monk, a scholar of Christianity, saw the Prophet ﷺ and recognised in him the attributes that had been prophesised in the previous Divine Revelations, and so he said, 'This is the Master of the Messengers; this is the Master of the worlds.' We have already mentioned this Ḥadīth, narrated by Tirmidhī, in detail in the section on the Seal of Prophethood.[452] Ibn Isḥāq narrated that Baḥīrā said to the Prophet ﷺ: 'Boy, I ask you by the right of Allāt and 'Uzzā[453] to answer the questions I have for you.' The Prophet ﷺ replied, 'Ask me naught by their right, for by Allah I hate nothing more than them.' Baḥīrā said to him, 'In that case, I ask you by Allah to answer the questions I have for you.' The Prophet ﷺ replied, 'Ask away.' Baḥīrā began to ask him ﷺ about his way of life, and his sleep, and his affairs in general, and he ﷺ answered him; and each answer was exactly what Baḥīrā was looking for. Qāḍī 'Iyāḍ said in *al-Shifā*: 'He only asked him by the right of Allāt and 'Uzzā to test him,' that is, to determine whether he ﷺ corresponded to the description prophesised in the Divine Scriptures of old, one attribute of which was the hatred of idols and false gods.

The Prophet ﷺ travelled to Syria a second time on a business trip for our Lady Khadīja when he ﷺ was twenty-five years of age. As Wāqidī and Ibn al-Sakan among other narrated, that our Lady Khadīja was a noble and wealthy merchant, and had trade links with Syria, and her caravan was as well-stocked as any of Quraysh. It was her practice to hire men to trade for her and pay them a cut of her takings.

---

[452] Volume 1, p. 201

[453] The pagan gods. [t]

Now Quraysh were a tribe of merchants, amongst whom he with no trade was considered inconsequential. And so Abū Ṭālib said to the Prophet ﷺ, 'Nephew, your tribe's caravan is set to leave for Syria, and Khadīja is hiring men to go and trade for her and take a cut of the profits. If you go to her, she will give you preference over any other, for she has heard of your honesty; and though I hate to see you go to Syria, and worry what the Jews there might have in store for you, I fear we have no alternative.' The Prophet ﷺ replied, 'Perhaps she will send for me and ask me to do so' – and this is a clear manifestation of his ﷺ honour, and high aspiration, and perennial dignity. Abū Ṭālib replied, 'Then I fear that she will seek out another!' But word of this conversation reached Khadīja, who had heard before this of his ﷺ honesty, trustworthiness and good character, and so she said, 'I had not known he wanted to do this!' She sent word to him, saying: 'I have sent for you because of what I have heard of your honesty, and your trustworthiness, and your good character; and I will pay you double what I have ever paid any man of your tribe.' The Prophet ﷺ told his uncle of this, and he replied, 'This is provision that Allah has destined for you.'

So he ﷺ set off, accompanied by Maysara, a slave-boy of Khadīja's, and went as far as Bostra, whereupon he sat beneath a tree in the marketplace near the cell of Nastūrā the monk. The monk looked to Maysara, whom he knew, and said, 'Maysara, who is that beneath the tree?' He replied, 'It is a man of Quraysh, one of those who guard the Sanctuary.' The monk said, 'None could sit beneath that tree but a Prophet.'[454]

---

[454] This may also be translated as 'None other than a Prophet is sitting beneath that tree', and indeed it has been translated thus elsewhere; however, as the author ﷺ here mentions, one narration has it, 'None but a Prophet could sit beneath that tree after 'Isā,' which suggests that Nastūrā was declaring that the act of his ﷺ sitting beneath the

He then asked Maysara, 'Is there some redness in his eyes?' Maysara said yes. 'Then it is he,' said Nastūrā, 'the last of the Prophets; if only I could live to see the day he is commanded to come forward!' And Maysara remembered his words well.

Then the Prophet ﷺ attended Bostra's market, and sold the goods he had brought with him, and bought others. A man contrived to argue with him about one of his goods, and said, 'Swear by Allāt and 'Uzzā!' He ﷺ replied, 'Never have I sworn upon those.' The man replied, 'Have it your way.' The same man then said to Maysara in confidence, 'This man is a Prophet: he is the one whom our rabbis find described in their Scriptures.' And Maysara remembered his words well. The caravan then moved on. Each day at noon during the journey, Maysara would see two Angels shading the Prophet ﷺ from the sun's rays. They arrived back in Mecca at noon. Khadīja was looking out of the window of her upstairs room, whereupon she saw the Messenger of Allah ﷺ coming on his camel, with two Angels shading him from above. She showed this to her maidservants, and they shared in her amazement. The Prophet ﷺ went to her and told her what they had made from the trade, and she was pleased. Later, when Maysara went to her, she told him of what she had seen. 'I saw the same, from the moment we left Syria!' said Maysara, and he told her of what Nastūrā had said, and of the words of the man who had differed with him ﷺ about the sale. It emerged that the Prophet ﷺ had made double the profit Khadīja could have expected from her goods, and she paid him double what she had originally promised.[455]

---

tree in itself fulfilled a prophecy; hence I have attempted to translate his words in a manner that reflects this. [t]

[455] See *al-Mawāhib* and its *Sharḥ*, in which the narration is ascribed to Abū Nu'aym, Wāqidī and Ibn al-Sakan. See also Ibn Hishām's *Sīrah*, and *al-Rawḍ al-Unuf.*

# HIS MARRIAGE ﷺ TO KHADĪJA BINT KHUWAYLID IBN ASAD رضي الله عنها

In both the time before the coming of Islam and the time after it, our Lady Khadīja رضي الله عنها was known as 'the Pure One' (*al-Ṭāhira*) because of her virtue and honour. She was righteous and pure, and possessed of great intellect and acumen, as well as beauty, noble lineage, and wealth. According to the majority of scholars, our Lady Khadīja رضي الله عنها proposed to the Messenger of Allah ﷺ when he was twenty-five years old, and she herself was forty. She sent Nufaysa bint Munya to him to deliver her proposal.

Ibn Sa'd narrated by way of Wāqidī that Nufasya bint Munya said: 'Khadīja was a resolute, noble woman, and Allah Almighty had great honour and goodness in store for her. At that time, she was the noblest and wealthiest of the Quraysh, and all the men of her tribe were keen to marry her if they could, and many of them had asked for her hand, and offered her large dowries. After Muḥammad ﷺ returned with her caravan from Syria, having made a fine profit, she sent me secretly to him. When I met him, I said, "Muḥammad, what prevents you from marrying?" "I have not the means to marry," he answered. "If you were given the means," I said, "and bidden to marry one possessed of wealth, beauty, honour and abundance, would you not accept?" He said, "Who is she?" I replied, "Khadīja." I then returned and told Khadīja of our conversation, and she sent me back to him with an invitation to come to her." And so our Lady Khadīja sent Nufaysa to the Messenger of Allah ﷺ to make mention of her to see if he would accept her. Once she knew he would, she decided to speak to him directly about the matter. Ibn Isḥāq narrated that Khadīja رضي الله عنها proposed to the Prophet ﷺ, saying: 'Cousin, I love you on account of your kinship with me, and your fine standing amongst your people, and your trustworthiness and fine character, and your honest speech.'

The reason she offered herself in marriage to the Messenger of Allah ﷺ was what her slave-boy Maysara, who accompanied him to Syria, had told her about the wonders he saw, and the things she herself ؓ had seen when the Messenger of Allah ﷺ returned from the journey as she watched from her upstairs room.

Another reason for her offering herself was that mentioned by Ibn Isḥāq in *al-Mubtada'*, saying:

> The women of Quraysh had a feast day in which they would gather. On one such day, they were gathered together when a Jewish man came to them and said, 'Hordes of Quraysh, the times draws near when a Prophet shall come to you; if any of you should be able to provide a bed for him, let her do so.' They began to pelt him with stones, and rebuke him harshly. Khadīja, however, remained silent, and did not join the women in chiding him, and his words affected her deeply. When Maysara told her of the wonders he had seen, some of which she had seen for herself, she said, 'If what the Jew said was true, it can mean none other than this man.'[456]

The Messenger of Allah ﷺ then told his uncles of the matter, and they gave him their blessing and approved of the match.

**The official proposal:** The Prophet ﷺ went with his uncles Abū Ṭālib and Ḥamza[457] to Khadīja's father Khuwaylid ibn Asad. The leaders of Muḍār were present at the gathering, and Abū Ṭālib addressed them, saying:

---

[456] See *Sharḥ al-Mawāhib*, vol.1, p.200, and *Sīrat Ibn Hishām*.

[457] This according to Suhaylī's narration; Ibn Isḥāq says that only Ḥamza accompanied him ﷺ and made the official proposal.

> Praise be to Allah who has made us the scions of Ibrāhīm, the posterity of Ismā'īl, the heirs of Ma'add, and has made us the custodians of His House, and the servants of His Sanctuary, and has given us a place of pilgrimage, and a protected sanctuary, and has made us leaders of the people.
>
> My nephew, Muḥammad ibn 'Abdullāh, would outweigh any man in nobility, and honour, and grace, and intellect; and though his wealth may be slight, wealth is but a shadow that comes and goes, and a loan that must be repaid. Muḥammad is one of those whose kinship you all well know, and he has come to ask for the hand of your noble lady Khadīja.
>
> For her dowry, he offers a total of twelve and one half *ūqiyya*[458] of gold, part to be paid now and part later.[459] By Allah, great and glorious things are in store for him from now on.

So her father gave her in marriage, though it is said it was her paternal uncle 'Amr ibn Asad, or her brother 'Amr ibn Khuwaylid.

Khadīja went on to bear all the Prophet's ﷺ noble children but Ibrāhīm, who was the son of Maria the Copt.

---

[458] An *ūqiyya* is equal to the weight of forty dirhams, so this means a total of 500 dirhams' weight of gold, or around 1480 grams. (*Lisān al-'Arab*, xv. 401 and *Reliance of the Traveller*, w15.2) [t]

[459] Al-Muḥibb al-Ṭabarī said: 'The Chosen Prophet ﷺ gave Khadīja twenty she-camels for her dowry.' Zurqānī said of this, 'This does not contradict what Abū Ṭālib said about her dowry (in the above speech) because it is possible he ﷺ could have given her more besides this, so both (the gold and the camels) were her dowry.'

# HIS NOBLE CHILDREN ﷺ

It is differed as to the number of children he ﷺ had, but the strongest opinion, according to Qasṭalānī and others, is that they numbered seven:

**Three boys**: Qāsim, 'Abdallāh, who was also known as al-Ṭayyib wa al-Ṭāhir ('fine and pure'),[460] and Ibrāhīm;

And **four girls**: our Lady Zaynab, the eldest, and our Lady Ruqayya, and our Lady Umm Kulthūm, and our Lady Fāṭima al-Zahrā al-Batūl, may the blessings and peace of Allah be upon their father, and upon them all.All of his ﷺ daughters lived to see the coming of Islam, and embraced it, and were with the Prophet ﷺ in Medina after the Emigration. Our Lady Zaynab was the eldest of his ﷺ daughters, though it is differed as to whether she or Qāsim was born first. Our Lady Fāṭima was the most beloved to the Prophet ﷺ of all his family; for Tirmidhī narrated, with a sound chain of transmission on the authority of Usāma, that the Prophet ﷺ said: 'The most beloved of my family to me is Fāṭima.'[461]

And 'Ā'isha ﵂ is related to have said: 'I never saw anyone who so resembled the Messenger of Allah ﷺ in manner, conduct or speech, even in the way he stood and sat, than Fāṭima, daughter of the Messenger of Allah ﷺ.' 'Ā'isha ﵂ also said: 'When Fāṭima ﵂ went to see the Messenger of Allah ﷺ, he would stand to greet her, and kiss her, and bid her sit down in his place; and when the Prophet ﷺ went to see her, she would stand for him and kiss him, and bid him sit down in her place.

---

[460] It is also said that al-Ṭayyib wal-Tāhir was another of his ﷺ sons, not simply a nickname for 'Abdullāh; it is also said that Ṭayyib and Ṭāhir are the names of two different sons.

[461] Also narrated by Ḥākim.

'When the Messenger of Allah's ﷺ final illness came, Fāṭima came to see him, and leaned over him and kissed him, and then raised her head and began to weep. She then leaned over him again, and raised her head, and that time she was smiling. After the Messenger of Allah ﷺ had passed away, I said to her, "I saw you lean over the Prophet ﷺ, and when you raised your head, you were weeping; then you leaned over him again, and when you raised your head you were smiling. Why was this?" She replied, "He ﷺ told me that he would die from this illness, so I wept; then he told me that I would be the first of his family to follow him, and so I smiled." '[462]

Imām Aḥmad narrated that Thawbān ؓ said: 'When the Messenger of Allah ﷺ travelled, the last thing he would do before leaving was visit Fāṭima, and the first one he would visit upon his arrival home would be Fāṭima ؓ.'

Ḥāfiẓ Abū 'Umar narrated that when the Prophet ﷺ came home from a battle or a journey, the first thing he would do is go to the mosque and offer two units of prayer, and then he would go and see Fāṭima, and then his wives.

The Messenger of Allah ﷺ informed Fāṭima that she would be the foremost of all women in Paradise; one narration has it that he ﷺ called her the foremost of the women of all the worlds. Bukhārī and Muslim narrate that 'Ā'isha ؓ said: 'Fāṭima came walking along one day, her gait the image of that of the Messenger of Allah ﷺ. "Welcome, my daughter," he said, and then bade her sit to his right. He then spoke some words to her in confidence, and she wept; he then spoke more, and she smiled. I thought to myself that I had never seen sadness more

[462] Narrated by Tirmidhī, Abū Dāwūd and Nasā'ī, and Tirmidhī declared it a sound singular narration. (See *Sharḥ al-Mirqāt 'alā al-Mishkāt*)

quickly turn to joy, and so I asked her what he ﷺ had said. "I could not reveal the Messenger of Allah's ﷺ secrets," she replied. When he ﷺ had passed away, I asked her again, and she told me that he had said: "Jibrīl usually comes to revise the Qur'ān with me once a year, yet this year he has come to me twice. I think naught but that my time is near, and you shall be the first of my house to follow me; what a fine predecessor I am for you!" And so she wept. Then, he ﷺ said to her, "Are you not pleased to be the leader of the women of the worlds?" [463] And so she smiled on account of this.'

Nasā'ī and Ḥākim narrated, with a good chain of transmission on the authority of Ḥudhayfa ؓ, that the Prophet ﷺ said: 'One of the Angels asked leave of his Lord to greet me, and told me that Ḥasan and Ḥusayn are the leaders of the youths of Paradise, and that their mother is the leader of the women of Paradise.'[464]

## THE BEGINNING OF HIS PROPHETIC MISSION ﷺ

Allah ﷻ sent our Master Muḥammad ﷺ as a Messenger to the worlds after forty years of his blessed life had passed, according to the Ḥadīth narrated by Bukhārī and Muslim in which Ibn 'Abbās ؓ said: 'The Messenger of Allah was sent (as a Messenger) at the age of forty, and he remained in Mecca for thirteen years whilst the Revelation was being given to him. Then he was commanded to emigrate, and lived for ten more years after the Emigration, and passed away at the age of sixty-three.'

---

[463] One narration has it 'the leader of the women of Paradise'; Aḥmad's narration reads, 'Are you not pleased to be the leader of the women of this nation?' or 'the believing women?'
[464] See *Sharḥ al-Mawāhib*, vol.3, p.205.

This is the opinion of the majority. Imām Suhaylī said, 'This is the soundest opinion according to the masters of prophetic biography and tradition', and Imām Nawawī said, 'This is the correct opinion.'

His fortieth birthday was in the month of *Rabī 'al-Awwal.* His ﷺ prophethood began on a Monday; Muslim narrates on the authority of Abū Qatāda that the Prophet ﷺ was asked about the merits of fasting of Mondays, and he ﷺ replied, 'That was the day I was born, and the day I was sent.' Some of the scholars say that it was actually in the month of Ramaḍān, since the first revelations of the Qur'ān came in that month, as Allah says: ﴾The month of Ramaḍān, in which was revealed the Qur'ān…﴿[465] To be exact, this occurred on the Night of Power in the month of Ramaḍān, as is indicated by Allah's word: ﴾Lo! We revealed it in the Night of Power.﴿[466] This means that the beginning of his ﷺ prophethood came when he was forty years and six months old.

The rightly-guided scholars have been able to reconcile the two opinions, as Zurqānī and others have noted, by proposing that he ﷺ was first given Divine Inspiration in the form of dreams in the month of *Rabī' al-Awwal,* when he ﷺ reached his fortieth birthday; then Jibrīl عليه السلام came to him the following Ramaḍān.

Ḥāfiẓ al-Zurqānī said:

> Some of them support this with the Ḥadīth: "Dreams are one forty-sixth of prophecy", because the Revelation lasted for twenty-three years, six months of which (in this view) took the form of dreams, which is equal to one forty-sixth.

---

[465] Qur'ān 2:185
[466] Qur'ān 97:1

Bukhārī and Muslim (the wording here is that of Bukhārī) narrate that 'Ā'isha ﵂ said: 'The first Revelation that the Messenger of Allah ﷺ received took the form of true visions in his sleep (another narration, also of Bukhārī and Muslim, has it 'in the form of sound visions'[467]); and when he saw these visions they were as clear as the light of dawn. Upon this, he became drawn to solitary retreat.[468] He would seek solitude in the cave of Ḥirā' and devote himself to worship[469] there for many nights[470] before returning to his family. He would take provisions for his stay, and then return to Khadīja to replenish

---

[467] Ḥāfiẓ Zurqānī said: 'A true vision means one that does not lie, or one that needs no interpretation; or it means one that comes to pass exactly as it was envisaged, or whose interpretation also comes in a dream.' As for the term 'sound vision', this is more specific than 'true vision'; it means a vision of glad tidings, as Qasṭalānī mentions in his commentary on *Ṣaḥīḥ al-Bukhārī.*

[468] That is, Allah ﷻ caused him ﷺ to be drawn to solitary retreat. Khaṭṭābī said: 'This is because solitary retreat is a means of emptying the heart (of worldly things), and it aids meditation, and allows one to be detached from human comforts, and concentrate one's heart, and gather one's focus.' 'Ā'isha's phrase 'he became drawn to solitary retreat' shows that the Prophet's ﷺ love for solitude was inspired in him by Allah; it was not a personal desire, but rather a result of Divine Inspiration, as 'Asqalānī noted in *Fatḥ al-Bārī.*

[469] The word used in the Ḥadīth is *taḥannatha*, which means to abstain from the sins of idolatry, which means worship, since worship is the means to abstinence from sin.

[470] The exact number is provided for us in Bukhārī and Muslim's narration on the authority of Jābir, which states that the Prophet ﷺ said: 'I stayed in Ḥirā' for one month.' The narration of Ibn Isḥāq specifies that the month in question was Ramaḍān. Ibn Isḥāq also stated that the Prophet ﷺ would keep solitary vigil in Hirā' for one month a year, namely Ramaḍān.

them,[471] until the Truth[472] came to him whilst he was in the cave of Ḥirā'. The Angel came to him and said, "Recite!"[473] "I am not a reciter," he replied.'[474] 'Ā'isha ﵂ then continued the story

---

[471] Zurqānī said: 'This means he would take provisions for a few nights, and then return home when they were finished to replenish them. This shows that being constantly separated from one's family is not the Sunnah, because he ﷺ did not completely cut himself off in the cave, but rather returned regularly to his family to see to their needs, and then return to his worship.

[472] I.e. the Revelation, called the Truth because it came from Allah ﷻ.

[473] So the Angel, who by consensus was Jibrīl, told him to recite. Ḥāfiẓ Zurqānī said: 'The purpose of this instruction was to alert him ﷺ of what would be revealed to him, and what he would be instructed to recite. This is a proof that it is rationally conceivable that one could be commanded (by Allah) to do something that is currently beyond one's means, provided that one will be able to do it later.'

[474] 'Asqalānī said in *Fatḥ al-Bārī*: 'The word *mā* in the expression *mā ana biqāri* ('I am not a reciter') was negative, since if (as some say) it were interrogative (giving the meaning 'what should I recite?'), it would be incorrect to add the governing particle of *bi* (to the word *qari*, 'reciter') – even though Akhfash said this is permissible (in the Arabic language) – since this is a minority opinion. Actually, the use of the governing particle of *bi* added emphasis to the negation, giving the meaning "I do not know how to read". After he had said this three times, the Angel said to him, ﴾Recite in the name of thy Lord﴿ (Qur'ān 96:1), that is: Do not recite by your own power or knowledge, but rather by the power and aid of your Lord, for He shall teach you even as He created you and removed from you the clot of blood which contained the influence of Satan (which affects all men) when you were but a child, and taught your people to read so that they wrote with the pen after having been unlettered – and this was noted by Suhaylī.'

Zurqānī said: 'It is also said that the *mā* is interrogative, although 'Iyāḍ and Ibn Qarqūl deemed this weak because of the presence of the

as reported to her by the Messenger of Allah ﷺ: 'So he took hold of me and embraced me[475] until he had reached the limit of my endurance, and then he released me, and said, "Recite!" "I am not a reciter," I replied, and so he took me and embraced me a second time, until he had reached the limit of my endurance, and then he released me, and said, "Recite!" I said "I am not a reciter", and he took me and embraced me a third time, and then released me and said: ﴾Recite in the name of thy Lord, who created! He created man from a clot of blood. Recite; and thy Lord is the Most Bounteous, He who hath taught by the pen, taught man what he knew not.﴿[476]'

'Ā'isha's relation continues: 'Upon this, the Messenger of Allah ﷺ returned home, his heart quaking, and he went to Khadīja bint Khuwaylid and said, "Cover me! Cover me!"

---

governing particle of *bi* before the predicate, which cannot be used in the case of the interrogative *mā.* In response to this, I say that the narration of Abū al-Aswad on the authority of 'Urwa has it, "How should I recite", and Ibn Isḥāq on the authority of 'Ubayd ibn 'Umayr has it, "What should I recite?" These narrations suggest that the *mā* here was interrogative; and Akhfash said that the governing particle of *bi* could indeed be added to a predicate, and Ibn Mālik allowed it in the case of the phrase *biḥasbika Zayd* ('Zayd will suffice you'), where the governing particle *bi* is added to the predicate *ḥasbika* without changing the meaning.'

[475] In these embraces were many Divine graces, secrets and illuminations that Jibrīl ﷺ brought from the All-Knowing, Wise Lord, in a way that enveloped the soul, the heart, and the spirit. Ibn 'Abbās said: 'The Messenger of Allah ﷺ once held me close to his blessed chest and said, "O Allah, teach him the Book." ' By means of this, Ibn 'Abbās was given enlightenment and grace.

[476] Qur'ān 96:1-5

'She covered him with a cloth, and his awe abated, so he told her what had happened, and said to her, "I feared for myself."[477] Khadīja replied to him, "No, by Allah! Allah would never cause you to grieve; for you maintain your family ties, and you always speak the truth, and you help those in need, and you receive your guests with hospitality, and you strive to uphold the truth." Khadīja then took him ﷺ to her cousin Waraqa ibn Nawfal ibn Asad, who had converted to the Christian faith in the days of pagan ignorance. He knew how to write Hebrew, and would write as much of the Gospel in Hebrew as Allah decreed he should. (Muslim's narration says that Waraqa knew Arabic writing, and would write the Gospel in Arabic.)[478] He was an old man by this time, and had lost his sight. Khadīja said to him, "Cousin, listen to your nephew." "Nephew, what have you seen?" asked Waraqa. The Prophet ﷺ told him what he had seen. Waraqa replied, "This is the self-same Nāmūs[479] that

---

[477] That is, I feared that my body would not be able to bear the weight of the Revelation. This was because the Revelation came with a weight that the strongest men could not bear, but only those whom Allah ﷻ strengthened with the graces of prophethood. This is especially true of the Muhammadan Revelation, since it was of the highest level of Revelation there is. Allah ﷻ said: ﴿Indeed We shall load thee with a word of heavy weight.﴾ (Qur'ān 73:5) Bayhaqī narrated that 'Ā'isha ﵂ said: 'If the Revelation came to the Messenger of Allah ﷺ whilst he sat atop his camel, the weight of it would cause the animal to lower its head. One day the Revelation came to him while he rode his camel, and the weight forced it to sit down.'

[478] Ḥāfiẓ 'Asqalānī said: 'Both relations are correct, since Waraqa knew how to speak and write Hebrew, and so he would write Scripture in both Hebrew and Arabic, as he knew both scripts and both languages.'

[479] The word *nāmūs* means 'one who bears a secret'; here it meant Jibrīl ﵇, because he was the one who bore the secret of Divine

came down to Mūsā! Oh to be young once more! Oh to be alive when your people cast you out!" The Messenger of Allah ﷺ replied, "They will cast me out?" Waraqa said, "Indeed they shall, for no man comes with what you have come with save they are rejected. Yet were I to live to see your day come, I would surely help you with all my might!" It was not long after that Waraqa passed away.'

The Revelation then ceased for a time, said to be two and a half years or three years. After this pause, Allah ﷻ revealed the first verses of Sūrat al-Muddaththir. Bukhārī and Muslim narrate, on the authority of Jābir رضي الله عنه, that the Messenger of Allah ﷺ said: 'I kept a sacred retreat[480] in Ḥirā' for one month.[481] When my retreat had finished, and I had come back down the slope, I heard a call. I looked to my right and saw nothing, and then looked to my left and saw nothing, and then looked behind me and saw nothing. I raised my head, and saw something (i.e. Jibrīl). One narration has it, 'So I raised my eyes, and there was the Angel that had come to me in Ḥirā', sitting on a throne suspended between the heavens and the earth. I was awe-stricken by him, and so I turned and left.'Another narration adds: 'I returned to my family, and said, "Cover me! Cover me!" Then Allah Almighty revealed:

---

Revelation from Allah to His Messengers and Prophets. He is known as the Greatest Nāmūs.

[480] The Prophet ﷺ used the verb *jiwār* here rather than *i'tikāf* because, as Ibn 'Abd al-Barr says, the word *i'tikāf* specifically means a sacred retreat in a mosque, and Ḥirā' was not a mosque.

[481] That is, during the time when the Revelation ceased; this does not refer to the month he ﷺ spent in retreat before Jibrīl came to him with the first Revelation. Bayhaqī narrates with a *mursal* chain [see note 381, p.168] on the authority of 'Ubayd ibn 'Umayr that the Prophet ﷺ would keep a sacred retreat one month out of every year, namely in Ramaḍān.

﴾O thou who art wrapped in thy cloak, arise and warn! Thy Lord magnify; thy raiment purify; defilement shun.﴿[482] And so he ﷺ began to warn the people, and call them to Allah ﷻ.

It was the custom of Allah ﷻ to call upon His Dearest Beloved ﷺ in the Qur'ān, not by his name, but rather to refer to him by names that showed his honour and exalted status, and so He would say: ﴾O Prophet, We have sent thee as a witness…﴿[483] ﴾O Messenger, be not aggrieved by those who are quick to disbelieve…﴿[484]

He ﷻ would also call him using names that described his current situation, out of compassion and love for him ﷺ, as is the case with ﴾O thou who art wrapped in thy raiment…﴿[485] and ﴾O thou who art wrapped in thy cloak…﴿[486] This is a clear indication of the pre-eminence of this Noble Messenger ﷺ over the rest of creation. He would not call him by his name, as He called the other Messengers and Prophets: ﴾He said, 'O Ādam, tell them their names!'﴿[487] ﴾It was said to him, 'O Nūḥ, disembark with peace from Us…﴿[488] ﴾O Ibrāhīm , turn away from this…﴿[489] ﴾O Mūsā, fear not…﴿[490] ﴾And Allah did say, 'O 'Īsā, I shall cause thee to die, and raise thee up to Me…﴿[491]

---

[482] Qur'ān 74:1-5
[483] Qur'ān 33:45
[484] Qur'ān 5:41
[485] Qur'ān 73:1
[486] Qur'ān 74:1
[487] Qur'ān 2:33
[488] Qur'ān 11:48
[489] Qur'ān 11:76
[490] Qur'ān 27:10
[491] Qur'ān 3:55

# ALLAH ﷻ PROTECTED HIS MESSENGER ﷺ FROM THE EVIL OF THE DEMONIC CONSORT

Imām Muslim and Aḥmad narrated, on the authority of Ibn Masʿūd ◈, that the Prophet ﷺ said: 'There is not one of you save that he has been assigned a consort from the jinn and consort from the Angels.' 'Even you, O Messenger of Allah?' they said. 'Even me,' he ﷺ replied, 'but Allah Almighty aided me against it, and it submitted, and so it only commands me to do good.'

One narration replaces 'and it submitted' with 'and so I am safe' (this requires a very slight change in the Arabic, only a single short vowel [t]), which would give the meaning 'I am safe from its allure and its scheming.' Ḥāfiẓ al-Zurqānī said:

> Khaṭṭābī preferred the reading 'and so I am safe', whilst ʿIyāḍ and Nawawī preferred 'and it submitted', since it corresponds to his ﷺ next words, 'and so (it) only commands me to do good.' Dumayrī also declared this to be the preferred reading.
>
> There is absolute consensus that he ﷺ was protected from Satan; the reason he ﷺ made this statement was to warn others about the mischief of the demonic consort and it's whispering and tempting. He ﷺ let us know that the demonic consort is with us in order that we would take whatever precautions against it we could.

So the Prophet ﷺ was protected from all temptations and satanic insinuations, and so he only spoke the truth, and only said what was right, and only did those things that pleased his Lord ﷻ.

# ALLAH ﷻ PROTECTED HIS MESSENGER ﷺ FROM FAULTS AND ERRORS AND FORTIFIED HIM WITH THE TRUTH AT ALL TIMES

Allah ﷻ aided His Messenger, our Master Muḥammad ﷺ, with the truth, and fortified all his words and deeds throughout his life, whether he was pleased or displeased, and whether his mood was serious or jovial, and whether his health was well or ill. If he ﷺ became angry, his anger would not cause him to err from the truth; he was firm upon the truth whether he was angry or pleased, unlike the rest of humanity, whose anger might cause them to fall short of impartiality and speak falsely. For this reason, the Messenger of Allah ﷺ informed us that anger did not have the influence over him that it has over others, but that rather he maintained his perfect impartiality, and justice word and deed, at all times, whatever his mood.

Abū Dāwūd narrated that 'Abdullāh ibn 'Amr said: 'I used to write down everything I heard the Messenger of Allah ﷺ say in order to memorise it later. The men of Quraysh attempted to dissuade me from doing so, saying, "Do you write everything the Messenger of Allah ﷺ says, when the Messenger of Allah ﷺ is a human being who speaks out of both anger and contentment?" I therefore stopped writing, and mentioned this to the Prophet ﷺ. Upon this, he pointed his finger to his mouth and said, "Write, for by the One in whose hand rests my soul, naught comes out of this save the truth." ' Dārimī's narration has it: 'Write, for by the One in whose hand rests my soul, naught has ever come out of this save the truth.'

And indeed, nothing ever did, or ever would, come from his ﷺ mouth except the truth! Even his ﷺ jokes would be based on truth, not falsehood, as he ﷺ said: 'Indeed I joke, but I say naught but he truth.'

And he ﷺ said: 'I have nothing to do with imbeciles, and they have nothing to do with me', as we saw before when discussing his ﷺ jovial side.[492] Satan could not influence him ﷺ to err from the truth, for he was completely protected from this, as we saw earlier. Anger and other negative emotions could not make him stray from his perfect impartiality, or from cleaving to absolute truth in word and deed, which is why he said: 'Write everything you hear from me, for by Allah, naught comes out of this (his ﷺ mouth) save the truth.' His pure, upright soul led him to nothing but goodness, truth and sincerity, and so he said: 'I have nothing to do with imbeciles, and they have nothing to do with me'; and 'I have nothing to do with falsehood, and falsehood has nothing to do with me.'

And so our Master the Messenger of Allah ﷺ was always of sound opinion and Allah ﷻ protected him from erring in his decisions and judgements. How could it be otherwise, when Allah gave him such a completely sound intellect, and such comprehensive knowledge, and such precise reasoning, and such powerful intelligence, and such perfect insight into all things!

There are many narrations which prove the truth of this, and show that if he ﷺ formed an opinion on any matter, and any of the Companions disagreed and did otherwise, the result would always be to their disadvantage and misfortune.

For example, consider what took place on the day of Uḥud: The Prophet ﷺ chose fifty archers, placing 'Abdullāh ibn Jubayr in charge of them, and instructed them to stay in the exact position he appointed them, saying: 'Protect our backs. If you see us being slain, do not come to our aid; and if you see us plundering them, do not come to join us.'

---

[492] See Volume 1, p. 230.

Another narration has it that he ﷺ said: 'If you see that we have the upper hand over them, do not leave your positions; and if you see that they have the upper hand over us, do not come to our aid,' as can be found in the books of prophetic biography.

Aḥmad narrates in his *Musnad* that the Prophet ﷺ also said: 'Even if you see the birds pecking at us, do not move from your positions unless I send for you.'

Yet when the Muslims began to rout the idolaters, the soldiers under 'Abdullāh's charge began to say, 'The plunder! Our side has won, so what are you waiting for?' 'Abdullāh said to them, 'Have you forgotten what the Messenger of Allah ﷺ said to you?' They replied, 'By Allah, we will go and take our share of the plunder!' And so the idolaters breached the gap behind the Muslims that the archers had been defending, and fell upon the Muslims, and put many of them to flight – and this was a direct result of the Prophet's ﷺ instructions being disobeyed.

When we examined the superiority of the Prophet's ﷺ noble intellect,[493] we mentioned several examples to prove the soundness of his reasoning in all his public and private affairs, and in his dealings with his foes, and in all his military campaigns. The majority of scholars and researchers have affirmed that the Prophet ﷺ was Divinely protected from error, substantiating this with many proofs which can be found explained in detail in the books of exegesis (*tafsīr*) and legal theory (*uṣūl al-fiqh*). These scholars affirm that to ascribe any error to the Prophet ﷺ would require evidence to corroborate this, and no such evidence exists, whether in the form of a verse of Qur'ān or a Ḥadīth. Moreover, it is not related that any Companion ever ascribed an error to the Prophet ﷺ of any kind. Some scholars are of the opinion that it was possible for

---

[493] Volume 1, p.119

the Prophet ﷺ to make a mistake momentarily before being corrected by Divine Inspiration. They adduce as evidence for this the story of the captives of Badr, and the cross-pollination of the date palms, and possibly also the story of his ﷺ changing positions at Badr on the advice of Ḥubāb ibn al-Mundhir.

However, when these matters are subjected to careful scrutiny, it becomes clear that they do not constitute proof for this opinion; rather, in each instance the Messenger of Allah ﷺ was correct to do as he did, and there was no error of any kind on his ﷺ part. Let us explain each one in turn:

## THE STORY OF THE CAPTIVES OF BADR

As for the story of the captives of Badr, Aḥmad narrated in his *Musnad* that Anas ؓ said: 'The Prophet ﷺ asked the people's opinion about the captives taken at Badr, saying, "Allah Almighty has given you to decide their fate." 'Umar ibn al-Khaṭṭāb stood up and said, "O Messenger of Allah, strike their necks!" But the Prophet ﷺ turned away from him. Then, the Messenger of Allah ﷺ returned, and said, "O people, Allah have given you to decide their fate, and just yesterday they were your brethren." 'Umar again stood and said, "O Messenger of Allah, strike their necks!" But the Prophet ﷺ turned away from him, and repeated his words to the people. Abū Bakr al-Ṣiddīq ؓ then stood up and said, "Messenger of Allah, we think you should be lenient to them, and accept ransoms for them." Upon this, the concern left the face of the Messenger of Allah ﷺ, and so he relented towards them, and accepted ransoms for them. Then Allah Almighty revealed: ﴾Were it not for a prior decree of Allah, you would surely have been visited by an awful torment on account of what you took.﴿[494]

---

[494] Qur'ān 8:68

Aḥmad also narrated that the Prophet ﷺ asked the advice of Abū Bakr, 'Umar and 'Alī,[495] and Abū Bakr said: 'Prophet of Allah, these men are our cousins, and our kin, and our brothers, and I believe you should take ransoms for them, and use our gains from them as a means of amassing strength against the idolaters; and perhaps Allah may guide them, that they be added to our strength.'

The Prophet ﷺ then said, 'What say you, 'Umar?' He replied, 'By Allah, I do not agree with Abū Bakr. I believe you should let me take care of so-and-so he mentioned the name of a relative of his), that I might strike his neck, and let 'Alī take care of 'Aqīl, that he might strike his neck, and let Ḥamza take care of so-and-so, that he might strike his neck, so that Allah shall know our hearts are free of any partiality towards the idolaters; for these men are their leaders, and their champions.'

'Umar said afterwards: 'The Messenger of Allah inclined towards Abū Bakr's opinion, and not mine, and so he ransomed them. The next day, I returned to the Prophet ﷺ and Abū Bakr and found them weeping. "Why do you and your companion weep?" I asked, "for if I am moved to weep, I shall weep, and if not, I shall make myself weep that I might weep with you."

'The Prophet ﷺ replied: 'I weep for what I have been informed of your companions' punishment for accepting the ransoms; for their punishment has been shown to me more clearly than this tree (he pointed to a nearby tree).'

Allah then revealed: ﴾It is not for a Prophet to hold captives until he hath made great slaughter in the land.

---

[495] These two narrations show that the Prophet ﷺ sought advice from the people in general and also from these three in private. There is no record of what 'Alī's ﵁ advice was. (*Sharḥ al-Mawāhib*)

You would have for yourselves the gains of this world, whilst Allah would have for you the Hereafter; and Allah is Mighty, Wise. Were it not for a prior decree of Allah, you would surely have been visited by an awful torment on account of what you took; yet enjoy the spoils ye have won as lawful and good, and be mindful of Allah. Allah is forgiving, Merciful.﴿[496] By these words, Allah made battle-spoils lawful to them.[497]

This is the story of the captives of Badr, and there is nothing in the texts that relate this story to suggest that the Prophet ﷺ was wrong in doing what he did with the captives. Rather, anyone who reflects deeply on this story, and on the verses and reports connected to it, will see without doubt that the Prophet ﷺ was completely right to do as he did. There are several observations that can be made about these events:

1 – The Prophet ﷺ came to this decision because of taking counsel as he was commanded to do by Allah ﷻ when He said: ﴾Consult them about their affairs, and once thou art resolved, put thy trust in Allah.﴿[498]

2 – The Prophet ﷺ inclined to the opinion of those who preferred to take the ransom because it was the way of mercy and leniency, which reflects the station in which Allah placed him, according to His word: ﴾And we have not sent thee save as a mercy to the worlds.﴿[499] Even when he ﷺ had been injured at the Battle of Uḥud, and they bade him invoke Allah against the idolaters, he replied, 'I was only sent as a mercy. O Allah, guide my people, for they know not!'

---

[496] Qur'ān 8:67-69

[497] The like of it was also narrated by Muslim, Abū Dāwūd and Tirmidhī.

[498] Qur'ān 3:159

[499] Qur'ān 21:107

**3** – His ﷺ action was in agreement with what had already been predestined in the Primordial Decree, in which Allah ﷻ made the taking of battles-spoils lawful for him ﷺ alone, having forbidden this to all who came before him. Ibn 'Abbās ؓ explained the verse thus: ﴾Were it not for a prior decree of Allah﴿ i.e. in the Primordial Decree, stating that taking battle-spoils and captives is lawful for you (the Muslims), ﴾you would surely have been visited by an awful torment on account of what you took﴿, i.e. the captives. Ḥāfiẓ Ibn Kathīr said:

> It is also reported that the opinion of Abū Hurayra, Ibn Mas'ūd, Sa'īd ibn Jubayr, 'Aṭā', Ḥasan al-Baṣrī, Qatāda, and A'mash, was that the meaning is: Were it not that Allah had decreed the taking of battle-spoils to be lawful for this community, you would surely have been visited by an awful torment on account of what you took. This was also the opinion of Ibn Jarīr ؒ.

If it be objected that the verse only proves that battle-spoils are lawful, not ransoms, we say that ransoms are included in the meaning of battle-spoils, because they both constitute property taken from the disbelievers (through battle). This is borne out by the statement of the Prophet ﷺ: 'Battle-spoils were made lawful for me, after having been unlawful for all who came before me.' This Ḥadīth clearly shows the same special dispensation for him ﷺ that was given by the verse, as Zurqānī makes clear in *Sharḥ al-Mawāhib*. 'Allāmah Ālūsī ؒ says in his exegesis:

> Muḥyī al-Sunnah mentioned that it is narrated that when the first verse (8:67) was revealed, the Companions of the Prophet ﷺ were ready to relinquish the ransoms they had taken; then it was revealed: ﴾Yet enjoy the spoils ye have won as lawful

> and good...》 And so they recognised that this verse had made the ransoms lawful for them. So the meaning of 《the spoils ye have won》 is either ransoming specifically, or all battle-spoils in general, in which case the ruling included ransoming as one form of spoils.

4 – Just as the Prophet's ﷺ acceptance of the ransoms was in accordance with Allah's Primordial Decree, it was also in accordance with the Sacred Ordinance that would presently be revealed in the Qur'ān, namely Allah's words: 《Yet enjoy the spoils ye have won as lawful and good.》 How could something that was in accordance with both the Primordial Decree and the Sacred Law which was about to be affirmed, ever be deemed a mistake? This is further clarified by considering the fifth observation:

5 – The revelation of the lawfulness of taking battle-spoils, namely Allah's words 《Yet enjoy the spoils ye have won as lawful and good》, was an endorsement of the Messenger of Allah's ﷺ actions, and an affirmation of his sound judgement. If what he ﷺ had done was a mistake, how could Allah ﷻ give it sanction by making it part of the permanent Divine Law?

Even according to the opinion of those who believe that the Prophet ﷺ could make a mistake momentarily before being corrected by Allah, it could not be said what he ﷺ did with the captives of Badr was a mistake, since Allah ﷻ endorsed his action, so where is the error? Ḥāfiẓ Ibn Kathīr said in his exegesis:

> The ruling established here concerning captives remains applicable according to the majority of scholars, namely that the Imām is free to choose from the following options:

1: He can execute them, as was the case with the Banī Qurayḍa, or 2: He can ransom them for money, as was done with the captives of Badr; or exchange them for Muslim captives, as the Messenger of Allah ﷺ did with the slave-girl and her daughter who were captured by Salama ibn al-Akwa', exchanging them for an equal number of Muslim captives held by the idolaters, or 3: He can keep the captives as bondsmen.

This is the opinion of Imām Shāfi'ī and other scholars; the details of the scholarly difference of opinion on this matter can be found in the books of jurisprudence.

**6** – If what the Prophet ﷺ did with the captives at Badr had been an error, Allah ﷻ would have commanded him to return the ransoms, and seek forgiveness from Him for the wrong he had done by taking them; yet Allah endorsed his action and sanctioned it with His words ﴾Yet enjoy the spoils ye have won as lawful and good﴿. If it had been a mistake, Allah ﷻ would not have sanctioned it in this way.

**7** – If what he did with the captives at Badr had been an error, the Messenger of Allah ﷺ would not have expressed his joy at the grace Allah showed him by making battle-spoils lawful to him. Yet the Prophet ﷺ would often mention the things with which Allah ﷻ blessed him, the greatest and most distinctive of these blessings being the five that were reserved solely for him ﷺ. Bukhārī, Muslim and others narrated on the authority of Jābir ؓ that the Prophet ﷺ said: 'I have been given five that none before me were given: Every Prophet was sent to his people alone, whilst I have been sent to all men, the red and the black; and battle-spoils were made lawful for me, having been lawful for none before me...'

Commenting on this, Khaṭṭābī said:

> Those who came before (him ﷺ) were of two kinds: those for whom fighting was not permitted and so took no spoils, and those for whom fighting was permitted but not the taking of spoils, so that any spoils they were to plunder would be consumed by fire.

**8** – The Prophet's ﷺ decision to take ransoms for the captives was based on wisdom and sound planning, because any Sacred instruction that could have been revealed after it would either confirm the correctness of his ﷺ actions, which indeed was the case, praise be to Allah, or else it would command him to return the ransom and execute the prisoners, in which case this would have been done.

Yet had he executed the prisoners and then a Sacred directive had come to take ransoms for them, what could he ﷺ have done then? His hesitation in executing the captives was therefore the epitome of wisdom, and was plainly the correct decision – which is why Allah approved of it and sanctioned it thereafter.

Qāḍī Abū Bakr ibn al-'Arabī ؓ said in his *Aḥkām al-Qur'ān*:

> If it be asked whether the Prophet's ﷺ choosing to accept the ransoms along with the Companions who took this view was a fault on his part, we reply: Some people have imagined this to be the case, saying that this was an unintentional sin on the part of the Prophet ﷺ.
>
> Yet Allah forbid that this should be the case! All the Prophet ﷺ did was wait and see (what Allah's ruling would be)?

> It was not as though there had been no killings, for they had executed the ringleaders, and spread great slaughter in the land[500]; for on the day of Badr, they killed seventy of the idolaters' ringleaders, and then captured a further seventy; the Prophet ﷺ then waited to see if this constituted enough (slaughter) or not. This is clear for all fair-minded people.

**9** – How could it be judged that the Prophet ﷺ was wrong in his dealings with the captives of Badr, when he ﷺ was commanded to give the decision to his Companions, and then acted in accordance with this decision?

Tirmidhī, Nasā'ī, Ibn Ḥibbān and Ḥākim all narrate with a rigorously authenticated chain of transmission that 'Alī ؓ said: 'Jibrīl ؑ came to the Messenger of Allah ﷺ on the day of Badr and said, "Give your Companions the decision regarding the captives: if they wish they may execute them, and if they wish they may ransom them, on the understanding that a similar number of them (i.e. the Companions) shall be slain next year." And so they said, "We choose the ransom, and that we be slain." ' (That is, that seventy of them be slain in turn, and thus be martyred in Allah's cause.)

Ibn Sa'd also narrates with a *mursal*[501] chain from Qatāda that their reply was: 'We shall ransom them, and thus gain strength over them by their means; and next year seventy of us shall enter Paradise,' and then they ransomed them.

Ḥāfiẓ Qasṭalānī said: 'This shows that they only did what they had been permitted to do.'

---

[500] An allusion to the verse above (8:67). [t]

[501] See note 381, p.168

**10** – How could it be judged that the Prophet ﷺ was wrong in his dealings with the captives of Badr, when before the battle occurred he ﷺ had already taken ransoms for the captives taken by the raiding party of ʻAbdullāh ibn Jaḥsh that killed ʻAmr ibn al-Ḥaḍramī, and Allah ﷻ did not censure him for doing so?

It is narrated in the books of Prophetic biography that the Prophet ﷺ sent ʻAbdullāh ibn Jaḥsh in a raiding party to attack the caravan of Quraysh. They attacked at Nakhla, not far from Mecca, and killed ʻAmr ibn al-Ḥaḍramī and took ʻUthmān ibn ʻAbdullāh and Ḥakam ibn Kaysān prisoner. The others fled, and so the raiding party took the camels.

Quraysh offered the Messenger of Allah ﷺ ransoms for the two captives, and he ﷺ replied: ʻWe shall not ransom them to you until our two Companions return (meaning Saʻd and ʻUtba)[502], for we fear that you might harm them; if you should slay them, we shall slay your two Companions.'

After a number of days Saʻd and ʻUtba returned, so the Messenger of Allah ﷺ gave up the captives for forty *ūqiyya*[503] each.

Ḥakam ibn Kaysān elected to embrace Islam, and remained true to the faith, staying with the Messenger of Allah ﷺ until he was martyred at the Battle of Maʻūna Well.

As for ʻUthmān, he returned to Mecca and died there a non-believer.

---

[502] They had been members of the raiding party, but were late in returning.

[503] See note 457, p.208

This raid took place in the month of *Rajab*, or some say in *Jumādā al-Ukhrā*, and the Battle of Badr took place the following Ramaḍān. Both battles took place in the year 2 AH. Allah ﷻ did not censure the taking of ransoms for the men captured in this raid; if such a thing had been forbidden, He would surely have censured it.[504]

**11** – Allah's words ﴿It is not for a Prophet to hold captives until he hath made great slaughter in the land. You would have for yourselves the gains of this world, whilst Allah would have for you the Hereafter…﴾ does not in any way constitute a rebuke of the Prophet ﷺ, but rather it rebukes those who advised the Prophet ﷺ to accept the ransoms out of desire for the gains of this world, namely the wealth that would be given for the ransom, when he sought the advise of the people in general before seeking it in private from Abū Bakr, 'Umar and 'Alī, as we mentioned above. And so by His words ﴿ You would have for yourselves the gains of this world﴾, Allah meant the people who desired to gain wealth.

As for our Master the Messenger of Allah ﷺ, he did not accept the ransoms out of desire for the gains of this world – Allah forbid such a thing! The life of this world in its entirety had no value for him whatsoever, and he ﷺ himself said: 'What have I to do with this world? My place in this world is not more than that of a traveller who seeks rest beneath a tree and, then moves on and leaves it.' The mountain of Tihāma's weight in gold was offered to him and he refused it: what did he have to do with the gains of this world?

Similarly, Allah's words ﴿Were it not for a prior decree of Allah, you would surely have been visited by an awful torment on account of what you took; yet enjoy the spoils ye have won as

---

[504] See *Sharḥ al-Mawāhib* and *Sharḥ al-Shifā*.

lawful and good﴿ is a declaration from Him regarding the favour and blessing He bestowed upon this community by the grace of their Prophet ﷺ, and an announcement that it was already decreed in pre-eternity that battle-spoils were lawful for this community alone as a blessing and favour from Him by the grace of their Prophet ﷺ and his noble status in the sight of Allah ﷻ.

And so the Prophet ﷺ would later celebrate this honour and make mention of this blessing as one of the great honours with which Allah singled him out, saying: 'I have been given five that none before me were given: Every Prophet was sent to his people alone, whilst I have been sent to all men, the red and the black; and battle-spoils were made lawful for me, having been lawful for none before me…' as was mentioned above.

Just as it was the pre-eternal decree of Allah, and subsequent Sacred ruling of Allah, that he ﷺ alone would be sent to all people, and that the entire earth would be made a place of prayer for him alone, the same was true of the lawfulness of battle-spoils; it was a Sacred Law, based on wisdom and justice. So reflect upon this, and use your insight, and be truthful, and contemplate. And so Qāḍī Abū Zayd ؓ said:

> If it be said, 'Did Allah not censure His Messenger for accepting the ransoms; and did not the words of the Messenger of Allah ﷺ "Were punishment to have been sent down, none would have been spared save 'Umar" not indicate that Abū Bakr was wrong?' We reply: This cannot be believed, because the Messenger of Allah ﷺ acted on the advice of Abū Bakr, and if any action of the Messenger of Allah was sanctioned (by Allah), it must have been correct – and Allah sanctioned his action with His words ﴾yet enjoy the spoils ye have won as lawful and

good⟫. So the interpretation of the verse is as follows: 'It is not for a Prophet to hold captives until he hath made great slaughter in the land; yet you, O Messenger of Allah, have been singled out, as a favour to you, with a dispensation in the matter; and were it not for a prior decree of Allah ordaining this special dispensation, you would surely have been visited by an awful torment, as the correct decision would have been that which 'Umar advanced.' Or, another interpretation might be: 'It is not for a Prophet to take captives until great slaughter has been made; and you indeed made great slaughter on the day of Badr, and thus you had the right to take captives as did all the other Prophets (peace be upon them all). Yet the options concerning the captives were either to free them or to execute them, not to ransom them; and were it not for the prior decree of the permissibility of your (O Messenger of Allah ﷺ) taking ransoms, you would surely have been visited by an awful torment.' If the decision of the Prophet ﷺ had been incorrect, the command would have been to reverse it (i.e. to return the ransoms and kill the prisoners). Moreover, there is no suggestion here that the Prophet ﷺ was at fault, but rather the verse constitutes a declaration of the favour he ﷺ alone was granted from amongst all the Prophets, as though Allah ﷻ were saying: 'It was not for any Prophet save thee to do this.' As for Allah's words ⟪You would have for yourselves...⟫, this is addressed to those amongst them who desired such, and is not addressed to the Prophet ﷺ, who was Divinely protected from such things.[505]

---

[505] Quoted by Ibn al-Humām in his discussion of *ijtihād* in *al-Taqrīr wa al-Taḥbīr 'alā Taḥrīr al-Kamāl*, vol.3, p.297.

And Ḥāfiẓ Ibn Ḥajar said in *Fatḥ al-Bārī*:

> The early generations differed as to which of the two opinions was the correct one. Some of them said that Abū Bakr's opinion was correct, because it agreed with what Allah decreed about the matter; and because of the way things ultimately turned out; and because of the many captives who later entered Islam, some alone and some along with their children who were born after the incident; and because it manifested the triumph of mercy over wrath, as is known to be the way of Allah ﷻ with those for whom He has decreed His mercy.
>
> As for those who believe that the other opinion was correct, they adduce for evidence for this the fact that the taking of the ransoms was censured (by Allah).
>
> But the answer to this is that this censure does not prove that the second opinion was correct (i.e. rather the first was correct); rather the purpose of the censure was to indicate the error of those who preferred anything of the life of this world to that of the Hereafter, however small it may be.

That is, any censure that might be inferred from the verse was directed to those who sought by the ransoms merely the gains this world, who represented a number of those who advised that the ransoms should be taken when the Prophet ﷺ asked the people in general for their counsel before asking the elite amongst them in private, as was mentioned above.

# THE STORY OF THE DATE-PALMS

Muslim and Aḥmad narrate on the authority of Anas ﷺ that the Messenger of Allah ﷺ passed by some people cross-pollinating date-palms, and said to them: 'Were you not to do so, it would be well.' The trees then produced poor yields. The Prophet ﷺ passed by them again, and said, 'What has befallen your date-palms?' They replied, 'You said such-and-such.' He ﷺ replied, 'You know best the affairs of your world.' From this Ḥadīth, some people have understood that the Prophet ﷺ could be wrong about worldly matters, and have gone as far as to say, 'The Prophet was wrong about this, and wrong about that'!

But the truth has more right to be followed, and the truth is that the words and deeds of the Prophet ﷺ explain one another, and resemble one another; and Allah ﷻ protected him ﷺ from error just as He protected him from sin. So we say, and all success comes from Allah:

First of all, the Prophet ﷺ grew up in those blessed lands in which date-palms are grown, and was raised amongst people who knew well the art of cultivating them, and the careful processes that it required. How could it be imagined that he ﷺ would be unaware of the unchanging customs of date-palm cultivation, and the necessity of cross-pollination as a basic agricultural principle? It is not as though this was a secret of date-palm cultivation, or some kind of hidden knowledge relating to it. And so he must have known about it just as well as they did; but he wanted to teach them something which they could not have learned by themselves.

Secondly, the Noble Messenger ﷺ was possessed of great knowledge, and Allah ﷻ bestowed much information upon him, to the extent that he could speak in detail with the Companions about any subject.

Ṭabarānī narrates that Abū Dharr ﷺ said: 'When the Messenger of Allah left us, there was not a single bird flapping its wings in the sky save that he had taught us something about it.'

How could it be imagined that the Prophet ﷺ was not aware that date-palms need to be cross-pollinated as is the normal agricultural practice? It must therefore be that the Messenger of Allah ﷺ had something else in mind.

Thirdly, there occurred other incidents similar to this one from which we can deduce what the Prophet ﷺ had in mind, one of which is the Ḥadīth of the sheep's leg:

Aḥmad narrated in his *Musnad* that Abū Rāfi'[506] said: 'A sheep was roasted for the Messenger of Allah ﷺ and brought to him. He said, "Abū Rāfi', pass me the foreleg," and so I passed it to him. After a time he said, "Pass me the (other) foreleg," so I passed it to him. He then said again, "Pass me the foreleg." I said, "Messenger of Allah, has a sheep more than two forelegs?" He ﷺ replied, "Had you only been silent, you would have passed me as many forelegs as I asked for." The Messenger of Allah ﷺ used to favour the foreleg.'

Haythamī says in *Majma' al-Zawā'id*: 'This Ḥadīth was narrated by Aḥmad and Ṭabarānī with several chains of transmission, one of which has it that Abū Rāfi' said: "The Messenger of Allah ﷺ asked me to roast a sheep for him, so I did so..." Ṭabarānī narrated in *al-Awsaṭ* in a shorter form, and one of the narrations of Aḥmad is sound.'

---

[506] This is Abū Rāfi' the Copt, a servant of the Messenger of Allah ﷺ who embraced Islam, and died in the early days of the caliphate of the Commander of the Faithful, 'Alī ﷺ. (*Sharḥ al-Zurqānī*)

It is also narrated that Abū ‘Ubayd[507] said: ‘I cooked a plate of meat for the Messenger of Allah ﷺ, who said: “Pass me its foreleg,” so I passed it to him, and then he said, “Pass me its foreleg,” so I passed it so him, and then he ﷺ said, “Pass me its foreleg,” so I said, “Prophet of Allah, how many forelegs does a sheep have?” He ﷺ replied, “By He in whose hand is my soul, if you had been silent, you would have given me as many forelegs as I asked for.” ’

This incident was not the same one as the previous narration, as Ḥāfiẓ Zurqānī and others have pointed out.

It is narrated in *Majma‘ al-Zawā’id*, on the authority on Ibn Isḥāq, who heard from a man of the tribe of Ghifār at a gathering of Sālim ibn ‘Abdullāh, that the Messenger of Allah ﷺ was presented with a meal of bread and meat. He ﷺ said, ‘Pass me the foreleg’, and so it was passed to him, and he ate it. Then he said, ‘Pass me the foreleg’, so the other was passed to him, and he ate it. Then he said, ‘Pass me the foreleg.’ They said to him, ‘Messenger of Allah, there are only two forelegs!’ He replied, ‘By your father, had you been silent, I would have continued taking as many forelegs as I asked for.’[508]

So when the Prophet ﷺ said ‘Pass me the foreleg’ the third time, despite knowing well that a sheep has only two forelegs, he did so out of a wish to display a miracle of generous bestowal, and a clear proof of his prophethood; but since he did not find a suitable occasion for it, the miracle did not take place.

---

[507] Abū ‘Ubayd was a servant of the Messenger of Allah ﷺ. Some of the narrators of Ḥadīth have his name as Abū ‘Ubayda.
(*Sharḥ al-Mawāhib* iv. 328)

[508] Narrated by Aḥmad; its chain contains one narrator whose name is not mentioned. (*Majma ‘al-Zawā’id*)

And so Ḥāfiẓ Zurqānī said:

> The meaning of the Prophet's ﷺ words "Had you only been silent, you would have passed me as many forelegs as I asked for" is that this would have gone on as long as he was silent, because Allah would have created foreleg after foreleg as a miracle for him ﷺ; yet the attendant's human instinct for haste made him say, 'A sheep has only two forelegs', and so the Divine outpourings were cut off. For such a thing could only come from the Divine outpourings of the Beneficent ﷻ, as a generous gift to the Finest of His Creation ﷺ.
>
> If the attendant had only responded with proper manners, and remained silent and alert to this miraculous wonder, it would have been enough to merit his being blessed by having this Divine outpouring be channelled though his own hands; but he responded with incredulity, and so the grace went back whence it came, finding no suitable place to manifest itself, as no one deserves to witness such a miracle – for the mere witnessing of it is a great honour for the witness – except one whose submission is absolute, and who is without the slightest trace of independent mind or will.

The same was the case for the incident of the date-palms. When the Prophet ﷺ passed by the men cross-pollinating the palms, he wanted to honour them by showing them a miracle that went against the usual custom of tending palms by cross-pollination, and so ennoble them by making the trees bear fruit without any pollination; for he ﷺ was as well aware of the usual need to pollinate date palms as they were, because he ﷺ lived amongst them and knew their ways.

But when some of the hearts of these men did not accept this, and did not completely submit to his ﷺ words 'Were you not to do so, it would be well', but rather clung to their worldly knowledge of the art of date-palm cultivation, which is that their prosperity depends on pollination; and so the Divine plenitude found no place to manifest, and so returned whence it came.

And so after that, the Prophet ﷺ bade them return to their ordinary way of doing things, to which they clung and been unable to leave behind, and so said: 'You know best the affairs of your world', that is, return to working as your own knowledge of your worldly matters dictates.

The truth of what we have just stated and our understanding that he ﷺ did not make a mistake in this matter is attested to by what the great Shaykh and Gnostic, the author of *al-Ibrīz*, may Allah benefit us with his knowledge,[509] said when asked about the incident of the date-palms:

> His ﷺ statement 'Were you not to do so, it would be well' was a statement of absolute truth, and these words issued from him because of the certitude he possessed that Allah is the true Doer. This certitude is based on his witnessing of the diffusion of His actions in all existence without intermediary or means, so that not a seed settles, nor a hair moves, nor a heart beats, nor a vein pulses, nor an eye glimpses, nor an eyelid blinks, except that He is the direct Agent of these actions without any intermediary. This is a matter that the Prophet ﷺ witnessed for himself just as plainly as he saw or sensed anything else, and it never escaped his

---

[509] Sidī 'Abd al-'Azīz al-Dabbāgh ؓ. [t]

attention for a moment, neither when he woke nor when he slept; for his ﷺ heart, in which this witnessing took place, never slept. There is no doubt that for anyone who were to witness such a thing, all causality would fall away from his sight, and he would advance from faith in the Unseen to direct and firsthand witnessing; and he would witness firsthand the words of Allah ﴾And Allah created you, and all that you do﴿,[510] and be endowed with an absolute certitude that befits such a witnessing, which means to be certain of the absolute meaning of the verse so that the notion that any action could be the work of any but Allah never crosses his mind for the slightest moment. There is no doubt that a certitude of this nature would be enough to break the natural order, and influence the run of things; and it is the secret of Allah ﷻ; alongside of it there can remain no other cause or intermediary. And so if someone who occupies this station were to indicate the non-existence of causality, and were to ascribe an action directly to the Lord of lords, his words would be the absolute truth.

As for one who occupies the station of faith in the Unseen, he does not directly witness Allah's words ﴾And Allah created you, and all that you do﴿, but rather he witnesses the ascription of an action to the one at whose hands it occurs, and he is only pulled towards the meaning of the verse and the ascription of all actions to Allah by means of the faith that He has granted him. So he is pulled in two directions by two things: The first is his Lord, in the form of faith, which pulls him towards the truth;

---

[510] Qur'ān 37:96

> The second is his nature, in the form of his observing that actions are performed by others (but Allah), which pulls him towards falsehood.
>
> So he is always caught between these two things, but sometimes the side of faith is stronger, and so he is able to taste the meaning of the aforementioned verse for a moment or two; and sometimes the side of his nature is stronger, and so he forgets the meaning of the verse for a day or two – and at these times of forgetfulness, the certitude which can break the natural order is absent. And so that which the Prophet ﷺ alluded to did not come to pass, because there were those among the Companions (i.e. among the farmers) who at that time were not attuned to this overwhelming certitude, which filled his ﷺ entire inner being, and caused these words to leave his mouth; and he ﷺ spoke the truth. And when he ﷺ realised the reason why what he had mentioned had not come to pass, and saw that the surpassing of this obstacle was not within their capabilities at the time, he left them as they were, and said: 'You know best the affairs of your world.'

In any case, it cannot be said that the Prophet ﷺ was wrong in the case of the date-palms any more than it could be said he ﷺ was wrong when he said to Abū 'Ubayd, 'Pass me the foreleg' the third time. It was not a mistake, but was rather correct, and expressed a wish to honour the men with a miraculous act of blessing and increase; but it did not come to pass because of the presence of an obstacle and hindrance to it.

The equivalent of this is the cutting of the blessed increase from the skin of butter which the Prophet ﷺ had blessed, when Umm Mālik squeezed it. Muslim narrates in his *Saḥīḥ* on the authority of Jābir ﷺ that Umm Mālik al-Anṣārīyya owned a skin containing butter which she would reserve for the Prophet ﷺ; and when her children would come to her asking for butter, and she found they had none, she would go to the skin she reserved for him ﷺ and find that there was still butter in it. The skin continued to provide butter for her whole family until she squeezed it, whereupon it ran out. She went to the Prophet ﷺ to ask about this. 'Did you squeeze it?' he asked. She said yes. 'Had you left it, it would have remained,' he replied.

Muslim also narrates from Jābir ﷺ that a man from the countryside came to the Prophet ﷺ and asked him for food, so the Prophet ﷺ gave him a half *wasq*[511] of barley. He, his wife, and any guests they had continued to eat from it until he weighed it, whereupon it began to decrease, and so he went to the Prophet ﷺ and told him of this. 'Had you not weighed it,' said the Prophet ﷺ, 'You would have eaten from it (evermore), and it would have remained for you.' That is, it would have remained as long as they lived without ever decreasing. So the weighing of the barley spelled the end of the blessing. Imām Nawawī explained the wisdom behind this, saying:

> The scholars have said that wisdom behind this is that the squeezing (of the skin) and weighing (of the barley) were contrary to the principle of submission and absolute trust in Allah's provision, and were signs of planning and using one's own power, and an attempt to encompass the secrets of the decree and bounty of Allah Almighty; and the penalty for any who does such a thing is to have the blessing taken from him.[512]

---

[511] This is equivalent to just over 60 kilograms. (*Reliance of the Traveller*, w15.1) [t]

[512] *Sharḥ Ṣaḥīḥ Muslim*, xv. 41

Ḥāfiẓ al-Zurqānī said:

> This does not contradict the words of the Prophet ﷺ: 'Weigh your food, and you will find blessed increase therein', because this refers to those who fear foul play; or it means "weigh that which you intend to spend in charity, lest you spend more or less than you can afford, but do not weigh what remains"; or it means one should weigh when buying, or when entering the house (after buying).

## ḤUBĀB IBN AL-MUNDHIR AND THE BATTLE OF BADR

Ibn Isḥāq[513] narrates that on the day of Badr, the Prophet ﷺ went out (with the Muslim army) to reach the wells before the enemy, and when they came to the first well at Badr he bade them stop.

Upon this, Ḥubāb ibn al-Mundhir said: 'Messenger of Allah, has Allah inspired you to stop at this place, and not to go beyond it or stop short of it, or is it a matter of opinion and strategy of war?' The Prophet ﷺ said, 'It is merely a matter of opinion and strategy of war.'

'In that case,' said Ḥubāb, 'this is not the best place. Lead the men on to the nearest well to the enemy, and stop there; then let us stop up the wells that lie beyond it and build a cistern and fill it with water, so that we can drink but they cannot.' 'Your opinion is sound,' the Prophet ﷺ said.

---

[513] See *Sīrat ibn Hishām* and elsewhere.

Ibn Sa'd has it that Jibrīl descended and said, 'The correct stratagem is that of Ḥubāb.'
There is nothing in this Ḥadīth to indicate that the Prophet's ﷺ opinion was wrong, because it was not a case of a firm decision having been made, but was rather a matter of presenting the matter in order to obtain the opinions of the men of strategy and experience, in line with his ﷺ usual custom of presenting matters such as this to those Companions who were men of strategy, and seeking their counsel.

This is borne out by the direct words of the Prophet ﷺ to Ḥubāb 'Your opinion is sound.' The position of the Prophet ﷺ here was that of a man seeking counsel who presents a matter for discussion, making no firm decision about it. If the first position had been his own opinion or a firm decision on his ﷺ part, he would have commanded the Companions to stay there, and would have continued with his ﷺ plan.

# PART IV: THE TREMENDOUS BLESSINGS OF OUR MASTER MUḤAMMAD ﷺ

## THE OVERWHELMING BLESSINGS AND TREASURES THAT EMANATED FROM HIM ﷺ

THE MESSENGER OF ALLAH ﷺ overflowed with blessings and treasures, and secrets and illuminations, which he bestowed upon those who were ready and willing to receive them. Bukhārī narrated that Ibn ʿAbbās رضي الله عنه said: 'The Messenger of Allah ﷺ hugged me to his chest and said, "O Allah, teach him the Book." ' By means of this embrace and this prayer, Ibn ʿAbbās obtained a great understanding of the Book of Allah ﷾.

Bukhārī and others narrate that Abū Hurayra رضي الله عنه said: 'I said to the Messenger of Allah ﷺ, "O Messenger of Allah, I hear so many sayings from you that I forget them!" He replied, "Open your cloak." I opened it, and he gestured as if to scoop something into it, and then said, "Close it", so I closed it; I have not forgotten a thing since then.' This is the wording of Bukhārī; others have it: 'Then he ﷺ said, "Hold it to your chest", and so I did so; I have not forgotten a Ḥadīth since then.'

Abū Nu'aym narrated that Abū Hurayra ؓ said: 'The Messenger of Allah ﷺ said to me, "Would you not ask me for some of these spoils?" I replied, "I ask you to teach me something that Allah has taught you." So he took the cloak from my back and placed it evenly between him and me, and then spoke to me until I had taken in all his words, and then he said, "Gather it up and draw it to you." And so it became that I never forgot another word of what he said to me.'[514] So this was a blessing of memory for Abū Hurayra ؓ, so that he would never forget another Ḥadīth.

**Another example of this** is the blessing of the knowledge of judicature that he ﷺ bequeathed to our Master 'Alī ؓ when he sent him to Yemen:

It is narrated in the *Musnad* and the *Sunan* collections, and also by Bayhaqī and Ḥākim with a rigorously authenticated chain of transmission, that 'Alī ؓ said: 'When the Messenger of Allah ﷺ sent me to Yemen, I said, "Messenger of Allah, will you send me, a young man, to judge between them when I know nothing of judicature?" So he ﷺ struck my chest with his hand and said, "O Allah, guide his heart, and strengthen his tongue." By the One who splits the seed, I was never unsure about any judgement between two parties thereafter.' Ḥāfiẓ Ibn Kathīr also narrated it in *al-Bidāya* as reported by Abū Ya'lā.

Aḥmad narrated in his *Musnad* that Jarīr ibn 'Abdullāh said: 'I said to the Messenger of Allah ﷺ, "O Messenger of Allah, I have difficulty staying on my horse." So the Messenger of Allah ﷺ struck my chest hard enough that I could see the marks his fingers left, and then said, "O Allah, make him firm, and make him a guide, and guide him." '

---

[514] See *al-Iṣāba*, which mentions the other narrations of this incident.

**Another example of this** is the blessing of strength he bequeathed (the Companion) Safīna when he said to him, 'Lift, for you are a ship!' (The name Safīna literally means 'ship') Safīna said: 'On that day, were I to have lifted the load of a camel, or two, or three, or four, or five, or six, or seven, it would not have been heavy for me.'

**The Messenger of Allah ﷺ dipped his hand in water in order to place therein blessing and cure**: Imām Muslim and others narrate that Anas ؓ said: 'When the Messenger of Allah ﷺ prayed the dawn prayer, the servants of Medina would come with their pails filled with water, and he would dip his hand in every pail; and they would even come on cold mornings, and he would dip his hand in them.' And so they would seek blessings and cures from that water.

**The Messenger of Allah ﷺ would wash his hands and face, and rinse his mouth with water, and then recommend the water to be drank and used to wash the face**: Bukhārī and Muslim narrate (and the wording here is Muslim's) that Abū Mūsā al-Ash'arī ؓ said: 'I was with the Prophet ﷺ whilst he was staying at Ji'rāna, between Mecca and Medina, along with Bilāl. A Bedouin man came to the Messenger of Allah ﷺ and said, "Will you not give me, Muḥammad, that which you promised me?" The Messenger of Allah ﷺ replied, "Rejoice."[515] The Bedouin said, "How generous is this word of yours, 'Rejoice'!" The Messenger of Allah ﷺ turned to Abū Mūsā and Bilāl in a somewhat angry state, and said to them, 'This man has rejected glad tidings, so take them for yourselves.' They replied, 'We accept, O Messenger of Allah.' So the Messenger of Allah ﷺ asked for a vessel of water, and washed his hands and face and rinsed his mouth in it, and then said, 'Drink it, and pour it onto

---

[515] That is, 'Be patient and I shall give you what will cause you to rejoice.' (*Fatḥ al-Bārī*)

your faces and necks, and rejoice.' They took the vessel and did as he ﷺ bid them, and then Umm Salama called them from behind the curtain and said, 'Spare some for your mother in your jug!' and so they kept some aside for her. This was a great honour for Abū Mūsā and Bilāl ؓ, because the leftover water of the Prophet ﷺ imparted many treasures and illuminations, and many blessings and graces.

Bukhārī narrates that Jābir ؓ said: 'The Messenger of Allah ﷺ came to see me when I was ill. I was unconscious at the time [one narration has it 'he found that I had lost consciousness'], and so he performed ablutions (*wuḍū'*) and then poured the water he used over me. Upon this, I regained consciousness, and said, "Messenger of Allah, who has the right of inheritance, for I leave behind me none but distant relatives?" And so the Revelations concerning inheritance were revealed.'

Bukhārī and Muslim narrate that Abū Hurayra ؓ said: 'The Messenger of Allah ﷺ came out to us at midday. He was presented with some water, from which he made ablutions; and the people took the used water and wiped in on themselves. The Prophet ﷺ then prayed the midday prayer…'

Imām Aḥmad[516] narrates that Abū Juḥayfa ؓ said: 'I saw a red leather tent that belonged to the Messenger of Allah ﷺ, from which Bilāl came out to pour away the leftover water from the Prophet's ﷺ ablutions. The people rushed up to him; those who were able to get any of the water wiped themselves with it, and those who could not get any took the drips that fell from the hands of the others.'

---

[516] The exact same Ḥadīth with this wording is also narrated by Bukhārī and Muslim. [t]

Ṭabarānī narrates that 'Abd al-Raḥmān ibn al-Ḥārith ibn Abī Mirdās al-Sulamī said: 'We were with the Prophet ﷺ when he asked for some water, into which he dipped his hand and performed ablutions, and so collected up the water and drank it. The Prophet ﷺ said, "What made you do what you did?" We replied, "The love of Allah and His Messenger!" He said, "If you love that Allah and His Messenger should love you, honour your trusts, and speak the truth, and be good neighbours." '

So the Companions were eager to get the water he ﷺ washed from, and made ablutions from, out of their love for Allah and His Messenger, and out of conviction in what they knew of the unique favours with which Allah had blessed him ﷺ; and the Messenger of Allah ﷺ approved of their actions, and did not criticise them.

## HIS BLESSED TOUCH ﷺ

When the Messenger of Allah ﷺ touched someone in pain, that person's pain would disappear by Allah's leave. And when he touched an ill or injured person, that person would be cured by Allah's leave. And when he touched the chest of a weak or fearful person, that person would be given strength and security by Allah's leave. And when he touched the face of a Muslim, the vitality of youth would remain in that person's face however old he grew. Bukhārī narrates that Ṣā'ib ibn Yazīd said: 'My aunt took me to the Messenger of Allah ﷺ and said, "O Messenger of Allah, my nephew is in pain!" So the Messenger of Allah ﷺ touched my head and prayed for blessings for me, and then performed ablutions, and I drank the water.'

Ṭabarānī narrates that Abyaḍ ibn Ḥammāl related that he had a rash on his face which had severely affected his nose, and so the Messenger of Allah ﷺ called him over and touched his face; and before the day was over, his nose had become completely unmarked.[517]

'Aṭā', the freed slave of Ṣā'ib ibn Yazīd said: 'I noticed that my master Ṣā'ib ibn Yazīd's beard was white, yet the hair on his head was black, and so I said to him, "Master, why did the hair on your head never go white?" He replied, "The hair on my head never turned white; for when I was a boy playing with my friends, the Messenger of Allah ﷺ passed by and greeted us, and I returned his greeting. He asked my name, and I replied, 'Ṣā'ib ibn Yazīd the nephew of Namir.' He ﷺ then placed his hand on my head and said, 'Allah bless you.' The hair on the spot the Messenger of Allah ﷺ touched never went white." '[518]

Ḥanẓala ibn Ḥidhyam said: 'I went with my grandfather Ḥidhyam to the Messenger of Allah ﷺ, and he bade me to come to him, and touched my head, and said, "Allah bless you." '

The narrator who heard this from Ḥanẓala then added: 'I have seen Ḥanẓala take a man with a swollen face, or a sheep with a swollen udder, and say, "In the Name of Allah, and upon the place where rested the palm of the Messenger of Allah ﷺ", then touch that spot and then touch the afflicted person, and the swelling would disappear.'[519]

---

[517] Haythamī says in *Majma' al-Zawā'id*: 'It was narrated by Ṭabarānī, and its transmitters are all reliable according to Ibn Ḥibbān.'

[518] Haythamī says in *Majma' al-Zawā'id*: 'It was narrated by Ṭabarānī in all three of his collections… the transmitters in the *Ṣaghīr* and *Awsaṭ* collections are all reliable.

[519] Haythamī says in *Majma' al-Zawā'id*: 'It was narrated by Ṭabarānī in *al-Awsaṭ*, and by Aḥmad, and its transmitters are all reliable.' Zurqānī said: 'It was also narrated by Bukhārī in his *Tārīkh*, and by Abū Ya'lā, and by others.'

'Ā'idh ibn 'Amr ؓ said: 'I was hit by an arrow in the face when fighting for the Messenger of Allah ﷺ at the Battle of Ḥunayn. When the blood began to flow from my face to my breast, the Prophet ﷺ placed his hand there and prayed for me.'

Ḥashraj said: ' 'Ā'idh used to tell us all about this when he was alive; when he died and we washed him, we looked for the mark he had told us had been left by the Messenger of Allah's ﷺ hand, and found there a white blaze like the blaze of a horse.'[520]

It is related that 'Amr ibn Tha'laba al-Juhanī said: 'I met the Messenger of Allah ﷺ and greeted him, and he touched my head.' The narrator said: 'Amr lived to the age of one hundred, and the spot on his head where the Messenger of Allah's hand touched never went gray.'[521]

It is narrated that 'Abdullāh ibn Hilāl al-Anṣārī ؓ said: 'My father took me to the Prophet ﷺ and said, "O Messenger of Allah, pray for him." I shall never forget how the Messenger of Allah ﷺ placed his hand on my head, so that I felt its coolness, and prayed for me and sought blessings for me.' The narrator said: 'And I saw 'Abdullāh ibn Hilāl fasting the day and praying the night even into his old age', i.e. the vigour and resolve of youth remained with him.

It is narrated that 'Amr ibn Akhṭab al-Anṣārī said: 'The Messenger of Allah ﷺ touched my head and my beard and then said, "O Allah, make him beautiful." ' The narrator said: 'And so 'Amr lived to the age of over one hundred[522], and there was

---

[520] Narrated by Ṭabarānī, Ḥākim, and others.

[521] Haythamī said: 'It was narrated by Ṭabarānī, and its transmitters back to Abū Nu'aym are reliable.'

[522] Literally 'One hundred years plus between three and ten.' [t]

not a white hair in his beard, and his face was smooth and had no wrinkles until he died.'[523]

Imām Aḥmad narrated that Ibn 'Abbās ﷺ said: 'The Prophet ﷺ touched my head and prayed that I be given wisdom.' Aḥmad also related that Ibn Mas'ūd ﷺ said: 'I said, "O Messenger of Allah, teach me something of this discourse."[524] The Messenger of Allah ﷺ patted my head, and said, "Allah have mercy on you, for you are a learned young boy." '

By this blessed Prophetic touching of their heads, Ibn 'Abbās and Ibn Mas'ūd indeed gained great good and extensive knowledge.

Abū 'Aṭiyya al-Bakrī ﷺ is reported to have said: 'My family took me to the Prophet ﷺ when I was a young boy, and he patted my head.' The narrator added: 'I saw Abū 'Aṭiyya with a full head and beard of black hair when he was one hundred years old', i.e. his hair never turned grey by the grace of that blessed touch of the Prophet ﷺ.

It is related that Ḥārith ibn 'Amr al-Sahmī went to the Prophet ﷺ during the Farewell Pilgrimage whilst he ﷺ sat on his camel, 'Aḍbā'. Ḥārith was a tall man, and so he approached the Prophet ﷺ until his face was level with the Prophet's knee. Then, the Prophet of Allah ﷺ leaned down and touched Ḥārith's face. After that, the brightness never left Ḥārith's face until he died.[525]

---

[523] Narrated by Tirmidhī, who declared it sound, and by Ḥākim and Ibn Ḥibbān, as mentioned in *Sharḥ al-Mawāhib* and *Majma' al-Zawā'id.*

[524] I.e. the Qur'ān.

[525] Narrated by Ṭabarānī; its transmitters are all reliable, as mentioned in *al-Iṣāba.*

It is related that ʿAbdullāh ibn Yusr ﷺ said: ʿThe Messenger of Allah ﷺ laid his hand on my head, and said: "This boy shall live a century;" ʾ and he did indeed go on to reach one hundred years of age. And the boy had a growth on his face, and so the Prophet ﷺ said: ʿHe shall not die before this growth disappears from his faceʾ; and indeed this was the case.[526]

Yaḥyā ibn Abī al-Haytham said that he heard Yūsuf ibn ʿAbdullāh ibn Salām say: ʿThe Messenger of Allah ﷺ sat me in his lap and patted my head, and gave me the name Yūsuf.ʾ[527]

Baghawī narrates, on the authority of Ibn Wahb, that Yaʿqūb ibn ʿAbd al-Raḥmān al-Qārī said: ʿMy father took ʿAbd al-Raḥmān and ʿAbdullāh, the sons of ʿAbd, to the Messenger of Allah ﷺ. He blessed them, and touched their heads, and said about ʿAbdullāh: "This one will be a worshipper." Thereafter, whenever they shaved their heads the first place the hair would grow back would be the place the Messenger of Allah ﷺ touched.ʾ[528]

Ṭabarānī and Ibn al-Sakan narrate with a rigorously authentic chain of transmission that the Prophet ﷺ placed his hand on the head and face of Mālik ibn ʿUmayr; he went on to live along life, until the hair of his head and beard went gray, all except for the place where the Prophet ﷺ had touched his head and face.

Zubayr ibn Bakkār narrated in *Akhbār al-Madīna* that Muḥammad ibn ʿAbd al-Raḥmān ibn Saʿd said: ʿThe Prophet ﷺ

---

[526] Ḥāfiẓ Haythamī said: ʿIt was narrated by Ṭabarānī, and by Bazzār mentioning the growth only. The transmitters of Bazzārʾs narration are all rigorously authenticated, save Ḥasan ibn Ayyūb al-Haḍramī, who is reliable.ʾ

[527] Narrated by Aḥmad; its transmitters are reliable.

[528] Quoted in *al-Iṣāba*.

touched the head of 'Ubāda ibn Sa'd ibn 'Uthmān al-Zurqī and prayed for him; and he lived to be eighty years old without his hair ever turning grey.'

If we were to attempt to make mention of everything that has been narrated of this kind, the pen would be unable to list it all. The reports we have narrated here from many of the Companions ﷺ constitute the greatest evidence of the faith of the Companions ﷺ, young and old, and the strength of their conviction that our Master Muḥammad, the Messenger of Allah ﷺ was an overflowing river of treasures and blessings, and illuminations and secrets. They would strive for the opportunity for the Messenger of Allah ﷺ to touch their faces, or their heads, or their chests, or for him ﷺ to honour them with some of his noble saliva which was filled with blessings from Allah, or that he would honour them with his leftover food, or the blessed water he used to make his ablutions, or to drink the water he rinsed his mouth with – and all of this was so they might imbibe the blessings of these things into their own beings. They knew with complete certainty that this was all derived from the grace that Allah ﷻ imparted to His Dearest Beloved ﷺ, and the honour and blessing that He bestowed upon him ﷺ.

Allah ﷻ said: ﴾And the grace of Allah upon thee has been great.﴿[529] And He said: ﴾And the bounty of thy Lord exult.﴿[530] And He said: ﴾Lo! We have given thee Abundance. (*al-Kawthar*)﴿[531] Ibn 'Abbās ﷺ said that this means 'We have given unto thee great treasures'; amongst these treasures is the river of Kawthar in Paradise, and the Pool at the Resurrection, and more besides.

---

529 Qur'ān 4:113

530 Qur'ān 93:11

531 Qur'ān 108:1

# HE ﷺ WOULD TOUCH THE CHESTS OF HIS COMPANIONS TO STRENGTHEN THE FAITH IN THEIR HEARTS

**The story of Shayba ibn 'Uthmān al-Awqaṣī,** who embraced faith on the day of conquest of Mecca: 'Asqalānī said in *al-Iṣāba* that Shayba intended to assassinate the Prophet ﷺ at the Battle of Ḥunayn, and so Allah cast terror into his heart; and then the Prophet ﷺ placed his hand on his chest, and so faith became firm in his heart, and he fought on the side of the Prophet ﷺ, as was narrated by Ibn Abī Khaythama. *Al-Iṣāba* also mentions[532] that Shayba said: 'So I crept up on the Prophet ﷺ from behind, and drew closer and closer until all I had to do was smite him with my sword, whereupon something like a bolt of lightning struck me, and so I jumped back in terror. The Prophet ﷺ turned to me and said, "Come forward, Shayba." Then he placed his hand on my chest, and I raised my eyes to him, and lo, he was become more beloved to me than my very hearing, and my very sight.' So the Prophet ﷺ became more beloved to him than his own hearing and sight after he ﷺ placed his blessed hand on his chest, whilst before that he had been filled with such hatred that he tried to assassinate him ﷺ! Look at how this touch of the Prophet ﷺ changed him from one state to the other!

**The story of Abū Maḥdhūra**: The *Sunan* collections and the *Musnad* of Aḥmad narrate that Abū Maḥdhūra said: 'I went out in a group, and we were in one of the roads to Ḥunayn when the Messenger of Allah ﷺ was making his way back from there. The Messenger of Allah ﷺ came our way, whereupon his ﷺ muezzin made the call to prayer.

---

[532] As narrated by Ibn Isḥāq in *al-Maghāzī*, and Ibn Sa'd on the authority of al-Wāqidī, and also by Baghawī with a different chain of transmission.

'We were off the road, and when we heard the voice of the muezzin we raised our voices to disturb him and mock him. The Messenger of Allah ﷺ heard the noise, and so he sent for us, and we were all brought before him. He ﷺ said, "Which one of you did I hear raising his voice?" They all pointed at me, and they were truthful in doing so, and so he let them all go and kept me there. Then, he ﷺ said to me: "Get up, and sound the call to prayer." I stood up, and there was nothing I hated more than the Messenger of Allah ﷺ and what he was asking of me. I stood before the Messenger of Allah ﷺ, and he told me the words of the call to prayer himself ﷺ, saying, "*Allāhu Akbar, Allāhu Akbar...*" and so on. Then he ﷺ called me when I had finished making the call, and gave me a purse containing some silver. Then he placed his hand on my forelock, and then passed it over my face twice, and then twice over my hands, then over my chest to my navel, and then the Messenger of Allah ﷺ said: "Allah bless you." I said, "O Messenger of Allah, command me to make the call to prayer in Mecca!" He replied, "I command you thus." And so all the hatred I had held for the Messenger of Allah ﷺ vanished, and turned into love for him ﷺ.'

Another narration mentions that Abū Maḥdhūra would never cut or part his fringe after that, because the Messenger of Allah ﷺ had touched it, and he wanted to preserve its blessing. Look at how this touch of the Prophet ﷺ turned rancorous hatred into tender love.

**The story of Ḥarmala ibn Zayd** ؓ, and how the Messenger of Allah ﷺ took hold of his tongue and prayed for him, so that hypocrisy left his heart: Ṭabarānī narrated that Ibn 'Umar ؓ said: 'I was with the Prophet ﷺ when Ḥarmala ibn Zayd came along and sat before him ﷺ and said: "O Messenger of Allah, faith is here" – and he pointed to his tongue – "but hypocrisy is here" – and he pointed to his heart, "and it remembers Allah but a little." The Prophet ﷺ was silent, and so Ḥarmala repeated what he had said. And so the Prophet ﷺ took hold of the tip of Ḥarmala's tongue and said, "O Allah, give him a truthful tongue, and a grateful heart, and grant him to love me, and to love those who love me, and direct his affairs to what is good."

'Ḥarmala then said, "O Messenger of Allah, I have brethren who are hypocrites, and I was their leader; would you have me show them to you?" the Prophet ﷺ replied, "Whoever comes to us as you came to us, we shall seek forgiveness for them as we sought forgiveness for you; and whoever insists upon his sin, Allah will take care of them – and we shall not uncover anyone." '[533]

## THE PROPHET ﷺ TOUCHED THE FACE OF QATĀDA IBN MILḤĀN AND IT BECAME LIKE A MIRROR

Abū al-'Alā' ibn 'Umayr said: 'I was with Qatāda ibn Milḥān when a man walked by the other side of the house, and I saw him reflected in Qatāda's face! And whenever I saw him, it would seem as though there were oil on his face – for the Messenger of Allah ﷺ had touched his face.'[534] In *al-Iṣāba* it states that Ibn Shāhīn narrated that Ḥayy ibn 'Umayr said: 'The Prophet ﷺ touched the face of Qatāda ibn Milḥān, and when he became old, everything aged on him except his face. And I was with him when he died, and a woman passed by and I saw her reflection in his face as though it were a mirror.'

---

[533] Its narrators are rigorously authenticated according to *Majma' al-Zawā'id*; in *al-Iṣāba*, it is ascribed to Ibn Mandah and others.

[534] Narrated by Imām Aḥmad, and its transmitters are all rigorously authenticated (*Majma' al-Zawā'id*)

# THE MESSENGER OF ALLAH ﷺ HEALED THE EYE OF QATĀDA IBN AL-NU'MĀN WHEN IT WAS CUT OUT

Ṭabarānī and Bayhaqī (in *al-Dalā'il*) narrate that when Qatāda ibn al-Nu'mān's ﷺ eye was cut out at the Battle of Uḥud, the Prophet ﷺ came and returned it to its place, and it was sound once more. Ṭabarānī and Ibn Shāhīn also narrate on the authority of Qatāda that his eye was injured at the Battle of Badr, and came out so it hung on his cheek, and so the Prophet ﷺ returned it to its place and from then onwards it was the keenest of his eyes.[535] One narration of Ṭabarānī and Abū Nu'aym states that Qatāda said: 'I was using his face to shield the face of the Messenger of Allah ﷺ from the arrows, and the last arrow took out my eye, so I picked it up and ran to the Messenger of Allah ﷺ. When he saw it in my hand, his eyes filled with tears and he said, "O Allah, protect Qatāda as he protected the face of your Prophet, and make it the keenest and sharpest of his eyes." ' And indeed it was so. One narration has it: 'And that eye never became sore when the other did.'[536]

**And he ﷺ would touch the udder of a sheep, and so it would flow with milk in abundance:** Abū Qirṣāfa said: 'My Islam began when I was an orphan[537] living with my mother and aunt, and I was closer to my aunt. I used to have a few small sheep that I would tend. My aunt from often say to me, "Son, do not go to that man (meaning the Prophet ﷺ), lest he bewitch you and lead you astray." So I went out to the pasture and then left my flock to go the Prophet ﷺ, and stay and listen to him, and then I drove home my sheep, which were thin, and gave no milk. My aunt said to me, "What is wrong with your sheep that their

---

[535] See *al-Iṣāba.*

[536] *Sharḥ al-Mawāhib.*

[537] I.e. his father had died. [t]

udders are dry?" I said I did not know. Then I went back to him ﷺ a second day, and he did as he had done the first day, save that this time I heard him say, "O people, emigrate, and hold firmly to Islam, for emigration is still valid, as long as the struggle continues." Then I took my sheep back as I had done before. I then went back a third day, and stayed listening to him until I embraced Islam and swore allegiance to him ﷺ, and shook his hand, and told him of the problem of my aunt, and my sheep. So the Messenger of Allah ﷺ said to me: "Bring me the sheep." So I brought them to him, and he laid his hand on their backs and their udders, and prayed for blessed increase for them; and they became fleshy, and full of milk. When I took them back to my aunt, she said, "O son, this is the way to tend sheep!" I replied, "O aunt, I did nothing different than any other day; but I have a tale to tell you." I told her the story of how I had gone to the Prophet ﷺ, and about his own story, and the way he spoke. And so my mother and aunt said to me, "Come with us to him." So I went with my mother and my aunt, and they both embraced Islam and pledged allegiance to the Messenger of Allah ﷺ.'[538]

We have already seen the Ḥadīth of Umm Ma'bad al-Khuzā'iyya in Volume 1 of this book, and what took place when the Messenger of Allah ﷺ passed by her camp.[539] Another example of this was the incident when the Prophet ﷺ touched a sheep which had not yet been mated, when he ﷺ passed by Ibn Mas'ud as he tended sheep for 'Uqba: Imām Aḥmad narrates in his *Musnad* that Ibn Mas'ūd ؓ said: 'I was out tending sheep for 'Uqba ibn Abī Mu'īṭ, when the Messenger of Allah ﷺ and Abū Bakr came by.

---

[538] In *Majma' al-Zawā'id,* the author says: 'It was narrated by Ṭabarānī, and its transmitters are all reliable.' We mentioned the rest of this Ḥadīth in the section on the sweetness of the Prophet's ﷺ speech. (Volume 1, p. 75)
[539] Volume 1, p. 35

'The Prophet ﷺ said, "Son, is there any milk?" I replied, "Yes, but I am only entrusted with them."'[540] He ﷺ replied, "Is there any ewe which the ram has not yet mounted?" So I brought him such a ewe, and he touched its udder and milk began to flow from it, so he milked it into a pail and drank, and gave Abū Bakr to drink.' (Another narration adds: 'So he drank, and Abū Bakr drank, and then he ﷺ said to the udder, "Stop", and so it stopped.') Ibn Mas'ūd continued: 'Afterwards I went to him, and said, "O Messenger of Allah, teach me something of this discourse." (One narration has it "Teach me something of this Qur'ān.") The Messenger of Allah ﷺ patted my head, and said, "Allah have mercy on you, for you are a learned young boy." I then took from his ﷺ lips seventy chapters (of Qur'ān).'

## THE COMPANIONS WOULD KISS THE PROPHET'S ﷺ HAND AND BODY OUT OF REVERENCE FOR HIM ﷺ AND AS A MEANS OF SEEKING BLESSING AND ILLUMINATIONS

Usāma ibn Sharīk said: 'I went to the Messenger of Allah ﷺ and his Companions were around him as quiet and still as if they had birds perched on their heads. I greeted them and then sat down. When they got up to leave, they all kissed his ﷺ hand. And so I took his hand, and it was more fragrant than musk.'[541] And Ka'b Ibn Mālik is reported to have said that whenever he had to leave, he would go to the Prophet ﷺ and take his hand and kiss it.[542]

---

[540] I.e. they are not my sheep, so I do not have permission to give out their milk. [t]

[541] Narrated by Ibn Khuzayma and Ḥākim.

[542] Narrated by Ṭabarānī.

# THE COMPANIONS KISSED THE BLESSED HAND AND FEET OF THE PROPHET ﷺ

Ḥuṣayn ibn Waḥwaḥ al-Anṣārī reported that when Ṭalḥa ibn al-Barrā' ؓ met the Prophet ﷺ, he began to hug him and kiss his ﷺ feet, and then he said, 'O Messenger of Allah, command me with what you like, and I shall not disobey you.' The Prophet ﷺ was amused by the young man's words, so he said, 'Go kill your father!' Ṭalḥa went off to do it, and so the Prophet ﷺ called him and said, 'Come back, for I was not sent to break family ties.'[543]

Bayhaqī, Ṭabarānī and Abu Ya'lā narrate with a good chain of transmission that Mazīda ibn Mālik said: 'As the Prophet ﷺ was conversing with his Companions one day, he said, "There will presently come to you a group of travellers from among the finest men of the East." 'Umar ibn al-Khaṭṭāb went out to see, and found thirteen travellers. He asked them who they were, and they said that they ware from the tribe of 'Abd al-Qays. "What has brought you here?" 'Umar asked, "Trade?" They said no. "Indeed," said 'Umar, "the Prophet ﷺ mentioned you just now." So 'Umar walked with them to the Prophet ﷺ and said to them, "This is the one you want." So they jumped from their mounts, some walking, some quickening their pace, and others running, until they came to the Prophet ﷺ.' Zāri' ibn 'Āmir, who was one of these men, said: 'When we arrived in Medina, we quickly dismounted our horses and kissed the hand and foot of the Messenger of Allah ﷺ.'[544] Ashajj (their leader) waited until his trunk had been brought, whereupon he put on his two white garments and then walked to the Messenger of Allah and kissed his hand.

---

[543] *Al-Iṣāba* ascribes it with this wording to Baghawī, Ibn Abī Khaythama, Ibn Abī 'Āṣim, Ṭabarānī, Ibn Shāhīn, and Ibn al-Sakan; and the author mentions that others besides these narrated it also.
[544] Narrated by Abū Dāwūd (iv. 483) and Bayhaqī.

The Prophet ﷺ said to him: 'You are endowed with two qualities that Allah and His Messenger love: forbearance and patience.' Ashajj replied, 'O Messenger of Allah, did I attain to these qualities, or did Allah make them part of my nature?' He ﷺ replied, 'Allah made them part of your nature.' Ashajj said, 'Praise be to Allah, who endowed me with two qualities that Allah and His Messenger love!' Abū Ya'lā's[545] narration has it that Ashajj asked, 'Were these qualities mine from old, or are they newly developed?' The Prophet ﷺ said, 'They were yours from old.' So Ashajj said, 'Praise be to Allah, who endowed me with two qualities that Allah and His Messenger love!'

Another example of this was the blessings 'Amr ibn Abī 'Amr al-Mazanī sought from the foot of the Prophet ﷺ: *Al-Iṣāba* relates that it was narrated by Nasā'ī, Baghawī, Ibn al-Sakan, and Ibn Mandah with *'uluw*,[546] by way of Hilāl ibn 'Āmir, that Rāfi' ibn 'Amr al-Muzanī said: 'At the Farewell Pilgrimage, when I was five or six years old, my father took my hand and led me to the Prophet at Minā on the day of the sacrifice, where I saw him ﷺ sitting on a grey mule giving a sermon. I said to my father, "Who is that?" He replied, "That is the Messenger of Allah." So I approached him ﷺ and took hold of his shin, and moved my hand until it was between the sole of his foot and his shoe, so that I could feel its coolness on my palm.' He did this to seek the blessings of the Prophet's ﷺ foot.

Another example of this was how 'Abdullāh ibn Abī Sabaqa (or Sabaqah) kissed the Prophet's ﷺ shin and foot: Imām Baghawī narrates that 'Abdullāh ibn Abī Sabaqa al-Bāhilī ؓ said: 'I went

---

[545] See Zurqānī's *Sharḥ al-Mawāhib* iv. 16, and *Majma ' al-Zawā'id* vol.8, p.42

[546] A Ḥadīth narrated with *'uluw* means one which has a low number of transmitters in its chain, and therefore is more likely to be free of mistakes. ('Asqalānī, *Nuzhat al-Naẓr*, p. 147) [t]

to the Prophet ﷺ whilst he sat on his mule (Ibn Mandah's narration adds that this was during the Farewell Pilgrimage), and his foot was in the stirrup, so I hugged it, and he ﷺ tapped me with his whip. "Messenger of Allah," I said, "I must have retribution!" So the Prophet ﷺ handed me the whip, and I kissed his shin and foot.'[547]

## THE COMPANIONS KISSED OTHER PARTS OF HIS BLESSED BODY ﷺ

Abū Dāwūd, in the section of his *Sunan* concerning kissing the body, narrated on the authority of 'Abd al-Raḥmān Abī Laylā that Usayd ibn Ḥuḍayr was joking with the people and making them laugh, when the Prophet ﷺ poked him in his waist with a piece of wood. Usayd said, 'Let me take my retribution!' The Prophet ﷺ replied, 'Take it.' Usayd said, 'You are wearing a shirt, but I am not.' So the Prophet ﷺ lifted his shirt, and Usayd hugged him and kissed his waist, and said, 'That is all I want, O Messenger of Allah ﷺ.' Bayhaqī narrated in his *Sunan*, with a strong chain of transmission according to Dhahabī, that Abū Laylā said: 'Usayd ibn Ḥuḍayr was a pious, good-tempered, amiable man, and once when he was with the Messenger of Allah ﷺ, speaking to the people and making them laugh, the Messenger of Allah ﷺ poked him in the waist with his finger. Usayd said, "You hurt me, Messenger of Allah!" He ﷺ replied, "Then take retribution." He said, "O Messenger of Allah, you are wearing a shirt, whilst I am not." So the Messenger of Allah ﷺ lifted his shirt, and Usayd hugged him and then kissed his waist, and said, "My mother and father be your ransom, O Messenger of Allah, all I want is this."'[548]

---

[547] *Al-Iṣāba.*

[548] See *Kashf al-Khafā'* vol.2,p .41.

Ibn Isḥāq narrated, on the authority of Ḥabbān ibn Wāsi', that several elders of his tribe told him that on the day of the Battle of Badr, the Messenger of Allah ﷺ was organising the ranks, holding an arrow in his hand with which to direct them. When he came to Sawād ibn Ghaziyya ؓ, he poked him in his belly, and Sawād said, 'You hurt me, so give me my retribution!' So the Prophet ﷺ uncovered his midriff, but Sawād embraced him and kissed his belly. 'What made you do this, Sawād?' said the Prophet ﷺ, and he answered: 'O Messenger of Allah, here before us is what you see (i.e. the battle), and I desired that at my last moment with you, my skin should touch your skin.' So the Prophet ﷺ prayed for him and blessed him.[549]

Ḥāfiẓ 'Asqalānī said in *al-Iṣāba*:

> Ibn 'Abd al-Barr said that the person in this story was actually Sawād ibn 'Amr; but there is nothing to say that they are not actually two different stories, especially since their contexts are different: Baghawī narrated, by way of 'Amr ibn Salīṭ, on the authority of Ḥasan, that Sawād ibn 'Amr would use a perfume called *khalūq*,[550] which the Prophet ﷺ forbade him from using. One day he met the Prophet ﷺ, who was carrying a palm-leaf stalk, with which he prodded him in the belly. 'Give me my retribution, O Messenger of Allah!' he said, so the Prophet ﷺ uncovered his belly and said, 'Take requital,' whereupon Sawād threw the palm stalk aside and stooped and kissed the belly of the Messenger of Allah ﷺ.

---

[549] See *al-Bidāya wa al-Nihāya*, and *al-Iṣāba* vol.4, p.94.

[550] This is a perfume made from saffron and other ingredients, yellow or red in colour. The Prophet ﷺ forbade him from using it because it is a woman's perfume. (*al-Nihāya*)

## THE COMPANIONS WOULD SEEK BLESSINGS FROM THE RELICS OF THE PROPHET ﷺ IN HIS LIFETIME AND AFTER HIS PASSING

The Companions of the Prophet ﷺ would seek blessings from his relics and his leftovers, and his clothes, food, and drink, because of their certitude that his noble and hallowed relics were filled with blessings and treasures, simply because they were his ﷺ. We will give a few concise examples of this to stand for the many other instances:

## THE COMPANIONS SOUGHT BLESSINGS FROM THE CUT HAIRS OF THE PROPHET ﷺ AND WERE EAGER TO COLLECT THEM AND PRESERVE THEM

Muslim narrates that Anas ؓ said: 'I saw the Messenger of Allah ﷺ having his hair cut, and his Companions were circling around him, not wanting to let a single hair fall without landing in one of their hands.' They did this out of reverence for the hairs, and in hope of gaining blessings from them.

*Al-Iṣāba* narrates that Ju'shum al-Khayr pledged allegiance under the tree, and the Prophet ﷺ dressed him his shirt and his shoes and gave him some of his ﷺ hair. Bukhārī, Muslim and others narrate that Anas ؓ said: 'The Prophet ﷺ went to the stones (at Minā, on the pilgrimage) and pelted them, then returned to his camp at Minā and performed the sacrifice. Then he said to the barber, "Cut this," and pointed to his right side, and then his left; and then he gave the hair to the people.' As Ḥāfiẓ Zurqānī said, this was in order that they could seek blessings by it, and seek intercession to Allah through it because it was his ﷺ, and draw near to Him by means of it. Another narration has it that the Prophet ﷺ said to the barber, 'Here', and pointed to the right side of his head, and so the barber shaved it, and the Prophet divided the hair between those who were present; then he asked the barber to shave the left side, and he ﷺ gave this to Umm Sulaym bint Milḥān, the mother of Anas ؓ. The narration of Imām Aḥmad adds that the Prophet ﷺ then cut his nails, and divided them between those present. Another narration has it that the Prophet ﷺ gave the hair from the left side to Abū Ṭalḥa and had him share it amongst the people. Another narration has it that he ﷺ gave him the hairs from the right side, then the left, and said, 'Share it amongst the people.' Imām Nawawī said: 'This is evidence of the permissibility of seeking blessings from the hair of the Prophet ﷺ, and seeking to acquire it.' Abū 'Abdullāh al-Ubbī said:

> The fact that he ﷺ gave the hair to Abū Ṭalḥa does not contradict his ﷺ saying, 'Share it amongst the people,' since he may have given it to Abū Ṭalḥa to share it out. Let us consider the different narrations concerning the hair from the left side: One narration has it that he ﷺ shared it out as with the right side, another that he ﷺ gave it to Umm Sulaym, another that he gave it to Abū Ṭalḥā, and another that he ﷺ gave both sides to Abū Ṭalḥa. It may be that he ﷺ gave it to Umm Sulaym to pass on to her husband Abū Ṭalḥa, or that he ﷺ gave it to Abū Talḥa to pass on to his wife Umm Sulaym to share amongst the women.

That is, the hair from the right side went to the men, and that of the left side went to the women. Ḥāfiẓ Zurqānī said:

> The Messenger of Allah ﷺ only divided his hair amongst his Companions so that it would be a continuing source of blessing for them, and a reminder for them, as though he were indicating that

his time would soon come. And he ﷺ chose Abū Ṭalḥa to as a way of indicating this, for it was Abū Ṭalḥa who dug the noble grave, and bricked up its walls.

Bukhārī narrated that Muḥammad ibn Sīrīn said: 'I said to 'Abīda al-Salmānī, "We have some hairs of the Prophet ﷺ, which we got from Anas, or from Anas' family." 'Abīda replied, "That I could have a single hair of his would be more beloved to me that the world and everything in it." ' The narrations of Ismā'īlī has it that he said, '… more beloved to me than all that is gold and silver.' Bukhārī also narrated that Anas ؓ said: 'When the Messenger of Allah ﷺ shaved his head (at the Farewell Pilgrimage), Abū Ṭalḥa was the first to take some of his ﷺ hair.' The Prophet's ﷺ sharing out his noble hair at the Farewell Pilgrimage was an indication from him of the blessings and treasures that Allah had stored in his noble body, and the secrets and illuminations with which He distinguished him; and this was a matter of fact and reality, not supposition and fancy.

# KHĀLID IBN AL-WALĪD SOUGHT VICTORY IN HIS MILITARY CAMPAIGNS BY VIRTUE OF THE PROPHET'S ﷺ HAIR

Ja'far ibn 'Abdullāh ibn al-Ḥakam related that Khālid ibn al-Walīd ؓ lost his cap on the day of the Battle of Yarmuk. He sent men out to look for it, but they could not find it, so he sent them out again, after which they found it, and saw that it was a worn-out old cap. Khalid explained, 'The Messenger of Allah ﷺ performed 'Umra and shaved his head, and the people rushed to collect his shorn hairs. I was the first to get to his forelock, and I stowed it in this cap; and I have not attended a battle with it since save that I was given victory.'[551]

---

[551] Ḥāfiẓ Haythamī said: 'It was narrated by Ṭabarānī, and Abū Ya'lā narrated the like of it; its transmitters are all rigorously authenticated.'

Imām Aḥmad narrated that Muḥammad ibn ʻAbdullāh ibn Zayd reported that his father ʻAbdullāh saw the Prophet ﷺ at the site of the sacrifice dividing the meat between some men from the Helpers. There was none left for ʻAbdullāh and his companion, and so the Messenger of Allah ﷺ shaved his head and gave the hairs to ʻAbdullāh, and cut his nails and gave them to his companion. ʻAbdullāh told his son Muḥammad that he still kept the hairs, and his companion kept the nails.

## THE COMPANIONS SOUGHT BLESSINGS FROM THE FINGERPRINTS OF THE MESSENGER OF ALLAH ﷺ

Imām Aḥmad narrated, on the authority of Jābir ibn Samura ؓ, that when the Messenger of Allah ﷺ was given food and ate some of it, he would sent the rest to Abū Ayyūb al-Anṣārī ؓ, who would place his fingers in the marks left by the fingers of the Messenger of Allah ﷺ.

ʻOnce, the Prophet ﷺ was given a plate of food, and found that there was garlic in it, and so he ﷺ did not eat any of it. Then it was sent to Abū Ayyūb, and when he saw that the marks of the Prophet's ﷺ fingers were absent, and so he did not eat it, and went to him ﷺ and said, ʻO Messenger of Allah, I did not see the mark of your fingers on it.' He ﷺ replied, ʻI smelled garlic in it.' Abū Ayyūb said, ʻWhy did you send it to me without eating any?' He ﷺ replied, ʻThe Angel comes to me.'[552]

Ḥāfiẓ Haythamī said: ʻIts transmitters are rigorously authentic.' Muslim also narrated aversion of it in his *Ṣaḥīḥ*.

---

Jaʻfar heard it from several Companions; I do not know if he heard it directly from Khālid or not.'

[552] Or ʻthe Angel will come to me.'

## THE COMPANIONS SOUGHT BLESSINGS FROM THE LEFTOVERS OF THE PROPHET ﷺ

Bukhārī and Muslim narrate that Sahl ibn Sa'd ؓ said: 'The Prophet ﷺ was brought something to drink, and so he drank it. There was a boy sitting to his right, and on his left were the elders. He ﷺ said to the boy, "Do you give me leave to pass (the drink) to these others?"[553] The boy replied, "By Allah, O Messenger of Allah, I cannot give anyone my share of what is from you." So the Prophet ﷺ placed it into his hand.' The boy was 'Abdullāh ibn 'Abbās ؓ.

## THE COMPANIONS SOUGHT BLESSINGS FROM VESSELS WHICH THE PROPHET'S LIPS ﷺ HAD TOUCHED

Imām Aḥmad and others narrate that Anas ؓ said: 'The Prophet ﷺ went to see Umm Sulaym one day. There was a skin of water hanging in her house, and he ﷺ stood and drank from it. Afterwards, Umm Sulaym cut off the mouth of the skin and kept it; and we still have it.

So Umm Sulaym cut the part of the skin that the Prophet ﷺ had drunk from, and kept it in her house, in order to gain the blessings of the Prophet's ﷺ relic.

We have already mentioned (in Volume 1) how the Companions used the Prophet's ﷺ sweat as perfume, and sought blessings and cures from his ﷺ blessed saliva.

---

[553] He ﷺ asked because ordinarily the one on the right side would be the next to drink. (*Fatḥ al-Bārī*) [t]

# THE COMPANIONS SOUGHT BLESSINGS AND CURES FROM THE CLOTHS OF THE MESSENGER OF ALLAH ﷺ

Muslim narrates that 'Abdullāh, the freed slave of Asmā' bint Abī Bakr ﵄ said: 'One day, Asmā' brought out for us a *jubbah*[554] decorated with a pattern and hemlines, its collar and cuffs lined with brocade, and said: "This is the *jubbah* of the Messenger of Allah ﷺ, which was in the keeping of 'Ā'isha, and when she ﵂ passed away I took it. The Prophet ﷺ used to wear it, and now we wash it to treat the sick." '

One narration has it: 'We wash it to treat those who complain of illness, and we are cured by it.' That is, they were cured by virtue of its having been imbued with his ﷺ blessed sweat, and having clothed his ﷺ blessed, fragrant body.

Bukhārī narrates that Sahl ibn Sa'd ﵁ said: 'A woman brought a cloak with stitched hemlines and said, "Messenger of Allah, I give you this to wear." The Prophet ﷺ took it, having need of it, and wore it. He came out to us wearing it, and a man of the Companions saw it and said, "O Messenger of Allah, how fine this cloak is; give it to me to wear!" He ﷺ told him yes. Then he sat with us for as long as Allah decreed, and then went back and folded it up, and sent it to him.

'Once he ﷺ had gone, the others criticised the man, and said, "It was not good of you to ask the Prophet ﷺ for it when you saw that he was wearing it, and the he needed it; you know that he never refuses anything asked of him!" The man replied, "I hoped for its blessing, since the Prophet ﷺ had worn it; I hope to wear it as my burial shroud." '

---

[554] A long, loose outer garment with wide sleeves. [t]

# THE COMPANIONS SOUGHT BLESSINGS FROM THE PROPHET'S PHLEGM ﷺ AND THE WATER HE USED FOR ABLUTIONS

Bukhārī and Muslim narrate (and the wording here is that of Bukhārī), as part of the Ḥadīth of the Treaty of Ḥudaybīyya, that 'Urwa ibn Mas'ūd, who at that time was the envoy of the pagans in Mecca, began to watch the Prophet ﷺ very carefully.

He said later: 'By Allah, every time the Messenger of Allah expectorated phlegm, it landed in the hand of one of his followers, who then rubbed it into his face and skin.

'And when he (the Messenger of Allah ﷺ) commanded them, they obeyed instantly; and when he made ablutions, they almost fought one another to get to the water he used; and when he spoke, they lowered their voices, and they never looked directly at him out of their reverence for him ﷺ.'

'Urwa ibn Mas'ūd then returned to his people in Mecca, and said: 'O People! By Allah, I have been sent to kings, and to the Caesar, and Khosrau, and the Negus; by Allah, I never saw a king whose subjects venerate him like the Companions of Muḥammad venerate Muḥammad!

'By Allah, every time the Messenger of Allah expectorated phlegm, it landed in the hand of one of his followers, who then rubbed it into his face and skin!

'And when he (the Messenger of Allah ﷺ) commanded them, they obeyed instantly! And when he made ablutions, they almost fought one another to get to the water he used! And when he spoke, they lowered their voices for him! And they never looked directly at him out of their reverence for him! And indeed, he has made you a just proposal, so accept it.'

## THE PROPHET ﷺ CURED THE COMPANIONS WITH HIS BLESSED SALIVA

If the Prophet ﷺ spat onto a sick person, or blew or spat onto the place where they felt their ailment, they would be cured by leave Allah ﷻ, and there were many well-known instances of this. And so the Companions ؓ would eagerly seek to be cured by his ﷺ saliva.

One instance of this was when he ﷺ spat onto the eyes of 'Alī ؓ when they were badly infected to the extent that he could not walk without someone holding his hand to guide him, yet when the Messenger of Allah ﷺ spat into his eyes he was cured instantly: Bukhārī, Muslim and others narrate, on the authority of Sahl ibn Sa'd, that the Messenger of Allah ﷺ said on the day of Khaybar: 'Tomorrow, I will give my standard to a man by whose hand Allah will bring victory; he loves Allah and His Messenger, and Allah and His Messenger love him!' The next day, when the people woke, they all went to the Messenger of Allah ﷺ hoping that he would give it to them. He ﷺ said: 'Where is 'Alī ibn Abī Ṭālib?' They said; 'O Messenger of Allah, his eyes are ill.' He said: 'Send him to me.' So he was brought forward – or, in Muslim's narration, Salama said: 'The Messenger of Allah ﷺ sent me to 'Alī, and I came leading him, and his eyes were infected' – so the Messenger of Allah ﷺ spat in his eyes, and he was cured, as though he had never had any affliction.' Another instance of this was when the Prophet ﷺ spat onto the leg of Salama when it was injured at the Battle of Khaybar, and so he was healed instantly: Abū Dāwūd and others narrate that Yazīd ibn 'Abd al-Raḥmān said: 'I saw a scar on Salama's leg, and asked him what it was. He replied: "I was struck a blow at the Battle of Khaybar, and so the people gave the cry that Salama was injured, and I was taken to the Prophet ﷺ, who blew on me three times; and since then it has not bothered me to this day."'

And Ibn Ḥibbān narrated in his *Ṣaḥīḥ*, as did Ḍiyā' in *al-Mukhtāra*, that Ibn Mandah reported that the Prophet ﷺ spat on the leg of 'Amr ibn Mu'ādh al-Anṣārī when it was severed, and it was healed.[555]

Another instance of this was when he ﷺ blew into the mouth of Bashīr ibn 'Aqraba al-Juhanī and so cured his speech impediment: Isḥāq ibn Ibrāhīm al-Ramlī narrates in his *Fawā'id* that 'Aqraba al-Juhanī took his son to the Prophet ﷺ, who said, 'Who is that with you, 'Aqraba?' He replied, 'It is my son Buḥayr' The Prophet ﷺ said to the boy, 'Come here.' Buḥayr related the story: 'So I went to him and sat down on his right side, and he patted my head and said, "What is your name?" I said, "Buḥayr, O Messenger of Allah." He ﷺ said, "No, rather your name is Bashīr."[556] I had a speech impediment, and so the Prophet ﷺ blew into my mouth, and the impediment was cured. All the hair on my head turned white as I aged, except the part where his ﷺ hand had touched, which remained black.'[557]

Ṭabarānī narrated that Muḥammad ibn Ḥāṭib said: 'My mother brought me back from Abyssinia when my father Ḥāṭib died, and she brought me to the Prophet ﷺ. One of my hands had been burned by fire, and so my mother said, "O Messenger of Allah, this is Muḥammad, son of Ḥāṭib, your nephew,[558] and he has been burned by fire." I do not wish to lie about the Messenger of Allah ﷺ, so I say that I am not sure whether he blew on me or patted my head; then he prayed for blessings for me and for my progeny.'[559]

---

[555] See *al-Iṣāba.*

[556] The name Bashīr means 'one who brings cheer.' [t]

[557] See *al-Iṣāba.*

[558] Meaning here 'your kinsman.' [t]

[559] Narrated in *Majma' al-Zawā'id.*

After mentioning this story in *al-Iṣāba*, 'Asqalānī said that it was also narrated by Aḥmad, Ibn Abī Khaythama, and Baghawī on the authority of 'Abd al-Raḥmān ibn 'Uthmān, the son of Muḥammad ibn Ḥāṭib, who heard it from his father as told to him by his grandfather; this narration mentioned that Muḥammad's mother told him : 'I said, "O Messenger of Allah, this is Muḥammad ibn Ḥāṭib, the first boy to be named after you (in Abyssinia)." Then the Messenger of Allah ﷺ patted your head, and blew into your mouth, and prayed for blessings for you.' Another instance of this was how the blessed saliva of the Prophet ﷺ cured a woman of her propensity for foul speech: Ṭabarānī narrates on the authority of Abū 'Umāma ؓ that a foul-mouthed woman went to the Prophet ﷺ while he was eating dry meat and said, 'Will you not give me something to eat?' So he gave her some of what he had, but she said, 'No, I only want what is in your mouth.' So he ﷺ took it out and gave it to her, and she tossed it into her mouth and ate it; and after that, the foul and harsh speech the woman had been wont to use was never heard again.

## HIS BLESSED SALIVA ﷺ MADE WATER PURE AND SWEET

Imām Aḥmad, Ibn Mājah, Bayhaqī, and Abū Nu'aym narrate that Wā'il ibn Ḥujr said: 'The Prophet ﷺ was brought a pail of water and he drank from it, and then the water was poured back into the well' – or he said 'then he spat it back into the well' – 'and a scent like musk emanated from it.'

Abū Nu'aym also narrated on the authority of Anas ؓ that the Prophet ﷺ spat into a well in Anas' house, and from then on no well in Medina gave sweeter water. Bayhaqī narrated that Anas ؓ was asked about the well of Qubā'. He answered: 'That well was such that a man would only draw enough to water his donkey before it ran dry; but then the Messenger of Allah ﷺ came to it and asked for a large pail, and drew some water, and then either made ablutions with it or spat into it, and then had it poured back into the well. From then on, it never ran dry again.' Ibn Saʿd also narrated similar statement from Anas ؓ. Ibn al-Sakan narrated that Humām ibn Nufayl al-Saʿdī said: 'I went to the Messenger of Allah ﷺ and said, "O Messenger of Allah, we had a well dug for us but the water came out salty." So he gave me a skin of water and said, "Pour it in", so I poured it in, and the water became sweet; indeed it was the sweetest water in all Yemen.'

## THE COMPANIONS SOUGHT BLESSINGS FROM HIS BLESSED SALIVA ﷺ

Baghawī narrated in his *Muʿjam*, on the authority of Ibn ʿUmar ؓ, that ʿUmar ibn al-Khaṭṭāb ؓ used to call Ibn ʿAbbās to him and say, 'I saw the Messenger of Allah ﷺ call you over, and pat your head and spit in your mouth, and say, "O Allah, give him a deep understanding of the faith, and teach him interpretation."'[560] The Companions ؓ would also take their babies to the Prophet ﷺ so he could chew dates for them to suck, so they would imbibe his ﷺ noble saliva; and instances of this were manifold. One instance of this: It is narrated in the *Ṣaḥīḥ* collections of Bukhārī and Muslim that Asmā' bint Abī Bakr al-Ṣiddīq ؓ said, about when she came to Medina from Mecca whilst pregnant with her son ʿAbdullāh ibn Zubayr: 'I set off towards Medina at the end of my term, and camped in Qubā', where I gave birth. Then I went to the Messenger of Allah ﷺ, and he took my son and placed him in his lap, and

---

[560] Related in *al-Iṣāba*, where it is mentioned that Ibn Khaythama narrated it from Saʿīd, from Jubayr, directly from Ibn ʿAbbās, in a similar form.

called for a date and chewed on it, then spat into his mouth – and so the first thing to enter his belly was the saliva of the Messenger of Allah ﷺ – and then he gave him the softened date, and then prayed for him and blessed him; and he was the first child to be born in Islam' – that is, the first child to be born to the Emigrants in Medina.

It is also narrated in the *Ṣaḥīḥ* collections of Bukhārī and Muslim that Abū Mūsā al-Ash'arī ؓ said: 'A son was born to me, and so I took him to the Messenger of Allah ﷺ, who named him Ibrāhīm, and he chewed a date for him, and prayed for blessings for him, and then gave him back to me' – and the child was the first of Abū Mūsā's children. Bukhārī and Muslim also narrate, on the authority of Anas ؓ, that he took a son born to Abū Ṭalḥa ؓ to the Messenger of Allah ﷺ. Anas said, 'When the Messenger of Allah ﷺ saw me, he said, "It seems that Umm Sulaym has given birth." I said yes. So I put the child in his ﷺ lap, and the Messenger of Allah ﷺ asked for a Medinan date and he chewed it in his ﷺ mouth until it was soft, and then placed it in the baby's mouth, whereupon the baby began to suck it. Then the Messenger of Allah ﷺ said, "Look at how the Helpers love dates!" And he stroked the baby's head; and named him 'Abdullāh.' Zubayr ibn Bakkār narrated that Ibrāhīm ibn Muḥammad ibn 'Abd al-'Azīz said: 'When Abd al-Raḥmān ibn Zayd ibn al-Khaṭṭāb was born, he was the most delicate child ever born. And so his grandfather Abū Lubāba wrapped him in a cloth and took him to the Messenger of Allah ﷺ and said, "I have never seen a smaller baby than this." So the Messenger of Allah ﷺ softened a date for him, and stroked his head, and prayed for blessings for him. And when he grew, 'Abd al-Raḥmān was never seen in a group of people save that he was the tallest of them; and 'Umar gave his daughter Fāṭima to him in marriage.'[561]

---

[561] Mentioned in *al-Iṣāba* and elsewhere.

# THE COMPANIONS SOUGHT BLESSINGS FROM THE PROPHET'S ﷺ BLOOD

Ṭabarānī, Bazzār, Ḥākim, Bayhaqī, and Abū Nu'aym (in *Hilyat al-Awliyā'*) all narrate, on the authority of 'Āmir ibn 'Abdullāh ibn al-Zubayr, that his father Abdullāh ibn al-Zubayr said: 'The Messenger of Allah ﷺ performed cupping on himself, and then gave me the blood and said, "Take this, 'Abdullāh, and conceal it." (One narration has it that he ﷺ said, "Take this blood and hide it where no one will see it.") So took it away and drank it, and then went back to him ﷺ. He said, "What did you do with it?" I replied, "I hid it." He said, "Perhaps you drank it?" I said yes, so he ﷺ said, "Woe to you from the people, and woe to the people from you!" '

One narration has it: 'So the Messenger of Allah ﷺ said, "What made you do that?" I said, "I knew that your blood would never be touched by the Hellfire, so I drank it." So he ﷺ said, "Woe to you from the people, and woe to the people from you!" '

Dāraquṭnī narrated in his *Sunan* that Asmā' said: 'The Prophet ﷺ performed cupping, and gave his blood to my son 'Abdullāh, who drank it. Jibrīl came to the Prophet ﷺ and told him about it, so he said, "What did you do?" He replied, "I did not like to pour your blood away.' The Prophet ﷺ replied, "The Hellfire will not touch it", and patted his head, and said, "Woe to the people from you, and woe to you from the people!"

Sa'īd ibn Manṣūr narrates in his *Sunan*, on the authority of 'Amr ibn al-Ṣā'ib, that he heard that when the Prophet ﷺ was wounded in his noble face at the Battle of Uḥud, Mālik ibn Sinān, the father of Abū Sa'īd al-Khudrī, sucked the wound until it was clean and white. The Prophet ﷺ said to him, 'Spit it out', but he said, 'By Allah, I shall never spit it out!' then he swallowed it.

The Prophet ﷺ then said, 'If any would look upon a man of the denizens of Paradise, let him look upon this man.' Mālik was then martyred during the battle.

Ṭabarānī also narrated it, and his narration added that the Prophet ﷺ said, 'Whosoever's blood mixes with my blood shall not be touched by the Hellfire.'[562] Sa'īd ibn Manṣūr also narrated that he ﷺ said: 'If any would be pleased to see a man whose blood is mixed with my blood, let him look upon Mālik bin Sinān.'[563]

'Allāmah Qasṭalānī said:

> It is related in the book *al-Jawhar al-Maknūn fī Dhikr al-Qabā'il wa al-Buṭūn* that when Ibn al-Zubayr drank the blood of the Prophet ﷺ, the scent of musk emanated from his mouth, and remained there until he was killed, Allah be pleased with him.
>
> Ṭabarānī narrated that Safīna ؓ said: 'The Prophet ﷺ performed cupping, and then said, "Take this blood and bury it", to protect it from beast, birds, and people. So I went to a secluded place and drank it, and then told him ﷺ about it, and he smiled.'
>
> After relating this, Haythamī said: 'The transmitters of Ṭabarānī are reliable.'

---

[562] Haythamī said: 'I see no one in its chain of transmission whose weakness is agreed upon.'
[563] See Zurqānī, *Sharḥ al-Mawāhib* vol.4, p.228.

# THE COMPANIONS SOUGHT BLESSINGS FROM COINS TOUCHED BY THE HAND OF THE PROPHET ﷺ

Ḥāfiẓ Ibn Ḥajar entitled part three of *al-Maṭālib al-ʿĀliya* 'Seeking Blessings from the Relics of the Righteous', and then mentioned the following Ḥadīth: Muḥammad ibn Sūqa reported that his father said: 'I went to 'Amr ibn Ḥurayth to ask to rent a room in his house, and he replied, "Rent it, for it is a source of blessing for its owner, and for the one who stays in it." 'I said, "How so?" He answered, "I went to the Messenger of Allah ﷺ and found they had just slaughtered a camel, and he ﷺ had told them to divide it up. He ﷺ said to the one who was cutting it, 'Give 'Amr a piece of it'; but he forgot about me and did not give it to me. The next day, I went to the Messenger of Allah, who had a few coins before him. He ﷺ said to me, 'Did you take the share I told them to give you?' I replied, 'O Messenger of Allah, they did not give me anything.' So the Messenger of Allah ﷺ picked up some of the coins and gave them to me, and I took them to my mother and said, 'Take these coins that the Messenger of Allah held in his hand and then gave to me; keep them until we decide what to put them in.' Then time passed by, and I came to buy this house (with those coins)." '

Then Ibn Ḥajar related the Ḥadīth of Khālid ibn al-Walīd we mentioned above, in which he said: 'The Messenger of Allah ﷺ then shaved his head, and the people rushed to get the shorn hairs. I was the first to the forelock, and so I took a cap and stored the hair in its peak; and I never faced an enemy with it save that I was given victory.' Ibn Ḥajar then related the Ḥadīth of Ibn Sīrīn in which he said: 'I asked Umm Sulaym to give me some of the musk she would soak with the sweat of the Prophet ﷺ, and she gave me some'; and when Ibn Sīrīn died, he was embalmed with that musk.

## THE COMPANIONS SOUGHT BLESSINGS FROM THE PROPHET'S STAFF ﷺ

Muḥammad ibn Sīrīn relates that Anas ibn Mālik ﵁ had in his possession a short staff which had belonged to the Prophet ﷺ, and when he died, it was buried with him between his body and his shroud.[564]

Imām Aḥmad narrated in his *Musnad* that Ibn 'Abdullāh ibn Unays reported that his father 'Abdullāh ibn Unays ﵁ said: 'The Messenger of Allah ﷺ called me over and said, "I heard that Khālid ibn Sufyān ibn Nubayḥ is gathering people against me to attack me. He is now in 'Urna (near Mecca); so go and kill him." I said, "O Messenger of Allah, describe him for me so I will recognise him." He said, "When you see him, you will feel your skin crawl."[565] So I strapped on my sword and went out, and found him encamped at 'Urna surrounded by his women. When the time for the afternoon prayer came, I saw him, and I felt my skin crawl just as the Messenger of Allah ﷺ had said it would. So I approached him; and I feared that something would happen between me and him that would cause me to miss the prayer, so I prayed as I walked towards him, nodding my head in place of bowing and prostrating. When I had reached him, he said, "Who are you?" I said, "I am an Arab who has heard of you, and heard that you are gathering a force against this man, and so I have come." He said, "Indeed, that is my aim." So I walked with him for a while until I was able to draw my sword and slay him. Then I withdrew, and left his women to wail over him. Once I returned to the Messenger of Allah ﷺ, he saw me

---

[564] Mentioned in *al-Tarātīb al-Idāriyya*, quoting from *Jam' al-Jawāmi'*, wherein it is ascribed to Bayhaqī and Ibn 'Asākir; and also quoting from *Kanz al-'Ummāl*.

[565] This means that the skin trembles and contracts like the earth after a drought. (*Majma' al-Zawā'id*)

and said, "A face marked with success!" I said, "I slew him, O Messenger of Allah." "Indeed you did," he replied. Then the Messenger of Allah ﷺ stood up with me and took me into his room, and gave me a staff, saying, "Keep this with you, O 'Abdullāh ibn Unays." So I took it out to the people, and they asked me what it was. I said, "The Messenger of Allah ﷺ gave it to me, and told me to keep it." They said, "Perhaps you should go back to the Messenger of Allah ﷺ and ask him what it is for." So I went back to the Messenger of Allah ﷺ and said, "Messenger of Allah, why did you give me this staff?" He ﷺ answered, "It shall be a sign between you and I on the Day of Resurrection; a day when only the fewest of people will have something to lean on." ' So 'Abdullāh attached the staff to his sword, and kept it with him until he died, whereupon he instructed that it be wrapped with him inside his shroud, and buried with him.

Abū Ya'lā and Bayhaqī also narrated it, and Ṭabarānī also narrated on the authority of Muḥammad ibn Ka'b al-Quraẓī; his narration has it: 'So the Prophet ﷺ gave him a staff which he himself ﷺ used to use, and then said to him: "Lean on it until you meet me with it on the Day of Resurrection." So it was placed on his chest, and then the shroud was wrapped around them both, and they were buried together.'[566]

## THE COMPANIONS LIT THEIR WAY USING A STAFF GIVEN TO THEM BY THE MESSENGER OF ALLAH ﷺ

Qatāda ibn al-Nu'mān ؓ said: 'I went out one dark night and thought that I might go to the Messenger of Allah ﷺ and keep the night vigil with him and keep him company, so I went.

---

[566] The transmitters of this narration are all reliable.

'When I came to the mosque, the sky erupted in lightning, and the Messenger of Allah ﷺ saw me and said, "O Qatāda, what are you doing?" I said, "My mother and father be your ransom, I wanted to keep you company, O Messenger of Allah." He said, "Take this staff and protect yourself with it, and when you go out it will cast light ten (paces) before you, and ten (paces) behind you." Then he said to me, "When you enter your house, you will see something like a rough stone, so smite it before it speaks, for it is a demon."[567] So I struck it until it fled from my house.'[568]

## THE COMPANIONS SOUGHT BLESSINGS FROM THE SHOES OF THE MESSENGER OF ALLAH ﷺ

Bukhārī and Tirmidhī (in *al-Shamā'il*) narrate that 'Īsā ibn Ṭahrān said: 'Anas ibn Mālik brought out to us a pair of smooth leather shoes with straps. Later, Thābit al-Banānī told me that Anas had told him the shoes had belonged to the Messenger of Allah ﷺ.' So Anas ibn Mālik ؓ kept the shoes of the Messenger of Allah ﷺ for their blessings, and showed them to his guests in order to share with them the honour of these blessings.

'Abdullāh ibn Mas'ūd ؓ used to take care of the shoes, tooth-stick, and pillow of the Messenger of Allah ﷺ. Ḥārith and Ibn Abī 'Umar narrate on the authority of Qāsim ibn 'Abd al-Raḥmān, with a *mursal* chain of transmission,[569] that when the Prophet ﷺ stood up, 'Abdullāh ibn Mas'ūd would put his shoes on for him, and when he ﷺ sat, he would keep them in is

---

[567] Some narrations omit the phrase 'so smite it…'
[568] Narrated by Imām Aḥmad and Ṭabarānī, as mentioned in *Majma' al-Zawā'id*.
[569] See note 381, p.168

arms until he ﷺ stood, whereupon he would place them on his feet for him. The reason Ibn Mas'ūd kept the shoes of the Messenger of Allah ﷺ in his arms when he ﷺ sat was for the honour and blessing of it.

## THE COMPANIONS SOUGHT BLESSINGS FROM THE PLACE ON THE PULPIT WHERE THE MESSENGER OF ALLAH ﷺ SAT

Ibn Sa'd narrated in the first section of his *Ṭabaqāt* that Ibrāhīm ibn 'Abd al-Raḥmān ibn 'Abd, known as al-Qārī, saw 'Abdullāh ibn 'Umar ؓ place his hand on the spot on the pulpit where the Prophet ﷺ sat, and then put the hand to his face.
Ibn Sa'd also narrated that Yazīd ibn 'Abdullāh ibn Qusayṭ said: 'I saw some of the Companions of the Prophet ﷺ, when the mosque (of the Prophet ﷺ) had emptied of people, taking hold of the pommel on the pulpit behind the grave with their right hands, and then facing the Qibla and supplicating.'

Ibn Sa'd mentioned these reports under the heading: 'The Pulpit of the Messenger of Allah ﷺ.'

## THE FOLLOWERS WOULD SEEK BLESSINGS FROM THE HANDS OF THE COMPANIONS THAT HAD TOUCHED THE PROPHET'S ﷺ HAND

Imām Aḥmad narrates in his *Musnad* that Thābit ibn al-Banānī said to Anas ibn Mālik ؓ: 'O Anas, did you touch the hand of the Messenger of Allah ﷺ with your hand?' Anas said yes. Thābit said: 'Let me kiss it then.' So he kissed his hand because it had touched the hand of the Prophet ﷺ.

Imām Aḥmad narrated that 'Abd al-Raḥmān ibn Razīn arrived at Rabdha (near Syria) with his companions on their way to the Ḥajj, whereupon they were informed that Salama ibn al-Akwa', a Companion of the Messenger of Allah ﷺ, was there. 'Abd al-Raḥmān said: 'So we went to him and greeted him, and asked after him, and he said, "I pledged allegiance to the Messenger of Allah ﷺ with this hand of mine," and then he showed us his hand, and it was large. So we all stood and went to him and kissed him hand,' i.e. to seek the blessing of the trace of the Prophet's ﷺ hand. Bukhārī also narrated this incident in *al-Adab al-Mufrad*, with the wording, 'So Salama took out his hands and said, "I pledged allegiance to the Prophet ﷺ with these two hands…" '

Abū Nu'aym narrated in *Ḥilyat al-Awliyā'* that Yūnus ibn Maysara said: 'We went to see Yazīd ibn al-Aswad when he was ill, and while we there the Companion Wāthila ibn al-Asqa' ؓ came in. when he saw him, he stretched out his hand and took hold of Wāthila's hand and touched it to his face and chest, because he had pledged allegiance to the Messenger of Allah ﷺ. Wāthila ibn al-Asqa' said to him, "O Yazīd ibn al-Aswad, what do you think of your Lord?" He replied, "The best." Wāthila said, "Then be of good cheer, for I heard the Messenger of Allah say that Allah Almighty says, 'I am as My servant thinks of Me: if good, then good; and if bad, then bad.' " ' That is, if a servant thinks well of Allah, He will treat him accordingly; and if he thinks bad of Allah, his bad opinion will come right back upon him. O Allah, we ask You to grant that we always think well of You! The Companions ؓ would also treat with reverence the hands with which they had shaken hands with the Messenger of Allah ﷺ: Ṭabarānī narrates on the authority of Ḥakam ibn al-A'raj, that 'Imrān ibn Ḥuṣayn ؓ said: 'I have not touched my private parts with my right hand since I used it to pledge allegiance to the Messenger of Allah ﷺ.'

# THE COMPANIONS' LOVE FOR THE PROPHET ﷺ

Allah ﷻ says: ﴿Say: If your fathers, and your sons, and your brethren, and your wives, and your clan, and the wealth you have amassed, and trade whose failure you fear, and dwellings in which you find contentment, are dearer to you than Allah and His Messenger, and striving in His cause: then wait until Allah brings His matter to hand. Allah guides not iniquitous folk.﴾[570]

So Allah warned His servants of requital, and judged them to be iniquitous, if any of these objects of desire and love were dearer to them than Allah and His Messenger ﷺ, and striving in His cause! Rather, it is incumbent upon them that Allah and His Messenger be more beloved to them than all of that.

The greatest exemplar of those to whom Allah and His Messenger ﷺ were more beloved than anything else, and the clearest manifestation of this overwhelming love for Allah and His Messenger ﷺ was that of the Companions of our Master Muḥammad, as the Commander of the Faithful 'Alī ؓ said when he was asked about the love of the Companions ؓ for the Messenger of Allah ﷺ, answering: 'The Messenger of Allah ﷺ was dearer to us than our possessions and our children, and our mothers and fathers, and dearer to us than cold water to the thirsty man.'

The Companions attained to the standard of the Prophet's ﷺ words: 'None of you believes until I am dearer to him than his father, and his son, and the people entire', and his ﷺ words: 'Three things, he in whom they are present finds the sweetness of faith: that Allah and His Messenger are dearer to him than anything else…'

---

[570] Qur'ān 9:24

They strived to their utmost capabilities out of their faith in him ﷺ and love for him, and they put him before themselves, being just as Allah ﷻ commanded them to be when He said: ﴾And (it is not for them) to prefer their own lives to his life…﴿[571]

Rather they preferred his life to their own, and they loved him ﷺ more than they loved themselves; and the way they behaved proved this without doubt.

**Let us mention some aspects of this:**

## FIRSTLY: THE WAY THEY LOVED HIM ﷺ MORE THAN THEY LOVED THEMSELVES AND PUT HIM ﷺ BEFORE THEMSELVES

One example of this is the story of Zayd ibn al-Dathinna, as narrated by the authors of the prophetic biographies, and by Bayhaqī on the authority of 'Urwa: 'When the idolaters in Mecca took Zayd in al-Dathinna from the Sacred Precinct to Tan'īm in order to kill him (because they would not shed blood in the Sacred Precinct out of respect for it), they met Khubayb, and so he and Zayd exhorted one another to have patience, and to be steadfast in the face of the evils they would soon have to face. 'Abū Sufyān ibn Ḥarb (who was still an idolater at the time) said to Zayd, "By Allah, O Zayd, would you not like for Muḥammad to be here in your place now so that we could strike his neck, if it meant you could be safe at home?" Zayd replied, "By Allah, I would not even like for Muḥammad to remain where he is now and for a thorn to prick him, that I might thereby sit in my home!"

---

[571] Qur'ān 9:120

'Abū Sufyān said, "I have never seen anyone love anyone more than the Companions of Muḥammad love Muḥammad!" ' So Zayd preferred to be killed than for even the slightest harm to afflict the Messenger of Allah ﷺ. Ḥāfiẓ Zurqānī mentioned that another narration of this incident states that they asked Khubayb this question, and he replied: 'By Allah, I would not want the Messenger of Allah to secure my freedom by taking a single thorn in his foot!' There is no contradiction between the two narrations, but rather they asked both Khubayb and Zayd ibn al-Dathinna the same question.

It is narrated in the *Musnad* of Aḥmad, on the authority of Anas ﷺ, that Abū Ṭalḥa stood in front of the Prophet ﷺ at the Battle of Uḥud and shielded him as he fired his arrows. He was a skilled archer, and every time he loosed an arrow the Prophet ﷺ would lift up his face to watch where it landed. And so Abū Ṭalḥa thrust out his chest and said, 'My mother and father be your ransom, O Messenger of Allah, no arrow shall strike you! My neck is worth less than yours!' And he placed himself as a barrier in front of the Messenger of Allah ﷺ, and said, 'I am strong, O Messenger of Allah, so use me as you need, and command me as you will.' Another example of this: Bayhaqī and Ibn Isḥāq narrate, as mentioned in *al-Shifā* and elsewhere, that the father, brother, and husband of a woman of the Helpers were martyred at the Battle of Uḥud with the Messenger of Allah ﷺ. When she was told of this, she said, 'And how fared the Messenger of Allah ﷺ?', meaning to ask whether he had survived, and phrasing it in this way out of etiquette – but it is sometimes written in the annals that she said, 'What has been done to the Messenger of Allah ﷺ?' They said, 'All is well; praise be to Allah, he is as well as you could hope,' that is, he is safe, and has been given succour. She said, 'Show him to me, that I might look upon him.' When she saw him ﷺ, she said, 'Every calamity, after looking upon you, is a mere trifle.'

# SECONDLY: HOW THEY LOVED HIM ﷺ AND YEARNED FOR HIM ﷺ

... And could not bear to be parted from him; and how when they saw him ﷺ they were content, and at peace: Ṭabarānī narrates on the authority of 'Ā'isha ؂, and Ibn Mardawayhi narrates on the authority of Ibn 'Abbās ؂, that a man (it was either Thawbān, or 'Abdullāh ibn Zayd, he of the story of the azan) came to the Prophet ﷺ and said: 'O Messenger of Allah, I swear you are dearer to me than myself, and my family, and my possessions; and I keep thinking of you until I cannot rest unless I come to you.

'And then I thought of my death, and yours, and I realised that when you enter Paradise you will be taken up to the Prophets, and if I enter it I will not see you,' i.e. because you will be in a station that no one but you can hope to reach.

And so Allah ﷻ revealed: ❴And those who obey Allah and the Messenger will be with those whom Allah has blessed: the Prophets, and the veracious believers, and the martyrs, and the righteous; what fine Companions they are!❵[572] And the Prophet ﷺ called him over and read the verse to him.

Ḥāfiẓ Zurqānī said: 'The meaning of this companionship is that they will be able to see them and visit them in Paradise, not that they will share the same rank with them.'

Imām Baghawī narrated that Thawbān, the slave set free by the Messenger of Allah ﷺ, who loved the Prophet ﷺ very much and could not bear to be parted from him, one day met the Prophet ﷺ, who remarked that his face had changed colour.

---

[572] Qur'ān 4:69

Thawbān replied, 'O Messenger of Allah, I am suffering from no illness or ailment; but rather whenever I go without seeing you I miss you so severely until I finally meet you. Then I thought of the Hereafter, and I fear I will not see you there, for you will be taken up to the Prophets; and if I enter Paradise, I shall occupy a station lower than yours (and so see you infrequently), and if I do not enter Paradise I shall never see you again.'

And so the verse was revealed: ﴾And those who obey Allah and the Messenger will be with those whom Allah has blessed…﴿

So the Companions of the Prophet ﷺ were not content or at peace unless they could see him ﷺ, because of their love for him, and their faith in him!

In the same spirit, Imām Aḥmad narrated that Abū Hurayra ؓ said: 'I said, "O Messenger of Allah, when I see you my soul is content, and I am filled with joy; so tell me about everything!" He ﷺ replied, "Everything was created from water," ' i.e. the water of life mentioned in the verse: ﴾And His throne was on the water﴿;[573] and this means the water that contains all the constituents of life, unlike the water we know, which is only one of these constituents.

Abū Hurayra continued: 'So I said, "O Messenger of Allah, tell me of something that if I apply it, I will enter Paradise." He said, "Give abundant greetings of peace, and feed much food, and keep your family ties, and stand in prayer at night while others sleep; and enter Paradise in peace." '

---

[573] Qur'ān 11:7

# THIRDLY: THEIR CONTENTMENT TO BE IN THE COMPANY OF THE MESSENGER OF ALLAH ﷺ

... And their willingness to part with the world, and all the riches in it, if they had that: Bukhārī and Muslim narrate, on the authority of Anas ؓ, that Allah granted to His Messenger many battle-spoils from the tribe of Ḥawāzin, and so when the army stopped at Ji'rāna, the Messenger of Allah ﷺ began to send gifts to certain men of Quraysh of one hundred camels each. When they saw this, some of the Helpers said, 'May Allah forgive the Messenger of Allah ﷺ! He gives to Quraysh, and leaves us out, yet our swords are still wet with their blood!' That is, their swords were wet with the blood of the Qurayshi idolaters after the battle they had fought with them to win them over to Islam. And so the Messenger of Allah ﷺ was told what they were saying, and so he sent for the Helpers and bade them gather in a enclosure under a leather canopy, and called for no one but them to attend.

Once they had all gathered, the Messenger of Allah ﷺ went to them and said, 'What is this I have heard you are saying?' The wise men from amongst them replied, 'As for those of us of good sense, O Messenger of Allah, they say nothing at all; but some of the younger ones among us are saying, "May Allah forgive the Messenger of Allah ﷺ! He gives to Quraysh, and leaves us out, yet our swords are still wet with their blood!"'

So the Messenger of Allah ﷺ said: 'I give to men who are newly shed of their disbelief, that I might reconcile them. Are you not content that the people take with them their wealth, whilst you take the Messenger of Allah ﷺ home (to Medina) with you? By Allah, that which you take home is better than that which they take.' They replied, 'O Messenger of Allah, we are content.'

The Prophet ﷺ said to them, 'Then you shall find great blessing: be patient until you meet Allah and His Messenger, for I shall be at the Pool.'

Another narration, also of Bukhārī and Muslim, has it that the Prophet ﷺ said: 'Quraysh are fresh out of ignorance, and are recently met with defeat, and I wanted to win their hearts and reconcile them. Are you not content that the people take with them the things of this world, while you take the Messenger of Allah ﷺ home with you?' They said, 'Indeed (we are content).' Then he ﷺ said, 'If all the people went down one path, and the Helpers another, I would take the path of the Helpers.'

The narration of Aḥmad in his *Musnad* has it that the Prophet ﷺ said: 'Men of the Helpers, did I not find you lost and Allah guided you, did I not find you destitute and Allah enriched you, did I not find you as enemies to each another and Allah reconciled your hearts?' 'Indeed you did, O Messenger of Allah,' they replied. The Messenger of Allah ﷺ said, 'Will you not respond, O men of the Helpers?' they replied, 'What can we say, O Messenger of Allah, and how can we respond? All the favour was from Allah and His Messenger!'

He ﷺ said, 'By Allah, if you wished you could say – and say true, and be believed: "You came to us an outcast and we took you in, destitute and we enriched you, fearful and we gave you sanctuary." ' They said, 'The truth is with Allah and His Messenger.' So the Messenger of Allah ﷺ said: 'Are you moved in your souls, O men of the Helpers, by the trifles of this world by which I have reconciled the hearts of a people newly entered Islam, whilst I have entrusted you unto the Islam that Allah has apportioned you? Are you not content, O men of the Helpers, that the people take with them their sheep and camels, whilst you take the Messenger of Allah home with you?

'By He in whose hand is my soul, if all the people went one way, and the Helpers another, I would go the way of the Helpers; and were it not for the Emigration, I would be myself a man of the Helpers. O Allah, have mercy on the Helpers, and their children, and on their children's children!' And the people wept until their beards were wet with tears, and they said, 'We are content with Allah as our Lord, and with His Messenger as our share!' And then they went their separate ways.

## FOURTHLY: THEIR ARDENT DESIRE TO ACCOMPANY THE PROPHET ﷺ IN THIS WORLD AND THE NEXT

.. And their request for this at times when their requests would be answered:

Ibn Jarīr narrates, on the authority of Rabī', that the Companions of the Prophet ﷺ said: 'We knew that the Prophet ﷺ would enter a higher station of Paradise than any of those who followed him and believed in him, and so we wondered how it could be possible that they would meet him ﷺ in Paradise and see him. And so Allah Almighty revealed the verse: ﴿And those who obey Allah and the Messenger will be with those whom Allah has blessed…﴾'

This narration of the occasion for the revelation of this verse does not contradict the other accounts we have mentioned, as the one verse may have been revealed on several different occasions, since all of these occasions are of the same nature, namely the question asked by the Companions both collectively and individually about whether they would be united with the Messenger of Allah ﷺ in the Hereafter, so that they could continue to keep his company and never be parted from him.

**Another example of this**: Muslim narrated that Rabīʻa ibn Kaʻb al-Aslamī ﷺ said: 'I used to spend the night at the house of the Messenger of Allah ﷺ and bring him water for ablution and anything else he needed. One time, he said to me, "Ask (for something)." I said, "O Messenger of Allah, I ask for your company in Paradise." He ﷺ replied, "Or (would you like) something else?" I said, "That is all." He ﷺ said, "Then help me for you own sake by making much prostration." '

**Another example of this**: Ibn Abī Shayba narrated, on the authority of Abū 'Ubayda, that 'Abdullāh ibn Masʻūd ﷺ was asked: 'What was the supplication you made on the night when the Messenger of Allah ﷺ said, "Ask, and you shall be given"?' He replied, 'I said: "O Allah, I ask You for faith that never wavers, and joys that never cease, and the company of Your Prophet ﷺ in the highest station of Paradise, the Garden of Immortality[574]." '

Abū Nuʻaym narrated, on the authority of Abū 'Ubayda, on the authority of his father, that 'Abdullāh ibn Masʻūd said: 'When I was praying one night, the Prophet ﷺ came along accompanied by Abū Bakr and 'Umar ﷺ. The Prophet ﷺ said to me, "Ask, and you shall be given." ' 'Umar ﷺ later said, 'So I went to him (Ibn Masʻūd) and said, "What did you pray for?" He said, "I have a prayer that I almost never fail to make: O Allah, I ask You for faith that never fades, and joy that never ceases, and contentment that is never disturbed, and the company of Your Prophet Muḥammad ﷺ in the highest of the Gardens, the Garden of Immortality." '

And when Bilāl ﷺ was close to passing, his wife called out, 'O, what sorrow!' He said, to her, 'O, what rapture! Tomorrow I shall meet the beloved: Muḥammad and his Companions!'

---

[574] *Jannat al-Khuld.*

# FIFTHLY: THE TEARS SHED BY THE COMPANIONS ﷺ OVER THE PAIN OF BEING SEPARATED FROM HIM ﷺ

... And how they wept when they remembered the gatherings they had attended with him ﷺ; and how they wept when they thought of him ﷺ and the times when the Revelation was coming to him, and the treasures and illuminations that reflected upon them from him ﷺ; and how they wept when they remembered the pledges they had made to him ﷺ; and their intense weeping upon his ﷺ passing; and how they wept when visiting his ﷺ blessed grave – and all of this showed the extent of their deep love for the Prophet ﷺ.

**We shall mention a few concise examples of this:**

**1 – How they wept for the pain of being parted from him ﷺ:** It is narrated that when the Messenger of Allah ﷺ sent Mu'ādh ibn Jabal ﷺ to Yemen, he ﷺ came out with him to give him counsel as he set off, walking in the shade of his horse. Once he ﷺ had finished his counsel, he said, 'O Mu'ādh, you might not meet me again after this year, and you might return and come to my mosque and find there my grave.'

Mu'ādh wept for his sadness at being parted from the Messenger of Allah ﷺ. Then the Prophet ﷺ turned, and faced Medina, and said, 'The people who have the best claim to me are the pious, whoever they are, and wherever they are.'[575]

---

[575] Zurqānī said: 'It was narrated by Aḥmad and Abū Ya'lā, and its transmitters are reliable.' Haythamī said, 'It was narrated by Aḥmad with two chains of transmission, whose transmitters are rigorously authenticated, except for Rāshid ibn Sa'd and 'Āṣim ibn Ḥamīd, who are both reliable.'

**2 – How they wept when they remembered the gatherings they had attended with him** ﷺ: Bukhārī narrates that Anas ؓ said: 'Abū Bakr and 'Abbās passed by a gathering of the Helpers and saw that they were weeping.[576] One of the two[577] asked, "Why do you weep?" They replied, "We remembered a gathering the Prophet ﷺ attended with us." So one of the two went to the Prophet ﷺ and told him about this. And so the Prophet ﷺ came out, with a cloth wrapped around his head, and ascended the pulpit – and he never ascended the pulpit again after that day. He praised Allah and extolled Him, and then said: "I bid you all take care of the Helpers, for they are my trustees and my inner circle,[578] and they have discharged their responsibilities, and await their reward; so accept their good, and forgive their ill."'

**3 – How they wept when they thought of him ﷺ, and the time when the Revelation was coming to him** ﷺ: Imām Muslim narrated, on the authority of Anas ؓ, that Abū Bakr said to 'Umar ؓ after the Prophet's ﷺ passing, 'come with us to visit Umm Ayman ؓ, just as the Messenger of Allah ﷺ used to visit her.' So they went to her, and when they arrived she began to weep. 'Why do you weep?' they asked, 'do you not know that which is with Allah is better for the Messenger of Allah ﷺ?'

She replied, 'Indeed I know that which is with Allah Almighty is better for the Messenger of Allah ﷺ, but I weep for the end of Revelation from Heaven.' And what she said moved them, and they too began to weep. That is, they wept for their memories of the Messenger of Allah ﷺ, and the Revelation that visited him, and the constant blessing of those treasures and illuminations.

---

[576] This was at the time of the Prophet's ﷺ final illness.
[577] I.e. either Abū Bakr or 'Abbās ؓ.
[578] Literally 'they are my stomach and my linen-basket'.

Ibn Sa'd narrated, on the authority of 'Āṣim ibn Muḥammad, that his father Muḥammad said, 'I never heard Ibn 'Umar mention the Messenger of Allah ﷺ save that his eyes would begin to shed tears.' Ibn Sa'd also narrated that Anas ؓ said: 'Not a night goes by wherein I do not see my beloved ﷺ', and then he wept.

Another example of this: Ibn 'Asākir narrated, with a good chain of narration as stated by Ḥāfiẓ Zurqānī, that whilst Bilāl ؓ was encamped in Dariyyā (near Syria) he had a vision of the Prophet ﷺ (after his ﷺ passing) saying to him: 'Why this harshness, O Bilāl? Is it not time that you visited me?' So Bilāl woke up in a state of sorrow and distress, and mounted his horse and went straight to Medina and approached the grave of the Prophet ﷺ, and began to weep and press his face to it. Ḥasan and Ḥusayn ؓ then came along, and Bilāl began to hug them and kiss them. They said to him, 'We would be happy to hear you make the call to prayer you used to make for the Messenger of Allah ﷺ in the mosque.' So he climbed to the roof of the mosque and stood in the place he used to stand, and called: *Allāhu Akbar Allāhu Akbar*, and the people of the city let out a cry. When he called *Ashhadu an lā ilāha illa Allāh*, they were further stirred, and when he said *Ashhadu anna Muḥammad Rasūl Allah*, the women began to come out of their chambers, saying 'Has the Messenger of Allah been sent back to us?' And never was there seen a day in Medina more filled with weeping, after his ﷺ time, than on that day. This was because they were reminded of the Messenger of Allah ﷺ when they heard the call of his ﷺ muezzin.

Ibn 'Asākir also narrated, on the authority of Zayd ibn Aslam, that 'Umar ibn al-Khaṭṭāb went out one night to keep watch, and saw a house with its lamp lit, and so approached it. He found there an elderly woman spinning thread and saying:

*Benedictions of the righteous be upon Muḥammad,*
*The pure and the chosen ones pray for you.*
*You stood in prayer in the watches of the night.*
*All my hopes and wishes are one:*
*May the Hereafter unite me with my beloved.*

So 'Umar sat down and wept, and continued to weep until he could not keep from knocking on the door. The woman said, 'Who is it?' He answered, 'It is 'Umar ibn al-Khaṭṭāb.' She said, 'What have I got to do with 'Umar? What brings 'Umar here at this hour?' He said, 'Open, may Allah have mercy on you, you have no cause to worry.' So she opened the door and he went in, and said to her, 'Repeat for me the words you said earlier.' She repeated them, and when she finished he said, 'I ask of you to include me with the two of you (in the prayer)', so she added:

*And 'Umar as well: forgive him, O Forgiver!*

And so 'Umar was pleased, and left her.[579] This was also the way with the best of the second generation, and those who came after them ﷺ: Muṣ'ab ibn 'Abdullāh said: 'When Imām Mālik mentioned the Prophet ﷺ, his colour would change, until those with him found it difficult to bear. He was asked about this once, and replied: "Had you seen what I have seen, you would not find fault with me for what you see now! I have seen Muḥammad ibn al-Munkadir, the leader of the reciters of Qur'ān, in such a state that we had barely asked him about a Ḥadīth before he would weep so much that we felt pity for him! And Sayyid Ja'far al-Ṣādiq ibn Sayyid Muḥammad al-Bāqir used to smile much, but if the Prophet ﷺ was mentioned to him his skin would become pale in awe and respect! And I never saw Ja'far al-Ṣādiq relate the sayings of the Messenger of Allah ﷺ unless he was in a state of ritual purity. And I went to see him

[579] *Al-Mawāhib.*

many times, and found him either praying, or in silent meditation, or reciting Qur'ān; and he was one of the true worshippers, who feared Allah Almighty. And I used to visit 'Āmir ibn 'Abdullāh ibn al-Zubayr, and when the Prophet ﷺ was mentioned before him he would weep until there were no more tears left in his eyes. And Zuhrī was the most light-hearted of people, but when he mentioned the Prophet ﷺ, it was like you did not know him, and he did not know you (because of his respect and awe for the Prophet ﷺ). And when Qatāda, the exegete, had a Ḥadīth read to him, he would weep and tremble because of the overwhelming love and awe he felt."
' All of this was mentioned by Qāḍī 'Iyāḍ in his *Shifā*, and by Qasṭalānī in *al-Mawāhib*. And when 'Abd al-Raḥmān ibn al-Qāsim mentioned the Prophet ﷺ, his colour would change so he looked as though his blood had been drained from him, and his tongue would dry up in his mouth.

**4 – How they wept when they remembered the pledges they had made to him** ﷺ: Yaḥyā ibn Ja'da reported that some of the Companions of the Messenger of Allah ﷺ visited Khabbāb and said to him, 'Be of good cheer, Abū 'Abdullāh, for you shall meet Muḥammad ﷺ at the Pool!' 'How could this be?' he said, and pointed to the ceiling of the house and the floor – and there were a few luxury items and pillows in the room – 'when the Messenger of Allah ﷺ said: "Every one of you should be sufficed by a traveller's provision." ' So he wept out of fear that he had enjoyed more of the pleasures of this world than a traveller would pack for his provisions, contrary to the pledge Messenger of Allah ﷺ had asked of them.[580]

'Āmir ibn 'Abdullāh related that when death approached Salmān al-Khayr ؓ, they noticed that he was trembling. They

---

[580] Ḥāfiẓ Mundhirī said: 'It was narrated by Abū Ya'lā and Ṭabarānī with a good chain of transmission.'

said, 'What makes you tremble so, O Abū 'Abdullāh, when you have done such good in your life? You fought for the Messenger of Allah ﷺ in many virtuous battles, and many great conquests!' He replied, 'I tremble because when our Beloved ﷺ departed us, he counselled us thus: "Each one of you should be sufficed by a traveller's provision." And this is what makes me tremble." So they counted Salmān's wealth, and found it amounted to fifteen dirhams.'[581] So Salmān feared that he had gone against the counsel of his Beloved ﷺ by having more money in his possession than a traveller would take with him on a journey.

**5 – The intense weeping of the Companions when our Master Muḥammad the Messenger of Allah ﷺ passed away**: It is mentioned in *al-Mawāhib* that Ibn Mandah and Ibn 'Asākir (and the wording here is his) narrated that Abū Dhu'ayb al-Hudhalī said: 'Word reached us that the Prophet ﷺ was ill, and so the whole neighbourhood was stricken with fearful concern for him ﷺ. I spent a long restless night, only sleeping a little while before dawn, whereupon I heard a voice say to me:

*A grave misfortune has visited Islam*
*Between the date palms and the dwellings:*
*The Prophet Muḥammad is taken, and our hearts*
*Are flowing with floods of tears for him.*

'I woke up in a state of shock, and I knew that the Prophet ﷺ had passed away; so I set off for Medina, and found the people there weeping with a clamour like that of the pilgrims when they greet the House. I said, "What is this?" They answered, "The Messenger of Allah ﷺ has passed away!" '

---

[581] Narrated by Ibn Ḥibbān in his *Ṣaḥīḥ*, as mentioned in *al-Targhīb.*

Qasṭalānī said: 'His ﷺ passing was on a Monday, and there is no difference of opinion about this, at the same time of day as he had entered Medina when he emigrated, in the heat of midmorning. He ﷺ was buried on Tuesday; some say it was the night before Wednesday,[582] others that it was on Wednesday.'

Madīnī said in *Laṭā'if al-Ma'ārif*: 'His ﷺ passing was on a Monday in the month of *Rabī' al-Awwal*, and there is no difference of opinion about this. The scholars differ as to what exact day of the month this was. It is said that his ﷺ passing was on the first day of the month, or the second, or the twelfth, or the thirteenth, or the fifteenth. The prevalent opinion is that it was the twelfth of *Rabī' al-Awwal*.' Ibn Isḥāq and others narrate that the Prophet's ﷺ passing way on the twelfth of *Rabī' al-Awwal*, and this is the majority opinion.

Wāqidī narrated that Umm Salama said: 'We were gathered together weeping for the passing of the Messenger of Allah ﷺ, and we did not sleep. The Messenger of Allah ﷺ was still in our house, and we sought comfort by looking at him lying on the bed. As dawn broke, we heard the sound of shovels. Upon this, we let out a cry, as did all of Medina, and the whole city let out a single tremulous cry. Bilāl called for the dawn prayer, and when he mentioned the Prophet ﷺ he wept and sobbed, and our sorrow deepened, and the people all tried to get in (to where he ﷺ was buried), but the doors were closed on them.' (That is, they were not allowed to disturb the blessed grave while the burial was still taking place.) 'What a misfortune it was! No misfortune was there after it save that it became trivial in our eyes once we remembered losing him ﷺ.'[583] There is no doubt that the misfortune of his ﷺ passing was the gravest of all misfortunes.

---

582 I.e. Tuesday night [t]

583 Ibn Sa'd also mentions some of this story in his *Ṭabaqāt*.

Mālik narrated in his *Muwaṭṭa'* that the Prophet ﷺ said: 'Let the Muslims be consoled in their times of loss by (remembering) my loss.' Ibn Mājah narrated, on the authority of 'Ā'isha, that the Prophet ﷺ said during his final illness: 'O people, when any of the believers suffer a loss, let them be consoled by (remembering) my loss rather than the loss of any other; for none of my community shall ever suffer a loss more grievous than my loss.' Mālik narrated that Ibn 'Umar said: 'The people wept for the Messenger of Allah ﷺ when he died, and said, "By Allah, we wish we had died before him, and we fear we shall be subject to trials after him!"'[584]

Ṭabarānī narrated, on the authority of 'Ā'isha, that Ṣafiyya bint 'Abd al-Muṭṭalib composed this eulogy for the Messenger of Allah ﷺ:

*O Messenger of Allah, you were our only wish,*
*And you were kind to us, and never harsh;*
*And you were merciful, a guide and a teacher;*
*Let any who would weep today, weep for you!*
*Upon my soul, I do not weep for the Prophet's death,*
*But I weep for the trials that shall come thereafter.*
*For the loss of Muḥammad, and for the love of him,*
*My heart feels as though it is burned and branded.*
*May Allah, the Lord of Muhammad, send blessings*
*Upon a grave newly settled in Yathrib.*
*I see here Ḥasan, whom you have left orphaned,*
*Crying and calling for his grandfather to come.*
*For you, Allah's Messenger, I would gladly ransom*
*My mother, aunts, uncles, my self and all I have!*
*You were steadfast always, you delivered the Message,*
*You died strong in faith, and pure as daybreak.*
*If only the Lord had kept you here among us*

---

[584] See *al-Bidāya.*

> We would rejoice; but His will was resolved.
> Upon you from Allah be peace, and good greetings,
> And may you enter the Gardens of Paradise joyfully![585]

### 6 – The tears shed by the Companions at the grave of the Prophet ﷺ, as they remembered his teachings and counsels:

Zayd ibn Aslam related that his father told him that 'Umar ؓ went to the mosque and found Mu'ādh weeping at the grave of the Prophet ﷺ. 'Umar asked him why he wept, and he replied, 'I heard a Ḥadīth of the Prophet ﷺ in which he said, "The slightest amount of ostentation (in worship) is idolatry, and whosoever shows enmity to the Friends of Allah has thereby declared war on Allah. Allah loves those who are inconspicuous, righteous, and pious: those whom if they are absent are not missed, and if they are present are not noticed. Their hearts are beacons of guidance. They endure all manner of difficult hardships." '[586]

Bayhaqī narrated that Ibn Abī Fudayk said: 'I heard some of the scholars whom I knew say that if someone stands at the grave of the Prophet ﷺ and recites the verse ❮Verily, Allah and His Angels send blessings on the Prophet. O you who believe, invoke blessings upon him, and give him greetings of Peace❯[587] and then says, "May Allah bless you, O Messenger of Allah" seventy times, an Angel will call to him: "May Allah bless you," mentioning him by name; and no need of his will go unfulfilled, nor any prayer unanswered, by virtue of the exalted status of the Beloved ﷺ with Allah, the Near, the Responsive.'

---

[585] Ḥāfiẓ Haythamī said: 'It was narrated by Ṭabarānī with a sound chain of transmission.' See also *al-Mawāhib* and its commentaries.

[586] Mundhirī said: 'It was narrated by Ibn Mājah, Ḥākim and Bayhaqī in *al-Zuhd*; Ḥākim declared it to be rigorously authentic, with no flaws in its chain of transmission.' (*al-Targhīb wa al-Tarhīb*)

[587] Qur'ān 33:56

# THE SECRETS, ILLUMINATIONS, BLESSINGS AND TREASURES THAT EMANATE FROM THE BLESSED GRAVE OF THE PROPHET ﷺ

In the section of his *Sunan* collection entitled *The Blessings Allah Bestowed on His Prophet ﷺ after His Death*, Imām Dārimī narrates that Abū al-Jawzā' Aws ibn 'Abdullāh said: 'The people of Medina suffered a dreadful drought, and so they complained of it to 'Ā'isha, who said: "Go to the grave of the Prophet ﷺ and open above it a window to the heavens so that there is no ceiling between it and the sky." They did as she said, and immediately we were given abundant rain, so that grass grew, and the camels so became fat that their skin split because of the fat, and thereafter the year was know as 'the Year of the Splitting.'

Another example of this was when the call to prayer was heard from the blessed grave of the Prophet ﷺ: Dārimī also narrated, in the same chapter, that Sa'īd ibn 'Abd al-'Azīz said: 'During the events of Ḥarra,[588] the call to prayer was not sounded in the mosque of the Prophet ﷺ for three days, nor was the *iqāma*. Sa'īd ibn al-Musayyib did not leave the mosque throughout that time, and he would only know the time of the prayer had come in by a humming sound he heard from the Prophet's ﷺ grave.'

Ibn al-Najjār also narrated it with the wording: 'The call to prayer was not sounded during the events of Ḥarra for three days, and all the people went out save for Sa'īd ibn al-Musayyib, who remained in the mosque. Sa'īd said: "When the time for the midday prayer came in, I heard the azan issuing from the grave, and so I offered two cycles of prayer; then I heard the *iqāma*, and so I offered the midday prayer.

---

[588] When Medina was attacked by Yazīd ibn Mu'āwiya. [t]

' "The *adhān* and *iqāma* continued to be sounded from the holy grave for every prayer until the three nights (of the events of Ḥarra) had passed." ' Allah granted Sa'īd ibn al-Musayyib a great honour by allowing him to hear this, and to take comfort from it.

Bayhaqī, Abū Ya'lā, Bazzār, and Ibn 'Udayy narrated (and Bayhaqī declared it to be rigorously authentic), on the authority of Anas ﷺ, that the Prophet ﷺ said: 'The Prophets are alive in their graves, praying.' This is further affirmed by the narration of Muslim (in his *Ṣaḥīḥ*) and Nasā'ī, on the authority of Anas ﷺ, that the Prophet said: 'On the night I was taken up, I came to Mūsā and found him praying in his grave by the red sand hill.'

**The Angels touch the blessed grave of the Prophet ﷺ for the blessing and honour of it**: Dārimī also narrated that Ka'b (al-Aḥbār) went to visit Ā'isha, and they spoke of the Messenger of Allah ﷺ. Ka'b said, 'Not a day goes by save that seventy thousand Angels descend and gather round the grave of the Prophet ﷺ to touch it with their wings.' The narration of Ibn al-Najjār and others has it: 'They touch the grave of the Prophet ﷺ (that is, they touch the noble grave with their wings for the blessing and honour of it) and send blessings upon the Messenger of Allah ﷺ, and when afternoon comes they ascend, and an equal number descend; and this will continue until the earth is rent asunder, whereupon he ﷺ will come out with seventy thousand Angels to bear him.'(Another narration of Dārimī has this last: '... to honour him.')[589] Ḥāfiẓ Zurqānī said: 'That is, they will magnify him ﷺ and extol his honour. It may be that Ka'b knew this from the previous scriptures, since he had been a rabbi.'

---

[589] It was also narrated by Ibn al-Najjār, Ibn Abī Dunyā, Abū al-Shaykh, and Qurṭubī in *al-Tadhkira*, as mentioned in *al-Mawāhib*.

# EPILOGUE

The compilation and writing of this book was completed on Monday, the 10th of *Rajab*, 1394 AH. It will, Allah willing, be followed by a book entitled *Our Master Muḥammad ﷺ: His Miracles and the Signs of His Prophethood.*

We ask Allah ﷻ to grant us health and success, and to bless our life and our works, and to make them all sincerely devoted to Him.

I also ask Allah ﷻ to accept from me my work, and to forgive my shortcomings in the authorship of this book regarding the Messenger of Allah ﷺ, and to excuse my sins and mistakes; for although my offering is slight, His mercy is ever to be hoped for.

And I ask Allah ﷻ, by the grace of His Noble Messenger ﷺ, to raise the rank of my father, and my master, and my spiritual guide, the great Shaykh, Teacher, Gnostic, Scholar of Ḥadīth and Exegete of Qur'ān, Muḥammad ibn Najīb Sirājuddīn رحمه الله to the highest ranks of the blessed saints, and to reward him on my behalf with the best reward, and to shower His unending blessings upon him, and upon us, and upon our brethren and loved ones, and the Muslims entire.

May the benedictions and salutations of Allah be upon our Master Muḥammad, the Leader of the Prophets and Messengers, and upon his noble Household and Companions, and all who follow them until Judgement Day; every time those of remembrance remember him, and every time those of forgetfulness forget him.

PRAISE BE TO ALLAH, LORD OF THE WORLDS

# BIBLIOGRAPHY


* Ālūsī, *Tafsīr Rūḥ al-Ma'ānī*
* Aḥmad b. Ḥanbal, *Musnad*
* Badruddīn al-'Aynī, *'Umdat al-Qārī*
* Ibn Athīr, *al-Nihāya fī Gharīb al-Ḥadīth*
* Ibn 'Allān, *Sharḥ Riyāḍ al-Ṣāliḥīn*
* Ibn 'Allān, *Sharḥ al-Adhkār*
* Abū Bakr b. al-'Arabī, *Tuḥfat al-Aḥwadhī*
* Abū Bakr b. al-'Arabī, *Aḥkām al-Qur'ān*
* 'Aẓīmabādī, *'Awn al-Ma'būd*
* Baghawī, *Sharḥ al-Sunna*
* Zubayr b. Bakkār, *Akhbār al-Madīna*
* Ibn 'Abd al-Barr, *al-Tamhīd*
* Bayhaqī, *al-Dalā'il*
* Bayhaqī, *al-Madkhal*
* Bayhaqī, *Shu'ab al-Īmān*
* Bayjūrī, *Hāshiyat 'alā al-Shamā'il*
* Bazzār, *Musnad*
* Bukhārī, *Adab al-Mufrad*
* Bukhārī, *Ṣaḥīḥ*
* 'Abd al-'Azīz al-Dabbāgh, *al-Ibrīz*
* Dāraquṭnī, *Sunan*
* Abū Dawūd, *Sunan*
* Abū Dawūd, *Marāsil*
* Ḍiyā', *al-Mukhtāra*
* Dhahabī, *Tārīkh al-Islām*
* Dhahabī, *Siyar*
* Haythamī, *Majma' al-Zawā'id*
* Ibn Hishām, *Sīrat Ibn Hishām*
* Ibn Humām, *al-Taqrīr wa al-Taḥbīr 'alā Taḥrīr al-Kamāl*
* Ibn Ḥajar al-'Asqalānī, *Fatḥ al-Bārī*
* Ibn Ḥajar al-'Asqalānī, *al-Iṣāba*
* Ibn Ḥajar al-'Asqalānī, *al-Maṭālib al-'Āliya*

* Ibn Ḥajar al-'Asqalānī *Nuzhat al-Naẓr*
* Ḥākim, *al-Mustadrak*
* Ḥākim, *'Ulūm*
* Ḥalīmī, *al-Shu'ab al-Īmān*
* Ibn Ḥibbān, *Ṣaḥīḥ*
* Ibn Ḥishām, *Sīrah*
* Ibn Isḥāq in *al-Maghāzī*
* Ibn Isḥāq, *al-Mubtada'*
* Ibn Isḥāq, *Sīrah*
* 'Irāqī, *al-Amālī*
* Abū al-Khayr b. al-Jazarī, *al-Ḥiṣn al-Ḥāṣin*
* Abū al-Khayr b. al-Jazarī, *'Urf al-Ta'rīf bi-Mawlid al-Sharīf*
* Qāḍī 'Iyāḍ, *Tartīb al-Madārik*
* Qāḍī 'Iyāḍ, *al-Shifā*
* Muḥammad b. Qāsim Jāsūs, *Sharḥ al-Shamā'il*
* Sibt Ibn al-Jawzī, *Mir'at al-Zamān*
* Ibn al-Jawzī, *al-Wafā'*
* Ibn Kathīr, *al-Bidāya wal-Nihāya (Tarīkh Ibn Kathīr)*
* Kattānī, *al-Tarātīb al-Idāriyya*
* Khafājī, *Sharḥ al-Shifā*
* Khaṭṭābī, *Ma'ālim al-Sunan*
* Khaṭṭābī, *al-'Uzla*
* Ibn Khuzayma, *Ṣaḥīḥ*
* Madīnī, *Laṭā'if al-Ma'ārif*
* Ibn Mājah, *Sunan*
* Ibn Mālik, *Alfiyya Ibn Mālik*
* Mālik b. Anas, *al-Muwaṭṭa'*
* Sa'īd ibn Manṣūr, *Sunan*
* Maṭrazī, *Sharḥ al-Maṣābīḥ*
* Mubārakpūrī, *Tuḥfat al-Aḥwadhī*
* Munāwī, *Fayḍ al-Qadīr*
* Munāwī, *Sharḥ Shamā'il al-Tirmidhī*
* Munāwī, *al-Taysīr*
* Mundhirī, *al-Targhīb wal-Tarhīb*
* Muslim, *Ṣaḥīḥ*

* Nasā'i, *Sunan*
* Nawawī, *al-Adhkār*
* Nawawī, *Riyāḍ al-Ṣāliḥīn*
* Nawawī, *Sharḥ Ṣaḥīḥ Muslim*
* Abū Nu'aym, *al-Ḥilya*
* Abū Nu'aym, *al-Riyāḍa*
* Ṣiddīq Ḥasan Khān,*Nuzul al-Abrār*
* Ibn Qāni', *Mu'jam al-Ṣaḥāba*
* 'Alī al-Qārī, *Jam' al-Wasā'il*
* 'Ali al-Qārī, *al-Mirqāt Sharḥ al-Mishkāt*
* 'Alī al-Qārī, *Sharḥ al-Shamā'il*
* Qasṭalānī said in *Irshād al-Sārī*
* Qasṭalānī, *al-Mawāhib*
* Qurṭubī, *al-Tadhkira*
* Ibn Rajab, *Jāmi' al-'Ulūm wal-Ḥikām*
* Ibn al-Sakan, *Saḥīḥ*
* Sakhāwī, *al-Maqāṣid al-Ḥasana*
* Taqī al-Dīn al-Subkī, *al-Sayf al-Maslūl*
* Suhaylī, *al-Rawḍ al-Unuf*
* Suyūṭī, *al-Jāmi ' al-Ṣaghīr*
* Shawkānī, *Tuḥfat al-Dhākirīn*
* Ṣāwī, *Ḥāshiyat Tafsīr al-Jalālayn*
* Ibn Abī Shayba, *al-Muṣannaf*
* Tirmidhī, *Shamā'il*
* Tirmidhī, *Sunan*
* Ṭabarānī, *Mu'jam al-Awṣaṭ*
* Ṭayālisī, *Musnad*
* Ṭībī, *Sharḥ al-Mishkāt al-Masābīḥ*
* Abū Ya'lā, *Ṣaḥīḥ*
* Ibn Udayy, *al-Kāmil*
* Zurqānī, *Sharḥ al-Mawāhib*

# ABOUT THE AUTHOR

THE Syrian city of Aleppo – also known as 'the city of scholars' – is considered by many to be the cradle of traditional Islamic scholarship. One of the greatest scholars it has ever produced was the Friend of Allāh ﷻ, Imām 'Abdallāh b. Muḥammad Najīb Sirājuddīn al-Ḥusaynī al-Ḥalabī ﵀, an extraordinary saint who dedicated his entire life to the service of Islām. His qualities were many and his skills outstanding. Imām 'Abdallāh was a renowned spiritual master, an expert in jurisprudence, a Ḥāfiẓ and scholar of Ḥadīth as well as a brilliant exegete of the Qur'ān. He was most famous, however, for his immense and intense love for our Master Muḥammad ﷺ, the Messenger of Allah.

A descendant of the Prophet's ﷺ grandson, our Master Ḥusayn b. 'Alī b. Abī Ṭālib ﵁ on his father's side, Imām 'Abdallāh was born into an honorable and pious family on the verge of the collapse of the Ottoman Sultanate in 1923 CE. During his childhood, Imām 'Abdallāh was surrounded by the love and care of his father, the esteemed Shaykh Muḥammad Najīb Sirājuddīn al-Ḥusaynī ﵀ who was himself a spiritual master and a leading jurist, exegete of the Qur'ān and scholar of Ḥadīth. Imām 'Abdallāh began his pursuit of knowledge at an early age and memorized the Qur'ān when only thirteen years old under the guidance of his father. At that time, he was studying Ḥadīth at the Islamic school of al-Khasrawiyya. There he studied under leading scholars of the time such as the great jurist Imām

Muḥammad Ibrāhīm al-Salqīnī, the Saintly Sūfī Shaykh 'Isā al-Bayanūnī, Shaykh 'Umar Mas'ūd al-Ḥarīrī, Shaykh Fayḍallāh al-Ayyūbī al-Kurdī, Shaykh Aḥmad al-Shammā' and several other prominent scholars. Imām 'Abdallāh also frequented other scholars who did not teach at his school, such as the jurist Shaykh Aḥmad al-Kurdī and Shaykh Muḥammad Sa'īd al-Idlībī. As he remained in their proximity, the great scholar of Ḥadīth and leading historian of Aleppo Shaykh Muḥammad Rāghib al-Tabbākh noticed his intelligence and intense devotion to the pursuit of knowledge and he decided to become his mentor. He continued his studies under the supervision of his father, Shaykh Muḥammad Najīb Sirājuddīn who always attracted large crowds to his lessons. In this environment Imām 'Abdallāh was given the opportunity to further develop his skills and increase his knowledge and his fame as a scholar soon spread throughout Aleppo. He began teaching Islām in various mosques, such as the Ḥamawī mosque where he tutored one hour in the morning, four times a week. Soon he was asked to teach at various colleges including the Sha'bāniyya school. He also taught many courses and lessons in various mosques including his own where he continued to impart knowledge upon the masses even when the funds that provided his payment were stopped.

Then came one year in which his father's age prevented him from continuing his classes. Imām 'Abdallāh, still only twenty-two years old, carried the heavy load of succeeding his father as a scholar. The demands of the public and the high level of his father's classes made this a great test for him, but by the Grace of Allāh he succeeded in it, and honouring this responsibility caused the admiration of the public for him. Following the vacuum caused by the closing of the Sha'bāniyya Islamic school, Imām 'Abdallāh felt the need to found a large Islamic school in Aleppo that would take charge of training future scholars and preachers.

He decided to revive religious teaching by founding the School of Islamic Teachings in 1958 CE. Its program combined legal courses, Islamic spirituality, the life and qualities of the Messenger of Allāh ﷺ as well as the sciences of Ḥadīth. In addition, he founded a Qur'ānic school whose mission it was to teach its students the Majestic Qur'ān. Generous scholarships were granted to the pupils in order to encourage the preservation of this knowledge.

Imām 'Abdallāh was known to be generous and helpful towards the poor, lenient towards the pupils of his school, and famed for his humility and devotion. As Imām 'Abdallāh became the leading scholar of Aleppo, he conveyed in his classes the quintessence of Islamic legislation and spirituality. In a moving voice, he often spoke of love towards the Messenger of Allāh ﷺ and the duty to follow his excellent manners. He promoted love for the Sunnah and revived it in his behaviour and exhortations. Shaykh Dr. Nūruddīn 'Itr mentions that he was "*extremely scrupulous and avoided any doubtful thing.*"

Imām 'Abdallāh was truly in love with the Messenger of Allāh ﷺ. He did not cease pointing out his qualities, his ethics and the nobility of his status in nearness of Allāh ﷻ, and did not accept anyone to be given the importance of our Master Muḥammad ﷺ. In light of this incredible love Shaykh 'Abd al-Raḥmān al-Shāghūrī ؓ once called him, "*the Pole of Prophetic love of our times.*"

Imām 'Abdallāh wrote nearly thirty books dealing with Islamic spirituality, creed, ethics and the noble manners of the Messenger of Allāh ﷺ, the sciences of Ḥadīth and Tafsīr of the Qur'ān. Perhaps his most famous work, however, was the book of which we have the translation before us today, *Our Master Muḥammad the Messenger of Allah* ﷺ.

Imām ‘Abdallāh’s students were numerous, many of them becoming prominent scholars themselves such as his son Shaykh Dr. Aḥmad Sirājuddīn, his nephew and son-in-law Shaykh Dr. Nuruddīn ‘Itr, Shaykh Dr. Sāmir al-Nass, Shaykh Muḥammad ‘Awwāmah and Shaykh Muḥammad al-Nīnowy, may Allah preserve them.

Following a surgical operation carried out toward the end of his life, the health of Imām ‘Abdallāh deteriorated. On the 4th of March 2002 CE (1422 H) he returned to his Lord. The news of his passing was announced throughout the Muslim world and covered it with a veil of sorrow. Imām ‘Abdallāh b. Muḥammad Najīb Sirājuddīn al-Ḥusayni al-Ḥalabi was buried in the Sha‘bāniyya complex, next to the graves of its Ottoman founders. May Allah sanctify the noble Imām’s secret.

# AUTHOR'S BIBLIOGRAPHY

* Ḥawla Tafsīr Sūrat al-Fātiḥa
* Ḥawla Tafsīr Sūrat al-Ḥujurāt
* Ḥawla Tafsīr Sūrat Qāf
* Ḥawla Tafsīr Sūrat al-Mulk
* Ḥawla Tafsīr Sūrat al-Insān
* Ḥawla Tafsīr Sūrat al-ʻAlaq
* Ḥawla Tafsīr Sūrat al-Kawthar
* Ḥawla Tafsīr Sūrat al-Ikhlāṣ
* Hadī al-Qur'ān al-Karīm ilā Ḥujjat al-Burhān
* Hadī al-Qur'ān ilā Maʻrifat al-ʻUlūm wal-Tafakkur
* Tilāwat al-Qur'ān al-Majīd
* Shahādah Lā Ilāha Illā Allāh, Muḥammad Rasūl Allāh ﷺ
* **Sayyidunā Muḥammad Rasūl Allāh** ﷺ
* Al-Hadī al-Nabawī wal-Irshādāt al-Muḥammadiyya ﷺ
* Al-Taqarrub ilā Allāh Taʻālā
* Al-Ṣalāt fīl Islām
* Al-Ṣalāt ʻalā al-Nabī ﷺ
* Ṣuʻūd al-Aqwāl wa-Rafʻ al-ʻAmāl
* Al-Duʻā'
* Tarjamat al-Shaykh Muḥammad Najīb Sirājuddīn al-Ḥusaynī
* Al-Īmān bi- ʻAwālim al-Ukhrā wa-Mawāqifuhā
* Al-Īmān bil Malā'ika
* Al-Adʻiyya wal-Adhkār al-Wārida
* Sharḥ al-Manẓūmat al-Bayqūniyya fī Muṣṭalaḥ al-Ḥadīth
* Adaʻiyyat al-Ṣabāḥ wal-Masā'
* Manāsik al-Ḥajj wal-ʻUmra
* Al-Ṣiyām
* Mawāqif Sayyidinā Muḥammad Rasūl Allāh ﷺ maʻa al-ʻĀlam
* Durūs Ḥawla baʻḍ al-Tafsīr Āyāt al-Qur'ān al-Karīm
* Muhāḍarāt Ḥawla Mawāqif Sayyidinā Muḥammad ﷺ